Virginia W

New Casebooks
*Collections of all new critical essays*

**NOVELS AND PROSE**

DAVID ALMOND
Edited by Rosemary Ross Johnston

MELVIN BURGESS
Edited by Alison Waller

ROBERT CORMIER
Edited by Adrienne E. Gavin

ROALD DAHL
Edited by Ann Alston & Catherine Butler

JOHN FOWLES
Edited by James Acheson

C. S. LEWIS: *THE CHRONICLES OF NARNIA*
Edited by Michelle Ann Abate & Lance Weldy

PHILIP PULLMAN: *HIS DARK MATERIALS*
Edited by Catherine Butler & Tommy Halsdorf

J. K. ROWLING: *HARRY POTTER*
Edited by Cynthia J. Hallett & Peggy J. Huey

J. R. R. TOLKIEN: *THE HOBBIT & THE LORD OF THE RINGS*
Edited by Peter Hunt

JACQUELINE WILSON
Edited by Lucy Pearson

**GENRE**

AMERICAN POETRY SINCE 1945
Edited by Eleanor Spencer

MEDIEVAL ENGLISH LITERATURE
Edited by Beatrice Fannon

**POETRY**

TED HUGHES
Edited by Terry Gifford

*Further titles are in preparation*

For a full list of published titles in the past format of the New Casebooks series, visit the series page at www.palgrave.com

# Virginia Woolf

*Edited by*

JAMES ACHESON

First published 2017 by
PALGRAVE

Palgrave in the UK is an imprint of Macmillan Publishers Limited, registered in England, company number 785998, of 4 Crinan Street, London, N1 9XW.

Palgrave® and Macmillan® are registered trademarks in the United States, the United Kingdom, Europe and other countries.

ISBN 978–1–137–43082–3 hardback
ISBN 978–1–137–43081–6 paperback

This book is printed on paper suitable for recycling and made from fully managed and sustained forest sources. Logging, pulping and manufacturing processes are expected to conform to the environmental regulations of the country of origin.

A catalogue record for this book is available from the British Library.

A catalog record for this book is available from the Library of Congress.

Printed in China

# Contents

Series Editor's Preface                                                          vii
Notes on Contributors                                                          viii
Acknowledgements                                                                 x
List of Abbreviations                                                            xi

Introduction                                                                      1
James Acheson

1  Mind–wandering and Mindfulness: A Cognitive
   Approach to *Mrs. Dalloway* and *To the Lighthouse*      16
   Melba Cuddy-Keane

2  Spirituality in *Mrs. Dalloway* and *To the Lighthouse*      32
   Heather Ingman

3  Victorian Roots: The Sense of the Past in
   *Mrs. Dalloway* and *To the Lighthouse*                          46
   Kate Flint

4  Modernism and Bloomsbury Aesthetics                          60
   Gabrielle McIntire

5  'Women Can't Write, Women Can't Paint':
   Art and the Artist in *To the Lighthouse*                        74
   Bonnie Kime Scott

6  On the Death of the Soul: a Jungian Reading
   of *Mrs. Dalloway*                                                    89
   Katherine Tarbox

7  On Not Being Able to Paint: *To the Lighthouse* via
   Psychoanalysis                                                       106
   Maud Ellmann

# Contents

8 *Mrs. Dalloway* and the War that Wouldn't End 125
Brian Finney

9 *Mrs. Dalloway* and the Reinvention of the Novel 139
*H. Porter Abbott*

10 *Mrs. Dalloway* and *To the Lighthouse*: The Novel as Elegy 152
*Daniel Bedggood*

11 'What is a woman? I assure you, I do not know': Woolf
and Feminism in the 1920s 165
*Patricia Moran*

12 The Warp and the Weft: Homoeroticism in *Mrs. Dalloway*
and *To the Lighthouse* 180
*Diana L. Swanson*

13 The Cambridge Woolf 195
*Jane Goldman and E. H. Wright*

*Further Reading* 209

*Index* 212

# Series Editor's Preface

Welcome to the latest series of New Casebooks. Each volume now presents brand-new essays specially written for university and other students. Like the original series, the new-look New Casebooks embrace a range of recent critical approaches to the debates and issues that characterise the current discussion of literature.

Each editor has been asked to commission a sequence of original essays which will introduce the reader to the innovative critical approaches to the text or texts being discussed in the collection. The intention is to illuminate the rich interchange between critical theory and critical practice that today underpins so much writing about literature.

Editors have also been asked to supply an introduction to each volume that sets the scene for the essays that follow, together with a list of further reading which will enable readers to follow up issues raised by the essays in the collection.

The purpose of this new-look series, then, is to provide students with fresh thinking about key texts and writers while encouraging them to extend their own ideas and responses to the texts they are studying.

*Martin Coyle*

# Notes on Contributors

**H. Porter Abbott** is Research Professor of English at the University of California, Santa Barbara. He is author of *The Cambridge Introduction to Narrative* and *Real Mysteries: Narrative and the Unknowable.*

**James Acheson** is former Senior Lecturer in English at the University of Canterbury in Christchurch, New Zealand. He is author of *John Fowles* and *Samuel Beckett's Artistic Theory and Practice.*

**Daniel Bedggood** is Senior Lecturer in English, Cinema Studies and Digital Humanities at the University of Canterbury, in Christchurch, New Zealand. He is currently working on a book on the revival of the utopian impulse in recent speculative fiction.

**Melba Cuddy-Keane** is Emerita Professor of English, University of Toronto–Scarborough. Her publications on Woolf include *Virginia Woolf, the Intellectual, and the Public Sphere* and the Harcourt annotated edition of Woolf's *Between the Acts.*

**Maud Ellmann** is the Berlin Professor of the Development of the Novel in English at the University of Chicago. She has written widely on modernism and psychoanalysis; her most recent book is *The Nets of Modernism: James, Woolf, Joyce and Freud.*

**Brian Finney** is Emeritus Professor of English at California State University, Long Beach, where he teaches courses on twentieth-century British literature. He is author of *Christopher Isherwood: a Critical Biography* and *English Fiction Since 1984.*

**Kate Flint** is Provost Professor of English and Art History at the University of Southern California and author of *The Woman Reader, 1837–1914*, *The Victorians and The Visual Imagination* and *The Transatlantic Indian 1776–1930.*

**Jane Goldman** is Reader in English Literature at the University of Glasgow. She is a General Co-editor, with Susan Sellers, of the Cambridge University Press edition of the writings of Virginia Woolf and editor of the CUP edition of *To the Lighthouse.*

**Heather Ingman** is Adjunct Professor of English at Trinity College, Dublin. She is author of *Women's Spirituality in the Twentieth Century* and *Irish Women's Fiction: From Edgeworth to Enright*.

**Gabrielle McIntire** is Associate Professor of English at Queen's University, Canada. She is author of *Modernism, Memory, and Desire: T.S. Eliot and Virginia Woolf*, and editor of *The Cambridge Companion to The Waste Land*.

**Patricia Moran** is Senior Lecturer in English at City University, London. She is author of *Word of Mouth: Body Language in Katherine Mansfield*, and of *Virginia Woolf, Jean Rhys, and the Aesthetics of Trauma*.

**Bonnie Kime Scott** is Emerita Professor of Women's Studies at San Diego State University and the University of Delaware. Her most recent book is *In the Hollow of the Wave: Virginia Woolf and Modernist Uses of Nature*.

**Diana L. Swanson** is Associate Professor of English and of Women's, Gender and Sexuality Studies at Northern Illinois University. She recently co-edited *Virginia Woolf: Writing the World* with Pamela L. Caughie.

**Katherine Tarbox** is a Jung scholar living and working in Maine, USA. She taught modern and postmodern British literature for twenty-five years, most recently at the University of New Hampshire.

**E. H. Wright** is Senior Lecturer in English at Bath Spa University in England. She is author of *Virginia Woolf: Brief Lives* and editor of *Bloomsbury Inspirations*.

# Acknowledgements

I would l like to thank, first and foremost, the contributors to this volume. Each wrote their essay specifically for this collection; their professionalism, intellectual energy and enthusiasm ensured that the project was a thoroughgoing pleasure. I would also like to thank my wife Carole for her stimulating conversation and many insightful suggestions.

I would like, too, to thank Professors Kathleen Wall, Suzette Henke and Susan Sellers for their support and encouragement when the project was in the planning stages, and my editor at Palgrave, Rachel Bridgewater, for her unfailingly helpful advice at every step of the way.

I wish to lament the passing of Thomas C. Caramagno (1946–2014), whose book, *The Flight of the Mind: Virginia Woolf's Art and Manic-Depressive Illness* (1992), is in my view the best account of Virginia Woolf's experience of mental illness to have been published to date.

Finally, I would like to thank the Mortimer Rare Book Room at Smith College, Northampton, Massachusetts, USA, for permission to reproduce Plate 38H from the Leslie Stephen Photograph Album, a photograph taken by Vanessa Stephen of Leslie and Julia Stephen reading, with daughter Virginia watching, 1893.

# List of Abbreviations

| | |
|---|---|
| *CE* | *Collected Essays,* ed. Leonard Woolf (London: Hogarth Press, 1966), 4 vols. |
| *D* | *The Diary of Virginia Woolf,* ed. Ann Olivier Bell assisted by Andrew McNeillie (London: Hogarth Press, 1977), 5 vols. |
| *E* | *The Essays of Virginia Woolf,* ed. Andrew McNeillie (vols I–IV) and Stuart N. Clarke (vols V–VI) (London: Hogarth, 1986–2011), 6 vols. |
| *O* | *Orlando* (1928; rpt. London: Penguin, 2011). |
| *L* | *The Letters of Virginia Woolf,* ed. Nigel Nicolson and Joanne Trautmann (London: Hogarth Press, 1975–80), 6 vols. |
| *MB* | Virginia Woolf, *Moments of Being,* ed. Jeanne Schulkind (1939–40; rpt. New York/London: Harcourt, 1985). |
| *MD* | *Mrs. Dalloway,* ed. Anne E. Fernald (1925; rpt. Cambridge: Cambridge University Press, 2015). |
| *MF* | 'Modern Fiction', in *The Essays of Virginia Woolf, Vol. 4, 1925–1928,* ed. Andrew McNeillie (1925; rpt. London: Hogarth Press, 1994). |
| *MrB* | 'Mr. Bennett and Mrs. Brown', in *The Captain's Death Bed and Other Essays,* ed. Leonard Woolf (1924; rpt. London: Hogarth Press, 1950). |
| *RF* | *Roger Fry: A Biography* (1940; rpt. New York: Harcourt, 1968). |
| *R/TG* | *A Room of One's Own/Three Guineas,* ed. Morag Shiach (1929, 1938; rpt. Oxford: Oxford University Press, 1992). |
| *TL* | *To the Lighthouse,* ed. David Bradshaw (1927; rpt. Oxford: Oxford University Press [World's Classics]), 2008. |
| *VO* | *The Voyage Out,* ed. C. Ruth Miller and Lawrence Miller (1915; rpt. Oxford: Blackwell [Shakespeare Head Press], 1995). |

# Introduction

## James Acheson

### Introduction: Virginia Woolf, novelist and essayist

Virginia Woolf's *Mrs. Dalloway* (1925) and *To the Lighthouse* (1927) are two of the twentieth century's most highly regarded novels. However, they were not universally acclaimed by contemporary reviewers, and to this day are regarded by many people as dauntingly difficult. One of the reasons for this is that they depart radically from the conventions of Victorian and Edwardian fiction: to understand why they are unconventional we must turn to two essays that Woolf wrote at about the same time, 'Mr. Bennett and Mrs. Brown' (1924) and 'Modern Fiction' (1925). What the essays reveal is that Woolf considered the inner world of the mind to be of greater interest than the outer world—the world at large—and for that reason believed that novels should reveal more of their characters' inner than of their outer experience. In practice this meant that she highlighted her characters' thoughts and feelings in her novels, presenting them in what William James refers to as a 'stream of consciousness'.[1]

Two chapters in the collection—one by Melba Cuddy-Keane and the other by Porter Abbott—discuss Woolf's narrative technique and help us to understand why *Mrs. Dalloway* and *To the Lighthouse* are written the way they are. However, the two novels confront us with other problems as well, problems that arise if we are unaware of the social and historical context within which they were written. Accordingly, six of the collection's chapters—the ones by Kate Flint, Gabrielle McIntire, Diana Swanson, Patricia Moran, Bonnie Kime Scott and Heather Ingman—examine the cultural milieu of the 1920s and the effect it had on Woolf's writing. The chapters by Brian Finney and Daniel Bedggood similarly consider the influence of the First World War, and the ones by Maud Ellmann and Katherine Tarbox reveal what there is to be gained by reading *Mrs. Dalloway* and *To the Lighthouse* in the light of two major twentieth-century psychologists, Sigmund Freud and Carl Jung. In the concluding chapter, Jane Goldman and E.H. Wright outline what has gone into the preparation of the new Cambridge University Press edition of Woolf's writings. Overall, what emerges from the collection's essays is that to understand Woolf's novels, we need to be aware of a good deal of background information, some of it biographical.

Virginia Stephen (she became Virginia Woolf when she married Leonard Woolf in 1912) was born in 1882 into an upper middle-class family, and typically for the time, was tutored at home, while her brothers were sent away to both school and university.[2] The rationale for this practice was that girls would only ever become housewives and mothers, while boys would eventually make their way in the world in the professions. The young Virginia Stephen was a bright girl who from an early age was allowed to read any book in her father's extensive private library. Her father, Sir Leslie Stephen, was the founding editor of the *Dictionary of National Biography*, and although he was a tyrannical paterfamilias, rather like Mr. Ramsay in *To the Lighthouse,* he nevertheless took an interest in his daughter's reading, and often asked her to tell him about the books that became so much a part of her life.

Significantly, Woolf's 1925 essay, 'Modern Fiction', reflects her interest in William James.[3] In *The Principles of Psychology* James comments that as babies we are daily assailed by a 'great blooming, buzzing confusion' of sense-data—sights, tastes, sounds, smells and tactile sensations—which, as we grow older, we learn to transform into intelligible perceptual wholes.[4] A Danish contemporary of James's, Edgar Rubin, theorised that we make sense of sense-data by distinguishing perceptually between 'the figure, the substantial appearance of objects, and the ground, the ... environment in which the [objects are] placed.'[5] Experiments performed by other early twentieth-century psychologists showed that the figure-ground distinction is invariably a simplification of what is perceived.[6] The world we know through perception is merely an approximation (because a series of approximations of sense-data in different situations) of the world as it really is.

In 'Modern Fiction' Woolf echoes James and his contemporaries when she calls upon us to

> Examine for a moment an ordinary mind on an ordinary day. The mind receives a myriad impressions—trivial, fantastic, evanescent, or engraved with the sharpness of steel. From all sides they come, an incessant shower of innumerable atoms; and as they fall, as they shape themselves into the life of Monday or Tuesday, the accent falls differently from of old ... Life is not a series of gig lamps symmetrically arranged; life is a luminous halo, a semi-transparent envelope surrounding us from the beginning of consciousness to the end. (*MF,* 160)

Here Woolf is saying, as James does, that our experience of the world is of an undifferentiated welter of sense-data. Initially it presents itself to us as a 'great blooming, buzzing confusion', but as we grow older it seems as orderly as a series of symmetrical gig lamps in a row of hackney cabs (the contemporary equivalent would be headlights in a row of taxis). The orderliness of the world, however, is spurious, for it derives from our perceptual faculties' simplification of sense-data. In 'Modern Fiction' Woolf says it is important to write not about the image of the world that the mind presents to us but instead about our initial impression of sensory experience: 'Let us record the atoms as they fall upon the mind in the order in which they fall, let us trace the pattern, however disconnected and incoherent in appearance, which each sight or incident scores upon the consciousness' (*MF*, 161).

In theory, simply recording sensations in this way would make for innovative fiction, but in practice a novel in which the author did nothing more than report the sights, sounds, smells, tastes and tactile sensations that his or her characters experienced would hold little appeal for even the most tolerant of readers. Woolf recognised that her novels would have to present not only her characters' sensations, but also their thoughts, memories, daydreams, hopes, fears and so on, and in *Mrs. Dalloway* and *To the Lighthouse* she relates them in a steady flow, as a stream of consciousness.[7] Thus at the start of *Mrs. Dalloway*, 'Clarissa's mind leaps from what she is about to do that day', says Melba Cuddy-Keane in Chapter 1 of this volume, 'to what others will be doing, to an imagined scene of children on a beach, and then to memories of girlhood. [Similarly, after] the first spoken words in *To the Lighthouse*, we plunge into the internal world of Mrs. Ramsay's son James, leaping from expected future joy (going to the lighthouse the next day) to present delight (cutting out a picture of a refrigerator, fringed in his mind with "heavenly bliss".' In a more conventional novel, the narrator would enter a character's mind and tell us in a logical sequence that, for example, 'Clarissa was looking forward to the events of the day, and to what her friends would be doing', and so on, or that, 'as James delighted in cutting a picture of a refrigerator out of a magazine, he was looking forward to sailing to the lighthouse next day'. Woolf departs from convention in her stream-of-consciousness rendering of her characters' thought processes, and many people coming to her novels for the first time find her approach to narration baffling.

Of special interest to Cuddy-Keane is the fact that Woolf's narrative technique is consistent with recent discoveries in the field of neuroscience. In particular Mrs. Ramsay's 'wool-gathering'—the term

Woolf uses to describe her character's mind-wandering—anticipates studies that show that this activity of mind enables 'creative solutions' and 'moments of inspiration'. This observation not only helps us to understand Mrs. Ramsay's thought processes more clearly but also suggests that *Mrs. Dalloway* and *To the Lighthouse* are all the more accessible the more closely we attend to the workings of our own minds.

## Inner and outer worlds

In her essays Woolf hints that her preference for writing about the inner world of the mind rather than the outer world—the world as revealed by perception—arises from her interest in the nineteenth-century German philosopher, Arthur Schopenhauer. To date, the influence of Schopenhauer has not been discussed at length by critics of Woolf, and this is no doubt because she mentions him by name in only a single book review.[8] Nevertheless, there are indications in 'Mr. Bennett and Mrs. Brown' that Schopenhauer lies behind much of her theorising about fiction. 'Sterne and Jane Austen', she says in this essay, 'were interested in things in themselves; in character in itself. ... But the Edwardians were never interested in character in itself. They were interested in something outside' (*MrB*, 99–100). Here Woolf's use of the term 'things in themselves' and her insistence on the importance of our inner lives recall Schopenhauer's use of the phrase 'the thing in itself', as well as his belief that introspection reveals truths of a higher order than perception.[9]

By 'the thing in itself' Schopenhauer means a blind striving force found everywhere in nature, a force he refers to as 'will'. The whole world is simply objectified will: will resides in all animate and inanimate objects and is responsible for their phenomenal characteristics. Will itself is, however, imperceptible: what perception reveals to us is only its indirect objectification, 'idea', a simplification of will's phenomenal manifestation. Of greater interest than our image of the world at large is our experience of the inner world of the mind, for whereas perception simplifies our experience of sense-data, introspection presents our thoughts and feelings to us in all their complexity.[10] Accordingly, Schopenhauer believes that the inner world should be the primary material of fiction; in an essay entitled 'On the Metaphysics of the Beautiful and on Aesthetics' he says,

> A [novel] will be of a so much higher and nobler kind, the more of *inward* and the less of *outward* life it portrays, and this proportion will

accompany all gradations of the [novel], as a characteristic sign. ... Art consists in the fact, that with the smallest possible expenditure of outward life, the inward is brought out into the strongest relief, for the inward is properly the object of our interest. The task of the novelist is not to narrate great events, but to make small ones interesting.[11]

Though Woolf's belief in the importance of inner experience may derive from other sources as well—from conversations with fellow novelists, for example—the above passage appears to have been an especially compelling influence. Schopenhauer's comments are consistent with both her theory of fiction in 'Modern Fiction' and 'Mr. Bennett and Mrs. Brown', and with her practice as a novelist in *Mrs. Dalloway* and *To the Lighthouse*—two novels in which she chooses 'not to narrate great events, but to make small ones interesting'.

In 'Modern Fiction' Woolf describes three Edwardian novelists, Arnold Bennett, H.G. Wells and John Galsworthy, as 'materialists' whose preoccupation with the outer world is to be deplored. In an oft-quoted passage in this essay, Woolf says that 'if a writer were a free man and not a slave, if he could write what he chose, not what he must, if he could base his work upon his own feeling and not upon convention, there would be no plot, no comedy, no tragedy, no love interest or catastrophe in the accepted style ... [in the modern novel]' (*MF*, 160). A writer is a slave to convention if he or she is content to describe the material world instead of focusing on the far more important thoughts and feelings of his or her characters. Bennett, Wells and Galsworthy write conventionally about outer experience: 'they write of unimportant things; ... they spend immense skill and immense industry making the trivial and the transitory appear the true and the enduring' (*MF*, 159). The true and the enduring are to be found, in Woolf's view, in the inner world of the mind, and it is the task of the novelist 'to convey this varying, this unknown and uncircumscribed spirit, ... with as little mixture of the alien and exterior as possible' (*MF*, 160–61).

The novelist who succeeds in doing this, Woolf stresses, will provide us with insight into 'the dark places of psychology' (*MF*, 162)— into 'life or spirit, truth or reality' (*MF*, 160), and ultimately into the essence of 'human nature' (*MrB*, 103) itself. But how is it possible to write a novel about the 'uncircumscribed spirit' in the absence of any reference to the material world? In Chapter 9, Porter Abbott draws attention to a contemporary reviewer's remark that 'only readers of preternatural intellect may discover a consecutive story' in *Mrs. Dalloway*.[12] The story is hard to follow because Woolf reveals the thoughts and feelings of all her major characters in the absence of the kind of structured plot favoured by the Edwardians. What she presents us with instead is a meandering, picaresque plot and an equally meandering subplot, each moving from one event to the next with every appearance of randomness. The randomness is, however, only apparent: Woolf takes pains to ensure that her novel is accessible to the reader willing to rise to the challenges that it presents. The claim that 'only readers of preternatural intellect may discover a consecutive story' in *Mrs. Dalloway* must be balanced against the fact that Woolf's experimental novels have always sold well and have never gone out of print.[13]

In *Mrs. Dalloway* Woolf reveals that the inner life of two of the main characters—Clarissa Dalloway and Peter Walsh—is of a kind that is familiar to most readers. Less familiar are the thoughts and feelings of Septimus Warren Smith, the ex-soldier who is suffering from the deferred effects of shell shock. Smith is clearly psychotic, and it is a tribute to Woolf's skill as a writer that she manages to convey his disturbed thoughts and feelings to us intelligibly. His hallucinations and his Messianic belief that he is the Chosen One are symptoms of Post-Traumatic Stress Disorder, a mental illness that has circumscribed his otherwise 'uncircumscribed spirit'. Seriously traumatised, he throws himself out of a window and dies impaled on the spikes of an iron fence below.

## The Bloomsbury Group, art and homosexuality

In Chapter 4, Gabrielle McIntire relates that from 1904 onwards, Virginia Woolf (Virginia Stephen as she then was) met regularly at her home in Bloomsbury with friends her brother Thoby had made at Cambridge. Eventually she and her guests became known as the Bloomsbury Group, a phrase not of their own devising (some of its members claimed that it had been invented by the press). Nevertheless they referred to themselves jokingly as 'Bloomsberries', and opened themselves to an impressive circle of intelligent young people. At first their conversations centred on G.E. Moore's *Principia Ethica* (1903), for Moore's interest in 'the good' was, as McIntire says, 'a problematic category' with significant implications for the theory and practice of art. In 1910 the Group's focus turned to Cézanne, one of the artists who featured in the first Post-Impressionist Exhibition organised by an older member of the group, Roger Fry. Under Fry's influence Woolf began to write in a style characterised by 'Post-Impressionist literary expressionism', says McIntire, 'with attention to fluctuations in mood and experience as intensely noted as the Impressionists had rendered fluctuations in light and shadow'.

Many of the Bloomsberries were homosexual, and found it a relief to be able to talk about their same-sex desires in the privacy of Woolf's home. Homosexual acts between men were at this time illegal, and only a few years after the publication of Woolf's two novels, a lesbian novel by Radclyffe Hall, *The Well of Loneliness* (1928), was put on trial for obscenity. The court deemed the book indecent, even though it contained no explicit sex scenes, and ordered that all copies of it be destroyed. It is thus not surprising that, as Diana Swanson observes in Chapter 12, Woolf only hints at the homosexual tendencies of Miss Kilman, Sally Seton and Clarissa herself in *Mrs. Dalloway,* and at Lily's same-sex attraction to Mrs. Ramsay in *To the Lighthouse.*

Lily lacks confidence, says Bonnie Kime Scott in Chapter 5, but she is aware of contemporary trends in art, and 'asserts her need to paint things as she sees them'. Her real-life counterpart is Virginia Woolf's artist sister Vanessa; the two often discussed art and literature together, and were influenced by the painter Walter Sickert, who recognised, Scott says, that 'painting and writing have much to say to each other'. Whether Lily Briscoe is familiar with the work of Sickert is unclear; however, she is ultimately able to counter Charles Tansley's misogynistic assertions ('Women can't paint, women can't write') in a painting that, when completed at the end of *To the Lighthouse*, is presented to us as a major achievement.

In Chapter 11, Patricia Moran focuses not just on women artists, but on the role of women more generally. She begins by commenting on *A Room of One's Own* (1929), the long essay in which Woolf argues that 'a woman must have money and a room of her own if she is to write fiction' (*R/TG*, 4), describing it as the 'capstone' of Woolf's thinking about women and writing in the 1920s. Another major essay is *Three Guineas* (1938), in which Woolf describes being approached for a donation by a pacifist group, a women's college and a group devoted to promoting the entry of women into the professions. As a pacifist and advocate of the rights of women she decides to donate a guinea to each. Oddly, though, Woolf insists in *Three Guineas* that the term 'feminist' has had its day: '… a word without a meaning is a dead word, a corrupt word', she says. 'Let us therefore celebrate this occasion by cremating the corpse. Let us write that word in large black letters on a sheet of foolscap; then solemnly apply a match to the paper' (*R/TG*, 302). She explains that women have won equality with men in having achieved the right to earn a living, and that further feminist striving is unnecessary. But although she spent the rest of her life using the term 'feminist' disparagingly, Woolf continued to take part in organised activities on behalf of women: both *A Room of One's Own* (1929) and *Three Guineas* grew out of talks she gave to women's groups; the women's library organisations received donations of books and money from her; and the Hogarth Press, established by the Woolfs in 1917, published numerous books by women authors.

## Freud and Jung

In Chapter 7, Maud Ellmann notes that Woolf wrote *To the Lighthouse* in the mid-1920s, some fifteen years before she claims to have started taking a serious interest in Freud. Yet '[so many] of Freud's theories map ... neatly onto *To the Lighthouse*', Ellmann adds, 'that the critic's task becomes almost too easy. [Key] Freudian concepts ... announce themselves on every page, making the novel something of a primer in psychoanalysis.' Certain concepts of the psychoanalyst Melanie Klein also find their way into the novel, though 'there is something knowing, even tongue-in-cheek' about Woolf's presentation of both Freudian and Kleinian theory. She seems, says Ellmann, 'to be poking fun at mind-doctors'. More illuminating than anything by Freud or Klein, Ellmann adds, is a book by Marion Milner, *On Not Being Able to Paint* (1950), a book whose title echoes Tansley's repeated 'Women can't write. Women can't paint'. Written some twenty-five years after *To the Lighthouse*, it is clearly not an influence on Woolf but instead presents an interesting parallel. Milner's reflections on her own artistic inhibitions parallel Lily Briscoe's in *To the Lighthouse*. At first Lily's canvas is a 'glaring, hideously difficult white space' (*TL,* 132), mocking her with a mirror of her own vacuity. She sees no point in working on a painting that, once completed, will be 'rolled up and stuffed under a sofa' (*TL* 131). If we ask in the light of this why an artist should bother to paint, Woolf's answer is neither Freudian nor Kleinian; instead, it is simply that creation provides the life of the artist with meaning and purpose, the act of painting or writing being more important than the result.

Though Woolf began to take a serious interest in Freud in 1939, there is no evidence that she ever read much, if anything, by the equally famous psychologist Carl Jung. Woolf and Jung were, however, 'contemporaries who shared the same ... unique pressures and conditions of late- and post-Victorian European culture', says Katherine Tarbox in Chapter 6. 'Both spent much of their creative energies analysing and writing about the ways that culture adversely affects an individual's psyche.' Thus *Mrs. Dalloway* presents us with the ongoing battle between the inner world of the mind and the outer world whose immense cultural power fields impinge on it—power fields that 'create society, gender roles, empire and war, and the sublimation of war, capitalism'. The patriarchy wields power over women and limits what they are allowed to do. 'Lady Bradshaw', says Tarbox, exemplifies the cost to women of male oppression. 'She has had to be "cramped, squeezed, pared, pruned" (*MD,* 90) to be what [the patriarchy] expects of her, illustrating Jung's observation that some people in the twentieth century seem to be "walking in shoes too small for them".'[14]

Jung believed that in every woman there is a masculine element, 'the animus', and in every man a feminine element, 'the anima'. Clarissa has subordinated her animus in the interests of being a society lady, and in the outer world of business, government and so on, lives through her husband Richard. Peter Walsh challenges her to take more of a part in the masculine world, but she rejects his offer of marriage because life with Richard is easier in prospect than the life of an independent woman. Septimus Warren Smith begins well as a young man under the influence of a teacher, Miss Pole, who puts him in touch with his feminine side. But 'his flower is crushed and torn apart in the war', says Tarbox, 'where to kill other people he must achieve "manliness" (*MD,* 77), the absence of feminine feeling'. So alienated is he from his sense of self after the war that he commits suicide rather than continue to be the psychological cripple it has made of him. The fact that Mrs. Dalloway is glad that he has killed himself becomes explicable once we recognise that she admires him for choosing death over the life of a hopeless psychotic.

## Woolf and the past

*Mrs. Dalloway* looks back not only to the effect that the First World War had on the 1920s but also to the influence of the Victorian era. As Kate Flint observes in Chapter 3 of this volume, by the 1920s Victorian views on religion and a variety of other subjects were being widely questioned. 'No age', she quotes Woolf as saying in a 1923 essay, 'can have been more rich than ours in writers determined to give expression to the differences which separate them from the past and not to the resemblances which connect them with it' (*E* III, 357). Woolf's examination of the differences between nineteenth- and early twentieth-century England takes the form of satire in *Mrs. Dalloway.* She mocks the prudishness of the Victorians—of the fathers who were horrified at the thought of

their daughters seeing a man naked—and the patriarchal pompos-
ity of some of the male characters, including Sir William Bradshaw,
who insists that his wife abide strictly by convention. Not only is
this a comment on the subjugation of women but also, says Flint,
on 'the cruel [Victorian] spirit' that is still at work in the Empire,
subduing native peoples and exploiting the natural resources of the
countries in which they live.

As a background to Heather Ingman's essay on Woolf and religion,
it is important to emphasise that *To the Lighthouse* is poignant rather
than satiric. In the 'Time Passes' section of the novel, in the midst of
describing how the Ramsays' holiday home is deteriorating under the
effects of rain, wind and human neglect, Woolf reports in parentheses,
as though they were inconsequential, the premature deaths of three of
the novel's characters—Mrs. Ramsay, Prue and Andrew. Here we are
reminded of the opening of the Old Testament Book of Ecclesiastes:
'What profit hath a man of all his labour which he taketh under the
sun? One generation passeth away, and *another* generation cometh: but
the earth abideth forever.'[15] At the start of Ecclesiastes the Preacher
observes, as Woolf appears to in 'Time Passes', that the life of a single
individual, a single generation or even a succession of generations is
trivial and meaningless. The Preacher himself is vexed that his life's
work will be in vain; however, in later verses he takes comfort in belief
in God, for he is convinced that God takes pleasure in human striving. 'Go thy way', he exhorts the reader, 'eat thy bread with joy, and
drink thy wine with a merry heart'.[16] We can, he suggests, be secure
in the knowledge that God confers meaning and purpose on human
endeavour.

But what if there is no God? In Chapter 2 Heather Ingman reveals
that Woolf was highly sceptical about God's existence, and it is consistent with this that her references to 'divine goodness' (*TL,* 105) and
'divine bounty' (*TL,* 109) in 'Time Passes' are ironic. Nevertheless,
Woolf recognised that human beings have a deep-seated need for
meaning in their lives, and in a world bereft of God, will search for
and adopt whatever might satisfy that need. At the end of the novel,
the language Lily Briscoe uses to describe the completion of her
painting suggests that she has substituted artistic creation for religious
belief: 'It was done; it was finished. Yes, she thought, laying down her
brush in extreme fatigue, I have had my vision' (*TL,* 170). Once completed, Lily's painting is expressive of some kind of mystical vision; yet
the fact that 'it was finished' is an echo of Christ's last words on the
Cross also implies that it is the product of an age in which not only
Christ but God Himself is dead.[17]

If the mention of mystical vision suggests that the lighthouse is a symbol of some kind of surrogate deity, we should be aware that Woolf emphasised in a letter to Roger Fry that, so far as she was concerned, the lighthouse had no symbolic significance:

> I meant *nothing* by The Lighthouse. One has to have a central line down the middle of the book to hold the design together. I saw that all sorts of feelings would accrue to this, but I refused to think them out, and trusted that people would make it the deposit for their own emotions—which they have done, one thinking it means one thing another another. I can't manage Symbolism except in this vague, generalised way. Whether its [sic] right or wrong I don't know, but directly I'm told what a thing means, it becomes hateful to me. (*L* III, 385)

The lighthouse confers order on Woolf's novel, just as God confers meaning and purpose on human life in Ecclesiastes. However, it is not intended to be a symbol of anything outside the novel: it is not meant to be an ordering principle replacing God in a world characterised by a marked decline of faith.[18]

The First World War contributed significantly to that decline. There were huge losses of men, and as Brian Finney reveals in Chapter 8, a secret War Propaganda Bureau was set up as early as 1914 to conduct a campaign that would justify the war being waged. Initially the Bureau placed advertisements in magazines and newspapers seeking to shame men into joining the armed forces ('What did you do in the war, Daddy?' ask two post-war children of their father in one advertisement). As time went on, and more and more men were lost, the Bureau began to characterise the war as a Holy Crusade against the Kaiser, who was presented as being in league with the devil. We see the effect of the propaganda, says Finney, in Siegfried Sassoon's famous poem, 'They'. In the first stanza a nameless Bishop says that the war has been a Crusade against 'the Anti-Christ', and that the soldiers returning from the trenches have undergone a change from ordinary men into glorious heroes. In the second stanza the soldiers he is addressing take an entirely different view. One has lost his legs, another is blind, a third has been shot through the lungs and will probably die, and a fourth has contracted syphilis. These are the changes they have undergone, the changes that propaganda overlooks. In the last line of the poem, the Bishop says: 'The ways of God are strange'. How, asks Sassoon, can a benevolent God have allowed His Crusaders to suffer the way they did? Finney notes that for Virginia Woolf, the war was never a Holy Crusade; instead, it was 'a preposterous masculine fiction' (*L* II, 76). The fact that she has Septimus Warren Smith conceive of himself, psychotically, as some kind of new Messiah, is evidence that she considered the Holy Crusade of the British propaganda machine to be a form of insanity.

It is partly because Woolf lamented the First World War's massive loss of life that she wondered about the need to invent a new name for her books to supplant 'novel'. 'A new — by Virginia Woolf', she says in *A Writer's Diary*.' But what? Elegy?'[19] In Chapter 10, Daniel Bedggood recalls that an elegy is a form of poetry fostered in classical literature, whose purpose is 'to lament and console', and in the case of Woolf's novels, to 'deal with problems attendant on return and survival in the wake of the Great War'. Septimus Warren Smith is a survivor of the horrors of trench warfare, and is set apart from the 'war-blind' civilians who surround him in 1923. In the midst of his visions of Messianic power Smith reveals what life was like at the battle front. His death, says Bedggood, 'reaffirms Clarissa's life, recognized as truly present at the end of *Mrs. Dalloway:* "for there she was"' (*MD,* 174). These are the final words of the novel, and 'they impart a kind of consolation … that cements the work as an ironic elegy in the face of death.' Similarly, Lily Briscoe's painting at the end of *To the Lighthouse* 'serves the elegiac purposes of restoring the absent dead and placing them back at the centre of the picture'.

## The Cambridge Woolf

It is clear that the reader of *Mrs. Dalloway* and *To the Lighthouse* will be rewarded by acquainting him- or herself with important background information about Woolf, and by reading her novels with the help of scholarly annotations. The new Cambridge University Press edition of Woolf's work assists in both respects, and in the final chapter one of the general editors, Jane Goldman, together with E. H. Wright, author of a recent book on Woolf, discuss what is involved in producing this scholarly new edition. The annotations in the Cambridge *Mrs. Dalloway* are especially helpful to readers wanting to know about events in Woolf's life, books she is known to have read and places with which she was familiar, and (as Jane Goldman puts it) 'the discoveries of past and present scholars of Woolf, in the hope that we might continue the dialogues they have initiated in published criticism'.

Woolf's recommendation to readers, stated in one of her essays, is 'to take no advice, to follow your own instincts, to use your own reason, to come to your own conclusions' (*EV,* 573). The annotations are thus designed to be helpful while at the same time offering the reader latitude for a variety of interpretations. Differences between the British and American first editions of *Mrs. Dalloway* are identified, and the novel's forerunners—the short story 'Mrs. Dalloway in Bond Street' and the novel *The Voyage Out*—are discussed in relation to it. In the Textual Notes successive alterations that Woolf made—additions, restructuring and deletions—are carefully specified. This chapter offers not only a wealth of information about the text of *Mrs. Dalloway*, but also considerable insight into what is involved in producing a scholarly edition of this famous novel, written almost a hundred years ago. All quotations from *Mrs. Dalloway* in the present collection are from Anne Fernald's Cambridge University Press edition; Jane Goldman is still working on the Cambridge edition of *To the Lighthouse*, and recommended that David Bradshaw's Oxford World's Classics be used in its place in this essay collection.

The importance of using good scholarly editions of Virginia Woolf's novels is only one of a number of issues raised in the Introduction and thirteen chapters of this collection. To understand *Mrs. Dalloway* and *To the Lighthouse* clearly, it is essential to examine their relationship to her two essays, 'Mr. Bennett and Mrs. Brown' and 'Modern Fiction', because the essays develop the theory of fiction that lies behind her practice as a novelist. In addition it is important to be aware of the historical context in which she wrote. The role of women in a patriarchal society plays a large part in her novels, as do the First World War, the decline of faith, the question of sexual identity, the relationship of her fiction to elegy and also the psychological theories of major figures like Freud and Jung. 'As we read Woolf's novels', comments Su Reid, 'we find ourselves to be participants in unresolved debates' about all these issues, 'and, more than this, we have to recognize and live out the complex activity of narration, of relating and explaining events that we frequently take for granted'.[20]

Of course there are other topics arising from the two novels that might have been discussed in the present volume, but there is only so much can be included in a book of this length. Readers who wish to find out more about Woolf's attitude to issues not covered here—her attitude to social class and race, for example—will do well to consult the 'Further Reading' section at the end of this volume. *The Cambridge Companion to To the Lighthouse,* which is listed there, was published after essays for my New Casebook had been commissioned; it contains an essay by Kathryn Simpson, entitled 'Social Class in *To the Lighthouse*', and another Urmila Seshagiri, '*To the Lighthouse* and the Art of Race', both of which are well worth reading. Similarly, readers of that volume will want to read Maud Ellmann's essay in this one, 'On Not Being Able to Paint: *To the Lighthouse* and Psychoanalysis', as well as Jane Goldman's essay, 'The Cambridge Woolf'. To say that the topics of the Ellmann and Goldman essays are not covered in *The Cambridge Companion to To the Lighthouse* is not to be critical of that volume. It is simply to say that no single essay collection can deal comprehensively with an author as talented as Virginia Woolf.

## Notes

1  See *The Principles of Psychology* (1890; rpt. Cambridge, Mass.: Harvard University Press, 1981), I, p. 233, where James comments that '[c]onsciousness … does not appear to itself as chopped up in bits. … It is nothing joined; it flows. A "river" or a "stream"are the metaphors by which it is most naturally described. *In talking of it hereafter, let us call it the stream of thought, consciousness, or subjective life.*'

2  Virginia Woolf's brothers were sent away to school and later to Cambridge University, whereas she was tutored at home. However, it has recently come to light that she attended some university courses at King's College London between 1897 and 1901. See Christine Kenyon Jones and Anna Snaith, '"Tilting at Universities": Woolf at King's College London', *Woolf Studies Annual* 16 (2010), 1–44.

3  In *Virginia Woolf* (Oxford/New York: Oxford University Press), p. 95, Michael Whitworth cites William James as a source for Woolf, noting that James's term 'stream of consciousness' became literary terminology in 1918 when May Sinclair used it to describe Dorothy Richardson's technique in her long novel *Pilgrimage*.

4  *The Principles of Psychology*, I, 462.

5  Robert I.Watson, *The Great Philosophers from Aristotle to Freud* (Philadelphia: J.B. Lippincott, 1968), p. 439.

6  Solomon E. Asch, 'Gestalt Theory', in *The International Encyclopedia of the Social Sciences*, ed. David Sills (London: Macmillan and the Free Press, 1968), VI, 168. Here Asch draws attention to the all-important Principle of Prägnanz, the principle that 'experienced perceptual wholes tend toward the greatest regularity, simplicity, and clarity possible under the given conditions'.

7  Whitworth, p. 95, rightly emphasises that 'as a literary term [the stream of consciousness] does not distinguish between the different kinds of consciousness and unconsciousness …', and that we should not conclude from the uses of this term that Woolf concerned herself strictly with the workings of the conscious mind.

8  In her chapter on Virginia Woolf in *Schopenhauer, Women's Literature and the Legacy of Pessimism in George Eliot, Olive Schreiner, Virginia Woolf and Doris Lessing* (Lewiston, New York: Edwin Mellen Press, 2001), pp. 69–88, Penelope LeFew-Blake draws attention to Woolf's 'To Read or Not to Read' (1917; rpt. *E* II, 155–57), a review of a book

by Viscount Harberton, entitled *How to Lengthen Our Ears: an Enquiry Whether Learning from Books Does Not Lengthen the Ears Rather than the Understanding* (London: C.W. Daniel, 1917). Woolf treats as preposterous Lord Harberton's insistence that nothing good comes of reading books, and is bemused by his self-contradictory admiration for Arthur Schopenhauer and Herbert Spencer. 'After all, then', comments Woolf, 'Lord Harberton is merely one of those cultivated people who play the innocent for a holiday. Still, one reader will give him the benefit of the doubt and take his advice to the extent of refraining for ever from the pages of Schopenhauer.' This last statement is, of course, ironic.

9   There are at least two reasons why Virginia Woolf did not acknowledge her interest in Schopenhauer more openly. One is that having mocked Lord Harberton in her review for believing that Schopenhauer can find 'the secret of the universe' (*E* II, 157), she may have felt uneasy about mentioning him by name in her own writing. Another may be that in the absence of any formal instruction in philosophy, she was afraid of being taken to task for making mistakes in print about Schopenhauer.

10  See *WWI*, II, 471: 'The knowledge of the will in self-consciousness is … not a *perception* of it, but a perfectly direct becoming aware of its successive impulses.'

11  'On the Metaphysics of the Beautiful and on Aesthetics', in *Selected Essays of Schopenhauer*, ed. Ernest Belfort Bax (1888; rpt. London: G. Bell, 1914), p. 304.

12  In the *Western Mail*, 14 May 1925 (*D* III, 21 n24).

13  See the General Editors' Preface to *MD*, p. xi.

14  C. G. Jung, *Modern Man in Search of a Soul*, trans. W. S. Dell and Cary F. Baynes (New York: Harcourt, Brace and World, 1933), p. 381.

15  King James Bible, Ecclesiastes 1: 3–4.

16  Ecclesiastes 9: 7.

17  Friedrich Nietzsche had proclaimed that 'God is dead' in an essay collection entitled *The Gay Science*, published in 1882.

18  On the other hand, in suggesting that Lily's art has arisen from some kind of vision, Woolf conveys that the artist finds meaning and purpose not in God but in the creation of works of art. This is a matter not of God creating man and taking pleasure in human striving, but of man creating a substitute for God. The lighthouse itself is arguably a work of art and (Woolf to the contrary) a symbol of artistic creation.

19  Virginia Woolf, *A Writer's Diary*, ed. Leonard Woolf (London: Hogarth Press, 1953), p. 80. The entry is dated 20 July 1925.

20  Su Reid, *Mrs. Dalloway and To the Lighthouse* (New York: St Martin's Press, 1993), p. 18.

# 1

# Mind-wandering and Mindfulness: A Cognitive Approach to *Mrs. Dalloway* and *To the Lighthouse*

Melba Cuddy-Keane

## Introduction: Wool-gathering

Responding, in 1931, to an article on fiction by Bloomsberrian Desmond MacCarthy, Virginia Woolf wrote, 'Oh I was annoyed with Desmond's usual sneer at Mrs. Dalloway—woolgathering' (*D* IV, 42).[1] In *To the Lighthouse*, Woolf herself used the offensive word with similarly deprecating connotations, but here Mrs. Ramsay employs it defensively to deflect her husband's intrusive criticism of her thoughts: 'He did not like to see her look so sad, he said. Only wool-gathering, she protested, flushing a little' (*TL,* 57). In *Orlando*, the word crops up humorously, to describe the indescribable process of writing: 'this mere wool-gathering; this thinking; this sitting in a chair day in, day out, with a cigarette and a sheet of paper and a pen and an ink pot'.[2] And in her diaries, Woolf self-identifies as a wool gatherer, describing her mind as 'woolgathering away about Women & Fiction' (the early title for *A Room of One's Own*), 'racing up & down the whole field of [her] lecture' (*D* III, 175).

In popular usage, 'wool-gathering' refers to wandering fancies or idle speculation, implying a profligate squandering of time. Yet the roots of this metaphor derive from the material process of roaming a countryside and picking up bits of sheep's wool caught on bushes and hedges—an important means of livelihood for those not privileged enough to own sheep themselves. As mind-wandering, wool-gathering might thus be productive work, playing a vital role in our ordinary lives. In roaming about, the brain may be rifling through its storage systems, scavenging for helpful bits of information, even pattern-making as it goes. Readying itself to spring into gear, the wandering mind might signify the idling, not the idle, brain.

To treat Woolf's 'wool-gathering' so seriously is of course to assume that writing (both fiction and life-writing) can tell us something about real-world cognition. But that proposition is not really strange. Neuroscience strives to tell us which brain regions are being activated, and by what *kinds* of thought, but even in science, actual thoughts are accessed, not by observation, but through self-reporting. People have to say or write down what they are thinking for their thoughts to be known. If verbal report is an imperfect medium, the imperfection is shared by literature and science alike. Modernist writers of fiction were furthermore fascinated by consciousness, and Woolf was a particularly fervent observer of her own mind. 'My own brain is to me the most unaccountable of machinery', she wrote, 'always buzzing, humming, soaring, roaring, diving, and then buried in mud' (*L* V, 140). She considered the mind a rich site for exploration, noting, 'I like going from one lighted room to another, such is my brain to me; lighted rooms' (*D* II, 310). Finally, writing about consciousness (and unconsciousness) was her express goal. Contrasting the stasis of painting to the 'action' of writing, she explained that writing achieves beauty by 'showing all the traces of the minds [*sic*] passage through the world',[3] while in her essay 'Modern Fiction', she urged aspiring writers to 'examine ... an ordinary mind on an ordinary day' and 'record the atoms as they fall upon the mind in the order in which they fall' (*MF,* 160). If her own fiction was similarly based on constant real-life examination, it is not unreasonable to suppose that we can gain insights into cognition from her characters' thoughts.

How, then, do Woolf's observations and representations compare to the psychological knowledge that we have today? Jonah Lehrer, a neuroscientist who recently popularised the cognitive approach to modernist literature, believes her insights hold up well. Lehrer describes modernist writers like Proust as 'artists who anticipated the discoveries of neuroscience' and asserts, 'Modern neuroscience is now confirming the self Woolf believed in.'[4] While we may not agree with Lehrer's interpretation either of the Woolfian or neuroscientific self, his general approach is a useful guide. For Lehrer, the artist proceeds by introspection, intuition and imagination to convey the experience of what consciousness is like. Subsequent scientific experimentation complements that intuition, helping us to understand how such consciousness operates physically in the brain.

When we turn to Woolf's positive approach to 'wool-gathering', however, we encounter a stumbling block. Most current psychological discussion treats mind-wandering as an insidious debilitating habit that we should attempt to avoid or control. Educators and cognitive behaviour therapists point to the detrimental effects of distraction and regard the mind's inability to stay focused on a task, in its extreme forms, as an attention disorder. Studies have demonstrated, for example, that 'participants who are caught mind-wandering more during reading tend to perform worse on subsequent comprehension tests', indicating that the ability to maintain attention 'may be a strong determinant of academic success or failure'.[5] The prescribed antidote is mindfulness training, on the principle that regularly practising sustained attention enhances our capabilities for non-distraction and improves our performance of tasks: 'participation in [a] mindfulness meditation class reduced mind-wandering during both a GRE reading comprehension test and a working memory test and improved performance on both of these measures' (Mooneyham and Schooler, 16).

The negative effects of mind-wandering are most salient, however, when the mind is *supposed* to be focused elsewhere, as when driving a car; mind-wandering may be a very different process during undemanding tasks, such as waiting your turn in a line, when paying minimal attention does not put us at risk. Differences also emerge from the nature of the thoughts involved. While 'perseverative cognition'—obsessively and repetitively ruminating about the past or worrying about the future—reflects our being stuck in a rut, imaginatively playing out a variety of future scenarios can help us better to plan for anticipated events.[6] Furthermore, constructive daydreaming need not involve consciously rehearsing for a future event; positive effects can also result from letting the mind drift off into seemingly unrelated thoughts. While the latter process may superficially resemble aimless speculation, an increasing number of studies suggest that in dreaming and semi-conscious daydreaming, the brain is actively engaged in 'offline cognition',[7] variously termed stimulus-independent thought (SIT), task unrelated imagery and thoughts (TUITs)—the anagram nicely bearing connotations of intuition—and self-generated thoughts (SGTs).[8] Whatever the terminology, the idea that mind-wandering can be, rather than escapism or distraction, a form of active cognition, supports the positive association of wool-gathering with writing claimed by Virginia Woolf.

## The form of Woolf's novels and the science of mind-wandering

The possibility of constructive mind-wandering has strong implications for our reading of *Mrs. Dalloway* and *To the Lighthouse*. On the first pages of both novels, we immediately confront the way thoughts hop about in time and space. Clarissa's mind leaps from what she is about to do that day, to what others will be doing, to an imagined scene of children on a beach, and then to memories of her girlhood. After the first spoken words in *To the Lighthouse*, we plunge into the internal world of Mrs. Ramsay's son James, leaping from expected future joy (going to the lighthouse the next day) to present delight (cutting out a picture of a refrigerator, fringed in his mind with 'heavenly bliss'). We then shift into his mother's mind, and follow her own leap from the present image of James to the imagined future of his becoming a judge. Such leaps both within characters' minds and between characters' minds can be discomforting, until we realise that the flexible freedom conferred by this inner world contrasts with the constraints of the outer (the weather's prevention of the imagined sail and Mr. Ramsay's 'no'). Early feminist criticism identified such associative logic or lateral thinking as a particularly female mode.[9] As the example of James suggests, however, Woolf did not limit such possibilities to women, although in her historical analysis of gender roles she argues that over the course of the nineteenth century, such thinking became identified primarily with women and largely repressed in men.[10] But Woolf turns around the pejorative conclusion that women are scatter-brained to suggest that women are more easily capable of mobile and flexible self-generated thoughts; then further, by employing such leaps in her narrative structure, she invites readers, irrespective of gender, to engage in such thought themselves. Reading such passages can be an enjoyable experience of freedom, if we can allow the linear plot to drop into the background (the hours, after all, chime throughout *Mrs. Dalloway* and one of the underlying structuring principles in *To the Lighthouse* is a journey). But if 'wool-gathering' is actually productive work, we might wonder, what is this flexibility for?

Although neuroscientific work on mind-wandering is still in its early stages, studies are beginning to link one particular neural network to forms of free-floating internally generated thought. Functional magnetic resonance imaging (fMRI) and other forms of tracking neural activity indicate that mind-wandering activates connected regions of the brain termed the default mode network, so-called because it was first serendipitously observed in so-called default conditions or 'resting states' before subjects began to work on an assigned task.[11] Some studies further show that mind-wandering has the potential to be creatively productive, providing a crucial 'incubation' period that enables 'creative solutions' and 'moments of inspiration', particularly when the 'thoughts or activities [are] not deliberately aimed at solving the problem [the conscious minds] were trying to solve'.[12] Rather than being overtly task-*oriented*, such thoughts can be task-*related*, responding to previously instigated dilemmas or 'unresolved longstanding conflicts' temporarily set aside. Mind-wandering has consequently been defined as 'a decoupling of attention from an immediate task context toward unrelated concerns' (Mooneyham and Schooler, 11). Much like the inspiration that can suddenly spring to mind when we think of a problem and then 'sleep on it', mind-wandering can indirectly generate a novel response once our conscious minds have set some question or situation as the scene.

To date, most attention has been paid to the *fact* that our minds are drifting away from the present, but cognitive researchers are increasingly tracking and differentiating the *kinds* of 'thought' that mind-wandering can involve. Early work tended to focus on literal and straightforward examples: replaying the past or rehearsing for the future. A current overview of recent work in the area, however, describes the experience as 'a complex and heterogeneous phenomena', involving 'associative or constructive processes'; analysis of these processes reveals 'multiple interacting dimensions', not only content features such as 'personal significance, temporal orientation, valence [positive or negative attributes and] social orientation' but also expressive characteristics such as 'level of specificity/detail, somatosensory awareness, and representational format (inner speech vs. visual imagery)'.[13] As researchers attempt to understand and describe the nature and the form of such thought processes, the goals of neuroscientific and literary analysis begin to converge.

Associative leaps and seemingly disconnected thoughts have been well recognised as features both in Woolf's characters' consciousnesses and in the form of her fiction itself.[14] H. Porter Abbott refers to her 'passages of aimless wandering' and 'intermittent narrative meanderings';[15] Laura Marcus analyses Woolf's 'wandering, digressive narrative voices';[16] and Rebecca Walkowitz identifies Woolf's development of 'narrative forms that are *evasive*'.[17] All three critics similarly read this style as enacting a mental freedom that opposes traditional constraints. Abbott argues that the form of *Night and Day* enacts the mind's 'unencumbered freedom to ramble',[18] countering the 'romance heroics' of the classic male narrative, governed by the trope of 'penetrating into an unexplored place' and extracting a 'long-buried prize'.[19] Marcus, who opposes unencumbered 'wool-gathering' to coercive 'shepherding',[20] argues that the former 'gives the mind the freedom to wander' and 'opens up imaginative possibilities', defying 'a rigidly analytical or logical line of argument' and the valorisation of social hierarchy and militarism embedded in 'the masculine point of view'.[21] For Walkowitz, Woolf opposes 'the wandering unpeacefulness of agitated thinking' to the 'unagitated attentiveness' essential to 'public triumphalism', showing 'how intellectual speculation, because it thwarts compliance, resists the passivity of wartime' and the unthinking acceptance of the categorical and hierarchical judgements embedded in patriotic thought.[22]

Such criticism usefully exposes the political resonances in the way we think and write, and it helps to show how Woolf's particular mode of writing promotes expansion rather than contraction of the mind. Walkowitz, for example, points to the way Woolf's narrative disrupts the inexorable march of linear progression through its tendency 'to stop, change direction, turn in on itself', and Walkowitz further connects 'strategies of [evasive] thought' to 'strategies of writing': 'poetic language, nick-naming, excitement, stammering, revision, and parataxis'.[23] But we have more to learn about how such thought actually works and, if it truly promotes freedom and openness, how that effect is achieved. Just how do the minds of Woolf's characters wander, and what makes their wandering different from the insidious debilitating habit educators deplore? What multiple dimensions does such thinking involve? If such thoughts are self-generated, what role, if any, does the immediate environment play? And perhaps most significantly, does such meandering take place in a context of 'remote concerns', and if so, does it yield new or creative responses? Is such thought *merely* liberating, or is it creative-productive as well?

## Mrs. Ramsay's wool-gathering

Mrs. Ramsay, being a self-confessed 'wool-gatherer', makes a good starting point for our analysis, and indeed Part I, section 5 of *To the Lighthouse*, focalised through Mrs. Ramsay, attracted the first sustained attention to Woolf's representation of consciousness many years ago. Writing in the 1940s about Woolf's mimetic internal reality, Erich Auerbach attributed the distinctive quality of 'modern narrative literature' to its rendering of 'the continuous ruminations of consciousness in its natural and purposeless freedom'.[24] Interlacing Auerbach's analysis now with the questions arising out of contemporary neuro-science, we can probe more deeply into the various forms Mrs. Ramsay's mind-wandering takes, asking how they differ, and how they interrelate.

Auerbach summarises the frame of external action in the novel's beginning: Mrs. Ramsay's attempt to measure the length of the stocking, for which she needs James to stand still. Consuming the first eight paragraphs, the performed action—as Auerbach indicates—takes place in just a few minutes or even seconds of actual time. We thus have a brief, immediate goal-oriented task—measuring the stocking—but one not so demanding of Mrs. Ramsay's attention that her mind is unable to rummage concurrently through other thoughts, both imagining the future and rehearsing the past. Catching sight of William and Lily together, her mind leaps to future planning (they must marry); returning to her current surroundings, she mentally surveys the house, its furniture, and its books, worrying about their growing shabbiness; thinking next of the need for closed doors and open windows, she remembers Marie, her Swiss *au pair,* staring out the window on the previous evening with tears in her eyes and speaking of the mountains at home but, Mrs. Ramsay guesses, thinking of her dying father— a complicated digression that mixes remembering the past with imaginatively constructing what another person feels. With thoughts so clearly decoupled from measuring the stocking, and so mobile in time, space, and person, Mrs. Ramsay is wool-gathering, yet her thoughts hover about a resistant problem, which Auerbach describes as 'the cruel meaninglessness of life whose continuance she is never-theless striving with all her powers to abet, support, and secure'.[25] Interfacing the inner and outer—two of these trains of thought, after all, are instigated by what Mrs. Ramsay sees around her—the immedi-ate task triggers or at least reinforces the nagging concern. Thinking of her silence when she looked at Marie, Mrs. Ramsay seems to feel the inadequacy of her response to the girl's sorrow, fearing that, like the stocking, she is coming up short. The incredible sadness at the end of the passage, which would be comic if instigated only by a short stocking, takes on deeper significance as a response to the shortness of life.

The opening section thus depicts a meandering that is not fully random and free; although associative and constructive, it circles around a central disturbance at the core. Also, while decoupled from the immediate task, it is still bound to immediate problems: an embodied image schema—in this case, measuring and coming up short—reveals a disturbing connection between overt action and mental state.[26] Mrs. Ramsay's mind-wandering thus seems more per-severative than creative, yet it also enacts the work of multi-tasking in a traditional woman's world. Shifting from James, to Lily, and then to Marie, Mrs. Ramsay monitors her surrounding environment, trying to detect if there is anything for others that she should do, or she pro-jects into the future, trying to anticipate her children's lives and needs.

However, a noticeable difference in mind-wandering occurs when Mrs. Ramsay is fully alone, when her thoughts are decoupled both from attention-demanding tasks and from her self-construction as a woman who must fulfil a responsible role. The experience is like '[l]osing personality', but loss of the world-oriented self opens a path to unbounded, expansive experience: 'this self having shed its attachments was free for the strangest adventures' (*TL*, 52–53). Mrs. Ramsay's thoughts now exhibit explorative, multi-directional mind-wandering; rather than the limited form of merely wandering away from the present, mind-wandering now involves imaginatively wandering, randomly and freely, about. As if in a dream, Mrs. Ramsay sees 'the Indian plains' and feels herself 'pushing aside the thick leather curtain of a church in Rome'; she experiences herself as 'a wedge-shaped core of darkness' that 'could go anywhere' (*TL*, 53). Rather than her actual thoughts, we are most likely reading, to use Dorrit Cohn's term, 'psycho-analogies' for internal experience, as Mrs. Ramsay responds to the need 'to think; well, not even to think. To be silent; to be alone' (*TL*, 52). Her mind slips into a mode of day-dreaming, sometimes termed *hypnagogia*—a semi-conscious state on the verge of consciousness, but not in the conscious realm. Hovering somewhere between thoughts and feelings, daydreaming takes her further and further away from herself, into a realm unbounded by human experience: a state in which Mrs. Ramsay 'became the thing she looked at', and when, being drawn to 'inanimate things; trees, streams, flowers', she 'felt they expressed one; felt they became one felt they knew one, in a sense were one' (*TL*, 53). Today this experience might be termed the extended mind: a state in which cognition is distributed into the environment. And for Mrs. Ramsay, its effects are two-fold: a diminishment of self-orientation and a feeling of merg-ing into a holistic universe. What is involved is a positive surrender to existence beyond the self, an expansion into life's embodiment in the world.

While free and unbounded, however, Mrs. Ramsay's experience still responds to remote concerns. The 'tasks' in the background of her mind-wandering are actions of gathering together: first picking up the scattered pictures that her son James has been cutting out of a catalogue, then knitting the skeins of wool into the stocking. And her need for a psychologically integrative experience seems answered when the troublesomeness of the daily world's 'fret', 'hurry' and 'stir' is soothed by the feeling of 'this peace, this rest, this eternity' (*TL,* 53). The translation of this feeling into consciousness, however, is problematic. The words that suddenly spring into her mind are, 'We are in the hands of the Lord' (*TL,* 53). Waking into consciousness implicates the habituated familiarities of language, prompting, out of her memories, a cliché that does not accord with her own belief. Yet interpreted as a response that reconstitutes in reductive conscious language a holistic experience at the semi-conscious level, the words capture the positive-constructive elements of her waking dream. If Mrs. Ramsay's remote concerns are her own inadequacies in solving life's problems and the inexorability of death, mind-wandering here enables her to consign responsibility to a universe larger than humanity, achieving a momentary peace through an acceptance of, and integration with, larger forces in the world.

**From mind-wandering to mindfulness**

If mind-wandering can thus lead through increasing expansion into a holistic moment of perception and awareness, then mind-wandering and mindfulness need not be antithetical forms. Indeed, Erich Auerbach interpreted Woolf's departures from the present narrative, which he termed 'excursus', as a 'transfer of confidence' from linear narrative to the 'random moment', revealing, in the process, 'nothing less than the wealth or reality and depth of life in every moment to which we surrender ourselves without prejudice' (552).[27] Mind-wandering might then be a route to mindfulness, but that claim requires us to recognise that, like mind-wandering, mindfulness takes different forms.

As cognitive scientists working in the area readily admit, studies of mindfulness, like mind-wandering, suffer from 'the absence of consensus about an operational definition'.[28] Just as mind-wandering can mean debilitating distraction or productive incubation, mindfulness can refer either to sustained task-focused attention or to receptive openness to 'what[ever] is occurring, before or beyond conceptual and emotional classifications about what is or has taken place'.[29] The first approach focuses on our 'ability to exert attentional and emotional control in the present moment, and, thereby, bring awareness to immediate experiences';[30] the second involves actually inhibiting our attentional drives by allowing 'spontaneous thoughts, images, sensations, memories, and emotions to emerge and pass freely without actively controlling or pursuing them'.[31] Studies thus distinguish between 'concentrative' and 'non-directed' meditation, between mindfulness training that seeks to enhance self-regulated attention for greater productivity and meditative practices that inculcate non-judgemental awareness of the present moment and 'the liberating insight of the emptiness of the self'.[32] Within the latter forms of meditation, distinctions can also be made between those practices that emphasise 'detachment' and those that foster 'acceptance and appreciation of one's "aliveness"'.[33]

Whereas distracted mind-wandering is antithetical to mindfulness focused on attention, exploratory mind-wandering and mindful awareness may actually interconnect. Both these latter processes involve suspension, or at least reduction, of logical, conscious control, and both differ 'from usual wakefulness, which is usually characterized by several biases, defenses, or ruminative thinking'.[34] Arguments for continuity are further supported by studies showing that 'nondirective meditation involves more extensive activation of the default mode network',[35] the brain regions similarly activated in resting state activity and self-generated thoughts.[36] Default mode activity furthermore appears to be inversely correlated with the activity of the frontoparietal control/dorsal attention network,[37] suggesting again that holistic mindfulness and exploratory mind-wandering both employ mental processes that contrast with attentional modes.

Cognitive studies of interactions among these various processes have focused on the well-recognised antithesis between distractive mind-wandering and concentrative mindfulness and, more recently, on the importance of being able to toggle back and forth between attentional and resting states. Woolf's novels push us further, however, to consider possibly positive interactions connecting the two *non-attentional* modes: exploratory mind-wandering and non-directed mindfulness. The digressions, wandering and evasiveness so strongly noted as features of her novels seem actually to enable the moments of holistic perception Woolf herself termed 'moments of being'.[38] Fiction may thus be revealing a significant connection: in certain forms, mind-wandering and mindfulness may be parts of one continuous stream.

## Peter Walsh's cognitive shifts

A short but highly condensed passage in *Mrs. Dalloway* offers, in striking miniature, a paradigmatic modelling of such processes at work. Peter Walsh has taken a taxi from Regent's Park to Lincoln's Inn Fields to consult with his lawyer, a direct task-oriented activity that the narrative significantly omits. Returning on foot to his hotel in Bloomsbury, he hears the bell of an ambulance, which the reader understands is the ambulance picking up Septimus's body after he flings himself from a window in his Bloomsbury flat. Peter and Septimus have encountered each other before—literally that day, in Regent's Park. A further imaginative encounter now takes place in Peter's thoughts. In the overt action, Peter is walking down a street he knows well, a low-resource-demand task that leaves his mind free to wander where it will. And impressively, in the space of one paragraph, his mind performs over twenty cognitive shifts. With some repetition and recurrence, he meanders through abstract reflections on the scene, observations of his immediate environment, imagining what has happened to the victim, observing what the traffic is doing, imagining what the drivers are thinking, remembering how people in India have judged his emotional nature and remembering previous incidents that day. Peter is cognitively mobile in time, space and person, evidencing empathetic and emotional capabilities far beyond the flattening, generalising tendencies that Walkowitz identifies with imperialist thought.[39]

Up to this point, Peter's thoughts appear to be conscious, though he is likely not thinking in such articulate words and sentences. When Peter recalls his visit to Clarissa that morning, however, a cognitive sea-change takes place: he falls into a day-dreaming, hypnagogic state, like Mrs. Ramsay in her solitude. The style and syntax of his internal narrative suddenly change, losing correspondence to external reality and logical sense. Feeling exhaustion due to 'the weight of the day', and 'its heat, its intensity', he follows 'the drip, drip, of one impression after another down into that cellar where they stood, deep, dark, and no one would ever know' (MD, 136). Who is standing and in what cellar? The reader has to make a sudden turn into the barely perceptible regions of non-conscious thought, running after the rapid transitions it enacts: 'he had found life like an unknown garden, full of turns and corners, surprising, yes; really it took one's breath away, these moments; there coming to him by the pillar-box opposite the British Museum one of them, a moment, in which things came together; this ambulance; and life and death' (MD, 136). The passage has taken us from reductive generalisation through free, exploratory mind-wandering to a moment of holistic awareness. And the process has a liberating, creative effect.

As I have mentioned, Peter is mind-wandering during an activity with a low attentional demand, thus safely and not with great risk. His mind-wandering also occurs in the context of remote concerns: the agitation he has been feeling all day lurks in the background, declaring itself briefly as 'that visit to Clarissa' (*MD*, 136). How can he hold together his contradictory feelings about her, his anger, his love? How can he resolve for himself who Clarissa really is, when she appears in such contradictory roles? The problems of the self, however, are through mind-wandering expanded outwards into the environment, into the realm of other minds, and into a mystical journey that involves a descent into a cellar and a sudden emergence into gardens. The outer world enters and transforms his thoughts: he watches 'as the ambulance turned the corner' and then in a process of what we might call embodied cognition makes a turn himself into a vision of life 'full of turns and corners' (*MD*, 136). The culminating experience is 'of things coming together', a holding together of contraries: Clarissa's nature, his feelings, and the supreme contraries that haunt the novel—'life and death' (*MD*, 136). His conflicts furthermore resolve in a sudden apprehension of acceptance, a mindful awareness that combines self-transcendence and a feeling of 'aliveness' (Chiesa and Malinowski, 413): 'It was as if he were sucked up to some very high roof by that rush of emotion, and the rest of him, like a white shell-sprinkled beach, left bare' (*MD*, 136). Compare Mrs. Ramsay's sensation of 'some sealed vessel in her brain whose bursting would flood her in delight as the sea 'rolled in waves of pure lemon' and 'raced over the floor of her mind' (*TL*, 55). For neither character does the moment offer permanent resolution: these are not linear narratives culminating in a final recognition scene, or anagnorisis. But these scenes do show the liberating effects of exploratory mind-wandering through the smooth transition to holistic mindfulness and its moment of insight and peace.

What are the implications, then, of such passages for reading each novel as a whole? The analysis here can certainly be extended to other scenes, comparing, for example, Mrs. Ramsay's quiet thoughts in solitude with Clarissa's when she is mending her dress—another low-resource-demand task—while the repetitive motion of her needle becomes the rhythm of waves, rocking her mind into a dreamy, hypnagogic state. For Clarissa, too, the irritations and imperfections of life and her own self are soothed by flowing outwards and merging into the world, allowing her temporarily to shed the burden of self-responsibility in a holistic awareness underpinning her belief that 'the unseen part of us, which spreads wide, the unseen might survive, be recovered somehow attached to this person or that, or even haunting certain places after death' (*MD*, 137). This apprehension of an extended self also links Peter's imagining of Septimus's death with Clarissa's projecting herself into Septimus's falling body, another wandering that leads to a full awareness of the richness of the moment and a meditative merging of self-transcendence and the feeling of 'aliveness'. One step back from the characters, we can consider the way the narrating consciousness in these novels leads us to wander in and out of other people's minds, and through houses—the Ramsays' house in the 'Time Passes' section and the Dalloways' house in the party scene. The 'Time Passes' section in particular is narrated in a kind of day-dreaming state from which we are abruptly wakened, with Lily, at its end.

Of course the close reading of these scenes isn't itself mind-wandering, but readers may be participating in, even temporarily surrendering their own mental processes to, the mental processes encoded in the wandering structures that operate in tandem with the linear plot. And such simulated mind-wandering can perhaps lead to a mindful experience of the whole, in a state somewhat removed from conscious, logical thought. In Woolf's own theories of reading, she often urged a surrendering immersion in the text, followed by more distanced analysis and critique; at other times, she wrote of conscious and non-conscious processes working almost imperceptibly together, with flashes of non-conscious thought forging the links that produce the apparent seamlessness of conscious thought.[40] But while Woolf reminds us in various ways of the need to toggle back and forth between attentional and non-attentional states, she clearly perceived a positive role for the non-attentional: exploratory wandering can facilitate moments of holistic mindful awareness that break up habitual rigidities and enable creative leaps. Thus the reader, I suggest, is solicited to share in Peter's creative leap at the end of *Mrs. Dalloway*. His final words, 'It is Clarissa' (*MD*, 174), sum up not one definitive discrete identity but a mindful apprehension of the whole of Clarissa, incorporating all her contradictions but also extending to everyone she has known and every place she has been, even people she doesn't know, and places she's never been. For the reader, the culminating experience of the novel may similarly be not a unified meaning but a mindful apprehension of the multi-faceted and complex whole of the novel that is given Clarissa's name. And from there, we may make our own creative leaps.

### Notes

1  'In the latest kind of novel—Virginia Woolf's, for example—events have become merely interruptions in a long wool-gathering process, a process, that is used chiefly to provide occasions for little prose poems.' Desmond MacCarthy (1931), 'The Bubble Reputation', *Life and Letters,* 7 (September), 182.

2  Virginia Woolf, *Orlando* (1928; rpt. London: Penguin, 2011), p. 187.
3  Virginia Woolf, *A Passionate Apprentice: The Early Journals, 1897–1909*, ed. Mitchell Leaska (London: Hogarth, 1990), p. 182.
4  Jonah Lehrer, *Proust was a Neuroscientist* (Boston/New York: Houghton Mifflin, 2007), p. 182.
5  B. W. Mooneyham and J. W. Schooler (2013) 'The costs and benefits of mind-wandering: A review', *Canadian Journal of Experimental Psychology*, 67.1, 12–13.
6  C. Ottaviani and A. Couyoumdjian (2013) 'Pros and cons of a wandering mind: A prospective study', *Frontiers in Psychology*, 4.524, 1–9.
7  Unlike the Freudian model, in which dreams are 'read' for symbolic significance, these cognitive approaches focus on the dream's constructive process as on-going interpretive activity. See E. J. Wamsley and R. Stickgold (2010) 'Dreaming and offline memory processing', *Current Biology*, 20.23, R1010–R1013.
8  SGT, as a broad category, includes thoughts that are overtly goal-directed, as long as achieving the goal requires internally directed thought. Mind-wandering, another subcategory of SGT, is decoupled from immediate tasks, although it may be indirectly responsive to remote concerns.
9  See Melba Cuddy-Keane, 'Narratological Approaches', in *Virginia Woolf Studies*, ed. Anna Snaith (Basingstoke/New York: Palgrave Macmillan, 2007), pp. 24–26.
10  See *R/TG*, pp. 124–37.
11  M. E. Raichle and A. Z. Snyder (2007) 'A default mode of brain function: A brief history of an evolving idea', *NeuroImage*, 37, 1083–1090.
12  B. Baird, J. Smallwood, M. D. Mrazek, J. W. Y. Kam, M. S. Franklin and J. W. Schooler (2012) 'Inspired by distraction: Mind wandering facilitates creative incubation', *Psychological Science*, 23.10, 1117–1122.
13  J. R. Andrews-Hanna, J. Smallwood, and R. N. Spreng (2014) 'The default network and self-generated thought: component processes, dynamic control, and clinical relevance', *Annals of the New York Academy of Science*, 1316, 32.
14  The diagram Woolf constructed for the three-part structure of *To the Lighthouse* reveals her as a conscious artist making decisions about form, but the leaps in time and space in the narrative, and the changing impression of pace imitate and instantiate meandering and momentary thought.
15  H. Porter Abbott, 'Old Virginia and the Night Writer', in *Inscribing the Daily: Critical Essays on Women's Diaries*, ed. Suzanne L. Bunkers and Cynthia A. Huff (Amherst: University of Massachusetts Press, 1996), pp. 242, 249.
16  Laura Marcus, 'Virginia Woolf and Digression: Adventures in Consciousness', in *Digressions in European Literature from Cervantes to Sebald*, ed. Alexis Grohmann and Caragh Wells (Chippenham, England: Palgrave Macmillan, 2011), p. 118.

17  Rebecca Walkowitz, 'Woolf's Evasion', in *Cosmopolitan Style: Modernism Beyond the Nation* (New York: Columbia University Press, 2006), p. 82.
18  Abbott, p. 249.
19  Ibid., p. 247.
20  Marcus, p. 123.
21  Ibid., pp. 119, 120, 122, 119.
22  Walkowitz, pp. 89, 92, 85.
23  Ibid., pp. 89, 95.
24  Erich Auerbach, 'The Brown Stocking', in *Mimesis: The Representation of Reality in Western Literature*, trans. Willard R. Trask (Princeton: Princeton University Press, 1953), p. 538.
25  Ibid., p. 531.
26  For connections between embodied and conceptual schemas, see Melba Cuddy-Keane, 'Movement, Space, and Embodied Cognition in *To the Lighthouse*', *The Cambridge Companion to Virginia Woolf's To the Lighthouse*, ed. Allison Pease (Cambridge: Cambridge University Press, 2015), pp. 58-68.
27  See H. Porter Abbott, this volume, for further discussion of Woolf's 'transfer of confidence' (Auerbach, 1953) from emplotted linear narrative to a meandering style, and Abbott's argument that both elements are nonetheless present in *Mrs. Dalloway* as 'conflicting narrative structures'. My own essay seeks to understand the cognitive processes involved on the non-linear side, suggesting, however, despite a tension, the need to 'toggle' back and forth between logical and associative modes.
28  A. Chiesa and P. Malinowski (2011) 'Mindfulness-based approaches: Are they all the same?', *Journal of Clinical Psychology*, 67.4, 405.
29  Ibid., 406.
30  R. S. Prakash, A. A. De Leon, M. Klatt, W. Malarkey and B. Patterson (2013) 'Mindfulness disposition and default-mode network connectivity in older adults', *Social Cognitive and Affective Neuroscience*, 8.1, 112.
31  J. Xu, A. Vik, I. R. Groote, J. Lagopoulos, A. Holen, Ø. Ellingsen, A. K. Håberg and S. Davanger (2014) 'Nondirective meditation activates default mode network and areas associated with memory retrieval and emotional processing', *Frontiers in Human Neuroscience*, 8.86, 2.
32  Chiesa and Malinowski, 411. Although focused and exploratory modes are generally antithetical, techniques in mindfulness training fall along a spectrum between the two poles, even shifting from one to the other. The practice of effortful, directed meditation, for example, can evolve, in skilled practitioners, into effortless non-directed meditation.
33  Ibid., 413.
34  Ibid., 406.
35  Xu *et al.*, 6.
36  See Andrews-Hanna et al.
37  P. J. Hellyer, M. Shanahan, G. Scott, R. J. S. Wise, D. J. Sharp and R. Leech (2014) 'The control of global brain dynamics: opposing

actions of frontoparietal control and default mode networks on attention', *Journal of Neuroscience* 34.2, 451–61.

38  Virginia Woolf, *Moments of Being*, ed. Jeanne Schulkind (New York: Harvest, 1985).

39  Walkowitz also highlights the importance of this passage, which she suggests may be the climax of the novel. Rather than a single climax, however, the non-linear plot of consciousness offers multiple significant moments that accumulate in effect. The development of Peter's thoughts in this paragraph also reveals how far he travels beyond his initial response to the ambulance as 'one of the triumphs of civilization' (*MD*, 135)—a summation that, as Walkowitz points out, occludes the insensitivity of Septimus's doctors and the exploitation that enabled imperialist success.

40  For Woolf's views on conscious and non-conscious reading processes, see Melba Cuddy-Keane, *Virginia Woolf, the Intellectual, and the Public Sphere* (Cambridge: Cambridge University Press, 2003), pp. 122–132.

# 2

# Spirituality in *Mrs. Dalloway* and *To the Lighthouse*

Heather Ingman

## Introduction: Wrestling with Christianity

At the age of fifteen or sixteen, as she recalled in her diary, Virginia Woolf wrote a long essay on the Christian religion 'proving that man has need of a God; but the God was described in process of change' (*D* III, 271; entry for 8 December 1929). The topic of spirituality in Woolf's fiction may seem counterintuitive, given that Woolf was surrounded by agnostics and sceptics all her life and frequently expressed marked hostility to institutional religion, particularly as embodied in a patriarchal Church of England. Her letters and diaries reveal, however, that despite her agnostic upbringing, Woolf continued to read the Bible and wrestle with Christianity throughout her life. She was unafraid to use language that had connotations of the sacred, explaining once to Ethel Smyth: 'irreligious as I am (to your eyes) I have a devout belief in the human soul' (*L* IV, 208).

The fact that Woolf occasionally employed vocabulary with religious resonances has begun to attract the attention not only of literary critics but also of theologians.[1] General studies by scholars such as Pericles Lewis, Suzanne Hobson and Erik Tonning have queried the equation of modernism with secularism.[2] Their linking of the interiority of modernism with writers' exploration of realms beyond the everyday has an obvious bearing on Woolf's attention in her work to moments of heightened consciousness. As described in her unfinished memoir, 'A Sketch of the Past' (1939–40), these intense, visionary moments producing feelings of insight into the mystery of the world akin to those of the mystics, but without their corresponding religious revelation, were essential to Woolf's view of life and her sense of herself as an artist.[3]

Although Woolf cannot be allied with any orthodox religious belief, scholars have discerned biblical influences and Christian iconography in both *Mrs. Dalloway* and *To the Lighthouse*. In the former, Septimus's death may be interpreted as the ritual sacrifice of the scapegoat/Christ figure redeemed and given meaning by Clarissa Dalloway. Other biblical echoes include the Edenic paradise (Bourton) from which Clarissa has been excluded and the eucharistic communion represented by Clarissa's party, offering the possibility of healing and reconciliation to a post-war world.[4] In *To the Lighthouse* Mrs. Ramsay may be likened to a Christ figure presiding over a ceremonial Last Supper before the outbreak of the First World War, and there are biblical echoes in the expiatory pilgrimage to the lighthouse and in Lily's Madonna with Child painting.

These biblical echoes have, however, to be balanced against passages that display hostility to institutional religion, notably in *Mrs. Dalloway* in the portrayal of Miss Kilman, whose evangelical Christianity is linked, in Clarissa's eyes, with an imperialistic urge to dominate and convert. She particularly resents her influence over her daughter. For Clarissa the danger of a religion like Miss Kilman's is that it destroys 'the privacy of the soul', the interior private world that she identifies with her elderly neighbour opposite quietly climbing the stairs to her room (*MD*, 113). Yet in *To the Lighthouse* Charles Tansley's atheism is portrayed as equally unattractive, part obsequious imitation of Mr. Ramsay's scepticism, part product, like Miss Kilman's religion, of class resentment.

A close reading of both novels suggests that, although Woolf borrows language from the Bible and from Christian liturgy, her work is resistant to ideological rigidity of any kind. Woolf's feeling that it was impossible to 'write directly about the soul' (*D* III, 62; entry for 27 February 1926) may have been partly prompted by her reading of recently translated Russian authors such as Chekhov and Dostoevsky, whose treatment of spiritual questions she praises in 'Modern Novels' (1919), contrasting them favourably with the materialism of her Edwardian predecessors.[5] She comes back to this point about the importance of the soul in Russian writers in 'The Russian Point of View' (1925), published as she was working on *To the Lighthouse*. The language of the original holograph draft of *To the Lighthouse* is more specifically religious than that of the final version. In this first draft Lily is a church-going Christian, Charles Tansley's atheism is subject to lengthy attack, and Mr. Bankes reflects on the decay of religious belief, which he associates with that sceptical follower of Hume, Mr. Ramsay.[6] In the final version of the novel, Woolf's language tends towards greater subtlety and indirection and it is in writing about the elusiveness of the soul that Woolf is at her most distinctive. At the same time her treatment of spirituality incorporates many intellectual influences characteristic of the modernist era.

## Ritual

One of these influences is Jane Harrison's work on matriarchal civilisations. It is noticeable that both in *Mrs. Dalloway* and *To the Lighthouse* women preside over the eucharistic ritual, dispensing hospitality and food to their guests. In reality, women were barred from the priesthood, an exclusion for which Woolf takes the Church of England to task in *Three Guineas*. Jane Harrison, like many of the Cambridge Ritualists, was interested in investigating ancient rituals and the myths that developed from them, building on James Frazer's discussion of religion from an anthropological perspective in *The Golden Bough* (1890). Woolf met Harrison on several occasions and her library contained a copy of Harrison's *Ancient Art and Ritual* (1913), in which she defined ritual as a collective experience aimed at the public good. Harrison's definition provided a bridge between art and religion that was to influence Woolf to the end of her career. In *Mrs. Dalloway* and *To the Lighthouse* Woolf draws on Christian iconography but augments it with Greek models in which women were permitted to act as priestesses.

Harrison's studies of Greek mythology led her to trace the way in which in Greek religion the mother goddess came to be robbed of her power: Demeter and Kore, mother and maid, were not, she explained, two women originally, but aspects of one goddess, representing woman before and after maturity. In *Mythology* (1924) and in the earlier *Prolegomena to the Study of Greek Religion* (1903), Harrison linked the decline of the power of the mother goddess to the thwarting of women in the patriarchy and argued that retrieving her power would liberate women's creativity. In *Mythology*, Harrison depicts matriarchal societies as communal, co-operative and life-giving, encouraging women's independence and creativity and fostering egalitarian relationships between women and men. For Harrison retrieving ancient matriarchal societies was not merely a historical exercise, but part of her search for the primal female principle in the collective unconscious.

Harrison's work confirmed for Woolf certain ideas she had been groping towards for years concerning the connection between the retrieval of the buried mother in a patriarchal society, the daughter's consequent sense of empowerment and female creativity. In *Mrs. Dalloway* the power of the mother goddess, embodied in the plaster cast of Ceres, has been destroyed during the war. The goddess's power lies so deeply buried in this post-war society that it lingers in the minds of the characters only as a faint, far-off memory, surfacing occasionally in brief moments of sympathy between women, connecting imagery of waves and flowers, an old beggar woman's semiotic babble and in Peter's dream of an all-encompassing maternal figure who will 'shower down from her magnificent hands, compassion, comprehension, absolution' (*MD*, 51). The novel depicts a society based on a mind/body dualism that is the opposite of the goddess's world as portrayed by Harrison. Septimus separates himself from his mother and attempts to cultivate manliness by joining the army where his suppression of bodily desire is demonstrated in his inability to mourn the loss of his homoerotic relationship with Evans. He thwarts Rezia's urge to maternity and, by bringing her to England, cuts her off from her female-centred world in Italy. In his madness Septimus is tormented by messianic notions that he must replicate Christ's sacrifice by killing himself in order to save the world. It is because he is able to see himself only in terms of a suffering Christ figure that he feels despair and Christianity thus becomes implicated in his insanity and eventual suicide.

Clarissa too internalises her society's suppression of female power. She feels that her body has no value now that it is past childbearing. Unlike Septimus, however, she does not repress her same-sex desire, remembering her kiss with Sally Seton as the high point of her life. Religious vocabulary becomes entwined with the erotic as Clarissa recalls 'the revelation, the religious feeling' (*MD*, 32) inspired by Sally's kiss. However, the kiss between Clarissa and Sally is ended by Peter's determination to separate them: the ancient matriarchal world of the goddess, a community of women-identified women, is glimpsed and then destroyed. Though embattled as she is in a matricidal society, Clarissa partly succeeds in expressing her impulse to create and connect, to bring people together and offer healing after the lacerations of the recent war. In this sense her party may be seen as acting out Harrison's definition of ritual as a collective experience aimed at ensuring the continued existence of the group. It also functions as a lingering remnant of Harrison's ancient matriarchy: significantly, it is at the party that Clarissa's mother is mentioned for the only

time in the novel. And it is at the party that Clarissa empathises with
Septimus's suicide and turns it into something meaningful, displacing
the father God of Judaeo-Christian tradition and accepting the son's
sacrifice.

In *To the Lighthouse* Mrs. Ramsay, like Clarissa, resists belief in an
external patriarchal God, yet remains committed to doing good for
its own sake, to acts of charity to her neighbours, to promoting harmony in her household of husband, children and guests. Like a pagan
goddess, Mrs. Ramsay is on the side of life, marriage and fertility,
encouraging the marriage of Minta and Paul. It is she who is able to
restore her husband to life after his moments of self-doubt and she
who makes William Bankes, who worships her, believe she can subdue
chaos and triumph over barbarity. She presides over her children's
lives like a divinity, so that, sitting beside her, young James 'endowed
the picture of a refrigerator as his mother spoke with heavenly bliss'
(*TL*, 7). Her role at dinner, like Clarissa's at the party, has overtones
of the administration of the sacraments; indeed the voices round the
dinner table remind Mrs. Ramsay of 'a service in some … cathedral'
(*TL*, 89). The lighting of the candles, Mrs. Ramsay's sacramental gestures as she holds her hands over the *boeuf en daube* prior to distribut-
ing it in an echo of Christ blessing the bread and the wine, Augustus
Carmichael holding his napkin like a long white robe, chanting and
then bowing to Mrs. Ramsay as she departs, all echo the liturgy of the
mass. As in Jane Harrison's work, ritual is in the service of the public
good. Mrs. Ramsay feeds her family spiritually, binding them into a
sacred community; as soon as she absents herself 'disintegration' sets
in, recalling the fate of the disciples after Christ's death.

Yet if Mrs. Ramsay is a goddess, she is a flawed one. Deeply sexist and in awe of masculine intelligence, she is not an empowering
maternal figure for her daughters who have 'infidel ideas' of a different life from hers, travelling, not always taking care of some man.
Mrs. Ramsay presides over lives she does not fully understand, urging
Minta and Paul into a marriage that will fail. Moreover, what power
she has is defeated by the war, during which her eldest son is killed,
her eldest daughter dies in childbirth and her own death is reported,
casually, in parentheses. In Part II of *To the Lighthouse* war, which in
*Three Guineas* Woolf was to equate with masculinist thinking, is a
time when the mother goddess is absent, a period of fragmentation,
darkness and destruction. Here it is the mother figure, Mrs. Ramsay,
who is the scapegoat, worn out by sacrifice on behalf of the race, as
Lily angrily acknowledges: 'Giving, giving, giving, she had died …'
(*TL*, 124).

**Visionary moments**

If Jane Harrison influenced Woolf's use of communal rituals in her fiction, many different intellectual influences may be discerned in Woolf's description of those moments of insight she experienced personally and which she lent to her characters. The books of Woolf's aunt, Caroline Stephen, on Quaker mysticism in which she argues for the authority of the individual's visionary experiences may have had some influence on Woolf's formulation of her 'moments of being'.[7] In 'A Sketch of the Past', Woolf describes such moments as intense, almost sacred moments of vision or ecstasy that disrupt everyday life momentarily transforming all around and revealing, or seeming to reveal, a pattern to life. She contrasts these moments with 'non-being', the greater part of life that is lived unconsciously. These visionary moments began in childhood when she experienced 'the most important of all my memories', that of lying in bed in the nursery in St Ives listening to the waves. 'It is of lying and hearing this splash and seeing this light, and feeling, it is almost impossible that I should be here; of feeling the purest ecstasy I can conceive' (*MB*, 65).

Woolf links these moments specifically to her vocation as a writer and various literary, rather than theological, influences have been adduced here—Plato, Wordsworth, Proust and Walter Pater:

> Perhaps this is the strongest pleasure known to me. It is the rapture I get when in writing I seem to be discovering what belongs to what; making a scene come right; making a character come together. From this I reach what I might call a philosophy; at any rate it is a constant idea of mine; that behind the cotton wool is hidden a pattern; that we—I mean all human beings—are connected with this; that the whole world is a work of art; that we are parts of the work of art. (*MB*, 72)

This intuition, she explains, has given 'scale' to her life, a belief that life is perpetually being lived 'in relation to certain background rods or conceptions'. In passages such as these, Woolf evokes her moments of being as the inspiration behind her vocation as a writer and she situates her task in groping after the pattern lying behind 'the cotton wool' of everyday life. She is adamant, however, that these private intuitions bear no relation to orthodox religion: a few lines earlier she declares 'certainly and emphatically there is no God'.

The problem for Woolf, unsupported as she was by any institutional faith, was where to find the authority for these private moments of vision. In *Mrs. Dalloway*, Septimus's breakdown, drawn from Woolf's own experience of insanity, causes him to perceive the connection of all living things.[8] He believes that birds sing messages to him and that the skywriting plane is signalling to him in secret code. He is convinced his messianic perceptions amount to the birth of a new religion. Septimus's ecstasies are clearly linked to his madness and to his conviction that he has been given a secret insight into life. They reveal Woolf's anxiety about her own bouts of psychosis and her fear that her visionary insights, and even her creativity, might in some way be connected with her illness. Indeed she was to write in her diary for 1930: 'I believe these illnesses are in my case—how shall I express it?—partly mystical' (*D III*, 287; entry for 16 February 1930). Given her fear that her moments of being might amount to no more than the vagaries of her own mind imposing patterns on life where there were none, Woolf was motivated to seek authority for them in the intellectual currents of the day.

Woolf was not alone amongst writers in the modernist era in being preoccupied with visionary insights: writers like W.B. Yeats, T.S. Eliot, Ezra Pound, May Sinclair, Mary Butts and H.D. were all interested in exploring mystical traditions that crossed religious boundaries, particularly Eastern religions and philosophies. Evelyn Underhill, one of the chief architects of the mystic revival during this period, displays in *Practical Mysticism* (1914) influences ranging from Henri Bergson to Rabindranath Tagore. Underhill argues that, far from being an esoteric pastime for an elite, mysticism is potentially within everyone's reach and, in simple, non-technical language, she outlines ways of training one's consciousness to reach new levels of awareness. Underhill's refusal to separate spirituality from everyday experience chimes in with Woolf's emphasis on immanence but, unlike Underhill's, the language Woolf uses to describe her mystic experiences slips away from any belief in a transcendent being. Woolf's visionary moments make most sense as private moments of insight linked not to religion but to the energising impulse behind her art.

The languages of science and psychoanalysis also fed into Woolf's conception of her moments of vision. For many, the emergence of Einstein's theories of relativity and even more those of quantum physics with its indeterminacy and stress on the interconnectedness between onlooker and nature, overturned nineteenth-century mechanistic and deterministic physics and invited spiritualised interpretations of science. This was notably the case of the astronomer, physicist and Quaker, Sir Arthur Eddington, whose influential study, *The Nature of the Physical World* (1928), argued that though the subjectivity and open-endedness embraced by quantum physics did not 'prove' religion, it did challenge the argument that religion was incompatible with science. The findings of quantum physics breaking down the old dualism between mind and matter were intruding into spaces that had previously been occupied by religion. In *Between the Acts* (1941), the old cronies remark: 'It's odd that science, so they tell me, is making things (so to speak) more spiritual … The very latest notion, so I'm told, is nothing's solid.'[9] However, a caveat must be entered as to the influence of wave and particle theories on the two novels under consideration here. Although Einstein's relativity and quantum theories were alluded to in newspapers from the early 1920s onwards, it was not until the 1930s that the popularising scientific work of Sir Arthur Eddington and Sir James Jeans was published that Woolf was able to use them in her subsequent fiction to affirm the validity of her modernist insights into the insubstantiality of the universe.[10] Nevertheless, scientific discussions which borrowed from the language of religion were very much part of the intellectual climate when Woolf was writing *Mrs. Dalloway* and *To the Lighthouse*.[11] The notion that the universe was less mechanistic, more uncertain than the Victorians had assumed gave Woolf confidence in her own belief that realism was not a style that accurately reflected her view of life.

It was not only the discoveries of quantum physics that paved the way to a more mystical view of the universe: psychoanalysis also provided a parallel with Woolf's interest in borderline areas of consciousness. The psychologist Henri Bergson's *Mind-Energy* (1921) contested the dualism of mind and matter and argued that there were times, for example during the mystic's trance, when the mind ran ahead of the body.[12] Bergson's distinction between linear clock time and internal psychological time, which is subjective and measured by the intensity of the moment, is relevant to Woolf's developing ideas. William James's influential study, *The Varieties of Religious Experience* (1902), looked at mysticism across religious traditions and this pluralistic view of religion led him to emphasise individual experience, rather than institutional religion, as central to the religious life.[13] In his exploration of the psychological basis for mystical experiences James argued that mystical states have to be directly experienced in order to be properly understood and that, although mystical states cannot usually be sustained for lengthy periods, some memory of their content always remains and influences the conscious life of the subject in practical ways. This focus on momentary and transient insights has much in common with Woolf's moments of being.

Woolf lends her fictional characters similar moments of insight when the characters feel at one with nature or believe they discern some purpose or pattern to life. Such moments are never associated with religious orthodoxy but are primarily motivated by a sudden and intense appreciation of life and linked to an individual's psychology. One such moment in *Mrs. Dalloway* is the kiss between Clarissa and Sally, referred to earlier. Like William James' description of mystical experiences this memory has remained with Clarissa all her life and such is the intensity of the moment that Clarissa, an avowed atheist, resorts to religious vocabulary to describe it.

The moment of visionary insight is explored further in *To the Lighthouse* in the description of the trance Mrs. Ramsay lapses into when she is alone. As she gradually lets go of her preoccupations and focuses on the rays from the lighthouse sweeping over the sea, Mrs. Ramsay sinks into a meditative state that allows her to shed the ego-centric self and merge with her surroundings:

> It was odd, she thought, how if one was alone, one leant to things, inanimate things; trees, streams, flowers; felt they expressed one; felt they became one; felt they knew one, in a sense were one; felt an irrational tenderness thus (she looked at the long steady light) as for oneself. (*TL*, 53–54)

The reader is reminded here, not only of classic accounts of mysticism, but also of the emphasis in quantum physics of the interconnection between the observer and the observed. Watching the light, Mrs. Ramsay becomes drawn in and feels at one with it until 'ecstasy burst in her eyes and waves of pure delight raced over the floor of her mind' (*TL*, 55). This moment of intuitive and emotional insight is distinguished both from Mr. Ramsay's ego-obsessed type of knowledge but also from conventional religious belief. The pious cliché, 'We are in the hands of the Lord', pops into Mrs. Ramsay's mind, irritating her: 'the insincerity slipping in among the truths roused her, annoyed her … How could any Lord have made this world?' (*TL*, 55). Woolf shows how difficult it can be to break the stranglehold of orthodox piety and move into a personal spiritual vision that more accurately reflects experience of the modern world. Times of war make this even more problematic: in Part II of *To the Lighthouse* the mystics lose faith in their visions and can articulate no answers.

Mrs. Ramsay's ability to sink into a meditative state is akin to Lily's intense artistic focus in Part III on her picture: 'Certainly she was losing consciousness of outer things' (*TL*, 132). Both women have the capacity, which Mr. Ramsay lacks, to shed egotistical preoccupations and lose themselves in experience of the other (the lighthouse, the painting). Citing the work of psychologists, Karen Armstrong has argued that mystical experiences may be seen, not as supernatural occurrences, but rather a 'quite normal, human activities for which some people have a special talent. The mystic has the ability to do certain things with his mind which is akin to the ability other people have to write poetry or compose music.'[14] It is in this light, rather than any link to established religion, that Woolf's mystic experiences, and those of her characters, make most sense.

## Immortality

The idea of an atheist discussing immortality might seem contradictory but the numerous deaths of close family members in Woolf's early years marked her with an acute awareness of the transience of life and a desire to salvage something from the devastation. Indeed she considered calling *To the Lighthouse* an elegy, for in it she raises her parents from the dead as a counter to the empiricists' arguments that people cease to exist when they are no longer there. At the very least, Woolf aimed to demonstrate, they survive in memory.

The society that Woolf portrays in *Mrs. Dalloway* and *To the Lighthouse* is one that profoundly fears ageing and death: Clarissa counts up the years, the sound of the waves makes Mrs. Ramsay start in terror at the ephemerality of life, and she covers up that *memento mori*, the boar's skull, so as not frighten Cam. It is, moreover, a society without much consolation. Whereas Septimus in his mystical madness looks for transcendent meaning everywhere, the death of Clarissa's sister in girlhood has led directly to her atheism and her conviction that there is no meaning in life unless it is created by ourselves. She has evolved what Peter calls her 'atheist's religion of doing good for the sake of goodness' (*MD*, 70), believing that one should mitigate the hardships of others without belief in God or hope for heavenly reward. Clarissa's acute awareness of the complex ways people survive in and through each other leads her to envisage spiritual connections between people who rarely, or never, meet: '… somehow in the streets of London, on the ebb and flow of things, here, there, she survived, Peter survived, lived in each other, she being part, she was positive, of the trees at home … part of people she had never met' (*MD*, 8). Michael Whitworth has detected here the vocabulary of unanism, a French school of writing that posited theories of group consciousness and was widely discussed in Britain before the First World War.[15] He points out that the vocabulary of unanism bears resemblance to the language used by contemporary spiritualists and mystics. As unanism advanced theories of emotional affinities that did not necessarily depend on physical proximity, so Clarissa's resurrection of Septimus at her party is achieved through her felt spiritual connection with the young man whom she has never met.

The theme of resurrection is not always taken seriously. In *Mrs. Dalloway* it is parodied in Peter's surprise at seeing Helena Parry, whom he had assumed to be dead, appear at Clarissa's party; in the beggar woman's song about meeting her dead lover on All Souls' Day when the spirits of the dead traditionally return; and in the recurrent refrain from *Cymbeline*, a play in which several characters thought dead are revealed to be alive. The theme is associated with irrationality: at the height of his madness Septimus believes there is no death and sees his friend Evans behind the park railings. Later he believes he himself has drowned and come back to life. Moreover, the argument for survival through others is undermined by the fragility of human life as well as by humans' capacity for forgetting or for distorting memory. Mrs. Ramsay believes that the Rayleys' marriage will be her testament but the marriage fails. Instead her memory is conserved in Lily's painting, an irony in view of Mrs. Ramsay's disparagement of Lily's artistry.

Clarissa's horror of final annihilation leads her to ponder the possibility of the disembodied human consciousness haunting not only other people's memories but places as well:

> It ended in a transcendental theory which, with her horror of death, allowed her to believe, or say that she believed (for all her scepticism), that since our apparitions, the part of us which appears, are so momentary compared with the other, the unseen part of us, which spreads wide, the unseen might survive, be recovered somehow attached to this person or that, or even haunting certain places, after death. Perhaps—perhaps. (*MD*, 136–37)

However, places may disintegrate in time just as much as people do, as Part II of *To the Lighthouse* suggests. With this in mind, Mark Häggbund argues that 'Far from redeeming death, [Mrs. Dalloway's] transcendental theory of survival bears time and loss within itself'.[16] If death can be transcended at all in Woolf it is only fleetingly.

The psychic traces surviving an individual's death form the background to Part III of *To the Lighthouse*. Without the presiding presence of Mrs. Ramsay, the house in the Hebrides seems to Lily Briscoe 'aimless' and 'chaotic', 'as if the link that usually bound things together had been cut' (*TL*, 122). She tries to recreate a structuring pattern through her painting and summons up the memory of Mrs. Ramsay to help her. At the height of Lily's struggle with her painting and despair over the randomness of life, in a scene that is not without echoes of interwar interest in séances and telepathy, Mrs. Ramsay comes in a vision to console her. In a reversal of the Demeter-Persephone myth, the daughter's desire raises the mother goddess from the underworld and she is able to complete her picture. The holograph specifically invokes the resurrection theme as Lily's intense focus on her painting is compared to 'that intensity and freedom of life which, for a few seconds after the death of the body, one imagines the souls of the dead to enjoy'.[17] The miraculous resurrection contains, though, the seeds of its own dissolution: Lily is aware that, just as the Rayleys' marriage failed, so her picture may hang forgotten in some attic.

Part III contains another kind of redemption. Mr. Ramsay, who is terrified of death, fearing in particular the consignment to oblivion of his life's work, undertakes the journey to the lighthouse in a spirit of expiation to his dead wife for his discouragement of the projected expedition in Part I. In the course of this pilgrimage towards the lighthouse he comes to accept death as an intrinsic part of life. When Macalister points out the spot where three men were drowned, rather than histrionically quoting from Cowper's poem about perishing each alone, he confounds Cam and James by simply murmuring to himself and scattering crumbs from his sandwich over the sea in what may be an echo of the funeral ceremony. Cam and James believe he is reflecting that death at sea is in the nature of things. Mr. Ramsay reaches the lighthouse in the end, through different means from Mrs. Ramsay's meditation. His achievement in acknowledging that evanescence is in the nature of things finds confirmation in Lily's echo of Christ's last words on the cross, 'It is finished', and in Mr. Carmichael who stands beside her 'like an old pagan god' and blesses mankind (*TL,* 169).

Woolf's experience of moments of being, her probing of what may survive of us and in general her interest in strange and unsettling states of mind, made her dissatisfied with the realist mode and thus the theme of spirituality in her work becomes entwined with the intellectual and aesthetic explorations of modernism. The ideologically rigid (Miss Kilman, Charles Tansley), the insane (Septimus) or the conventionally pious (Reverend Edward Whittaker) are convinced of a structuring pattern behind life. By contrast Woolf's seers (Clarissa, Mrs. Ramsay, Lily) are vouchsafed only glimpses: if there is a pattern it is always dissolving. As Lily recognises in Part III of *To the Lighthouse* truth can only ever be fragmentary: 'The great revelation had never come. The great revelation perhaps never did come. Instead there were little daily miracles, illuminations, matches struck unexpectedly in the dark' (*TL,* 133). By focused meditation (Lily in front of her painting, Mrs. Ramsay mesmerised by the light from the lighthouse) a vision may be granted but only momentarily.

At the time of writing *Mrs. Dalloway* Woolf was also composing her essay on Montaigne in which, reflecting on the theme of impermanence in Montaigne, she observed: 'Moment and change are the essence of our being; rigidity is death; conformity is death' (*E* III, 75).[18] For Woolf there was no overarching unitary truth: creating a system into which everything had to be fitted was one of her charges against D. H. Lawrence's work (*D* IV, 126; entry for 2 October 1932). Her own philosophy, as far as she had one, was worked out over the years in her diary: 'to adventure and discover and allow no rigid poses' (*D* IV, 252; entry for 14 October 1934). Nevertheless it is possible to argue that spirituality is at the heart of Woolf's vision, a spirituality outside churches and creeds, which will find full expression in *The Waves* with its portrayal of transitory human lives set against the recurring ebb and flow of the sea.

## Notes

1   See Donna J. Lazenby, *A Mystical Philosophy: Transcendence and Immanence in the Works of Virginia Woolf and Iris Murdoch* (London, New York: Bloomsbury Publishing, 2014).

2   Pericles Lewis, *Religious Experience and the Modernist Novel* (Cambridge: Cambridge University Press, 2010); Suzanne Hobson, *Angels of Modernism: Religion, Culture, Aesthetics, 1910–1960* (New York and London: Palgrave/Macmillan, 2011); Erik Tonning, *Modernism and Christianity* (London: Palgrave/Macmillan, 2014).

3   See *MB*, 64–159.

4   For more on Christian themes in *Mrs. Dalloway*, see Suzette Henke, '*Mrs. Dalloway*: The Communion of Saints' in *New Feminist Essays on Virginia Woolf*, ed. Jane Marcus (Lincoln: University of Nebraska Press, 1981), pp. 125–47; and Douglas L. Howard, '*Mrs. Dalloway*: Virginia Woolf's Redemptive Cycle', *Literature and Theology*, 12.2, 1998, pp. 149–58.

5   For more on Woolf's reading of the Russians, see R. Rubenstein, *Virginia Woolf and the Russian Point of View* (New York: Palgrave/Macmillan, 2009).

6   See Virginia Woolf, *To the Lighthouse: The Original Holograph Draft*, ed. Susan Dick (London: Hogarth, 1983).

7   See Jane Marcus, *Virginia Woolf and the Languages of the Patriarchy* (Bloomington and Indianapolis: Indiana University Press, 1987), pp. 115–35. Jane Goldman in *The Feminist Aesthetics of Virginia Woolf: Modernism, Post-Impressionism and the Politics of the Visual* (Cambridge: Cambridge University Press, 1998) criticises Marcus for aligning Woolf's 'moments of being' with mysticism. In turn, Donna J. Lazenby in *A Mystical Philosophy* takes Goldman to task for misunderstanding the nature of classical mysticism.

8 For an account of Woolf's bipolar disorder, see Thomas Caramagno, *The Flight of the Mind: Virginia Woolf's Art and Manic-Depressive Illness* (Berkeley: University of California Press, 1992).

9 Virginia Woolf, *Between the Acts* (Harmondsworth: Penguin, 1992), p. 118.

10 For Woolf's knowledge of popular science see Gillian Beer, '"Wireless": Popular Physics, Radio and Modernism', in *Cultural Babbage: Technology, Time and Invention*, ed. Francis Spufford and Jenny Uglow (London: Faber, 1996), pp. 149–66. In 'Relativity, Quantum Physics, and Consciousness in Virginia Woolf's *To the Lighthouse*', *Journal of Modern Literature*, 32.3 (2009), 39-62, Paul Tolliver Brown argues for parallels between early quantum physics and certain aspects of *To the Lighthouse*.

11 For the prevalence of discussions of the interrelationship between science, religion and the arts in magazines, newspapers and journals of the period, see Lara Vetter, *Modernist Writings and Religio-Scientific Discourse*, (New York: Palgrave Macmillan, 2010), pp. 1–29.

12 Henri Bergson, *Mind-Energy: Lectures and Essays* (London: Macmillan, 1921).

13 William James, *The Varieties of Religious Experience: A Study of Human Nature* (1902; rpt. Cambridge, Mass.: Harvard University Press, 1985).

14 Karen Armstrong, *The Gospel According to Woman* (London: Harper Collins, 1996), pp. 212–13.

15 Michael Whitworth, *Virginia Woolf* (Oxford: Oxford World Classics, 2005), pp. 145–48.

16 Martin Häggbund, *Dying for Time: Proust, Woolf, Nabokov* (Cambridge, Mass.: Harvard University Press, 2012), p. 67.

17 Virginia Woolf, *To the Lighthouse: The Original Holograph Draft*, p. 280.

18 The essay was originally published in the *TLS*, 31 January 1924.

# 3

# Victorian Roots: The Sense of the Past in *Mrs. Dalloway* and *To the Lighthouse*

Kate Flint

## Introduction: Past and present

In Virginia Woolf's essay 'How It Strikes a Contemporary'—published in 1923, the year in which *Mrs. Dalloway* is set—she wrote:

> We are sharply cut off from our predecessors. A shift in the scale—the sudden slip of masses held in position for ages—has shaken the fabric from top to bottom, alienated us from the past and made us perhaps too vividly conscious of the present. Every day we find ourselves doing, saying, or thinking things that would have been impossible to our fathers ... No age can have been more rich than ours in writers determined to give expression to the differences which separate them from the past and not to the resemblances which connect them with it. (*E* III, 357)

This sense of a great rupture is remarked upon in *Mrs. Dalloway* (1925) by Peter Walsh, the expatriate Indian administrator, recently returned to England and observing London on a gorgeous June day. Rather than locate the source of the split between past and present in the First World War, Peter places it a little later. 'Those five years—1918 to 1923—had been, he suspected, somehow very important. People looked different. Newspapers seemed different' (*MD*, 64). In *To the Lighthouse* (1927) the idea of an immense difference between pre- and post-war Britain is structurally written into the novel—two separate days, a decade apart, are joined by a deliberately impersonal representation of time's chaotic, careless, cruel passing.

But in *Mrs. Dalloway*, we are continually being invited to assess how deep the differences from the Victorian period may actually be. It is a novel about aging, in which characters in their fifties and sixties seem to take their sense of identity from the years when they were young adults. Woolf claimed that in writing the novel, she wished 'to criticise the social system, and to show it at work, at its most intense' (*D* II, 248). A good part of this critique depended upon her understanding of the long, tenacious reach of Victorian values—despite the shaking up of the class pyramid. Yet at the same time, she, with her compassionate as well as ironising treatment of her characters, is sympathetic to the tug of nostalgia.

For Woolf, 'Victorian' itself did not so much designate a temporally marked period corresponding to 1837–1901, the dates of Victoria's reign, as it signified a state of mind and an agglomeration of attitudes. The word is linked to possession of a confident public voice—'the sonorous Victorian trumpet' (*E* V, 146); ridiculous prudishness—'every Victorian family has in its cupboard the skeleton of an aunt who was driven to convert the native because her father would have died rather than let her look upon a naked man' (*E* V, 137)—coupled with a commitment, as here, to diverse forms of service; a style of furnishing—heavy, plush, dark. The Victorians, in Woolf's view, were dedicated to promoting and polishing surfaces, and this extended to their own self-presentations. Writing about Lytton Strachey's *Eminent Victorians* (1918), which debunked certain Victorian biographical myths, she notes how many of the 'remarkable figures' of the Victorian age 'had been grossly deformed by the effigies that had been plastered over them' (*CE* IV, 223). She admires her friend Strachey for being able to write true biography, to penetrate beneath public myths and façades. As she developed her own 'tunnelling process, by which I tell the past by installments, as I have need of it' (*D* II, 272) during the writing of *Mrs. Dalloway*, she incorporated a view of the Victorian past that savaged its smug rigidities.

Yet at the same time, Woolf understood the pull of this immediate past and its enduring presence in the memories of those who were now middle-aged—including herself. Writing of Henry James's recollections of London society in *The Middle Years* (1917), she had asked of 'the quality which seems to hang about those days and people as the very scent of the flower … Were they as beautiful as we like to remember them, or was it that the whole atmosphere made a beautiful presence?' (*E* II, 172). *Mrs. Dalloway* is a novel in which the present is always infused with a sense of earlier moments. Peter Walsh, despite acknowledging

England's outward changes, finds that memories come unbidden into
his mind. Like Clarissa Dalloway, who figures so strongly in these vol-
untary and involuntary reminiscences, he keeps returning—or being
returned—to the early 1890s. For both, it is as though they recognise a
better version of themselves, full of possibilities, when recollecting the
summer scenes at Bourton. Memories of Bourton, for them and others,
are highly personal, and animated by sensory impressions—yellow light,
cigarette smoke, flapping blinds, the toneless singing of Herr Breikopf,
the smell of mats, the sight and scent of tobacco flowers. They are filled
with people, too. Peter recollects, for example, Clarissa's Aunt Helena.
She is presented as a very distinct Victorian type, the botanical spinster, 'marching off in thick boots with a black tin collecting box slung
between her shoulders' (*MD*, 55). Now, walking through London on a
hot summer's evening, he feels, through 'intangible things you couldn't
lay your hands on—the shift in the whole pyramidal accumulation
which in his youth had seemed immovable. On top of them it had
pressed; weighed them down, the women especially, like those flowers
Clarissa's Aunt Helena used to press between sheets of grey blotting-
paper with Littré's dictionary on top, sitting under the lamp after dinner. She was dead now ... She belonged to a different age, but being so
entire, so complete, would always stand up on the horizon, stone-white,
eminent, like a lighthouse marking some past stage on this adventurous,
long, long voyage ...' (*MD*, 145).

Stone-white and eminent, this alabaster version of Aunt Helena
has all the immobility of the Victorian statues that populate the
public spaces of *Mrs. Dalloway*, recording England's recent imperial past and global dominance—from 'the Indian and his cross' in
Regent's Park (probably the Readymoney drinking fountain, the
gift of a Parsee from Bombay in 1869), to the statue of the Duke of
Cambridge in Whitehall (Queen Victoria's cousin, and the British
Army's commander-in-chief from 1856–1895), to 'the memorial to
Queen Victoria (whom he could remember in her horn spectacles
driving through Kensington), its white mound, its billowing moth-
erliness' that Richard Dalloway passes (*MD*, 105). This statue stands
where Woolf, in *Orlando* (1928), constructs an imaginary pyramid of
the worst excrescences of kitchsy Victoriana—crystal palaces, trousers,
whiskers, globes, maps and elephants. Aesthetic and political horrors
are thrown together in a wild installation. Generals and soldiers from
past wars have been commemorated as public sculpture, and some of
the human relics of Empire seem on their way to calcification. Peter
passes a retired Judge, presumably Anglo-Indian, 'sitting four square at
his house door dressed all in white' (*MD*, 147).

But Aunt Helena has not been turned into a memorial, after all. Indeed, 'Miss Helena Parry was not dead: Miss Parry was alive. She was past eighty. She ascended staircases slowly with a stick.' She is a guest at Clarissa's evening party. Her age has brought wisdom. Having spent time in Burma, botanising, 'she had no tender memories, no proud illusions about Viceroys, Generals, Mutinies—it was orchids she saw, and mountain passes, and herself carried on the backs of coolies in the 'sixties over solitary peaks ... an indomitable Englishwoman, fretful if disturbed by the war, say, which had dropped a bomb at her very door' (*MD, 159*). Helena Parry, her determined self formed in the high Victorian period, is alive and well in 1920s London. Indeed, if she is, all the same, to be read as a figure, it is not so much as an icon of the past as an allegory of the Victorian period's persistence in 1920s London—and in Woolf's own fiction.

Rupture and continuity: these contradictory assessments of one's relationship to the past endlessly preoccupied Woolf in the mid-1920s. This past was personal, literary and national. In *Mrs. Dalloway*, Victorian society continues through material objects, social practices, habits of thought and the memories of individuals. From the very beginning, the soundscape emphasises continuity. The streets are filled with the noise of brass bands and barrel organs, but also of motor cars and airplanes. Big Ben, sending out its leaden circles of sound into the June air, and providing a repeating sonic motif that links those who hear it, was first hung in the Great Tower of Westminster in the new Houses of Parliament in 1856 (then recast and rehung in 1858): it was originally to have been called Victoria or Royal Victoria. At the base of each of Augustus Pugin's clock dials on the bell's tower is the inscription DOMINE SALVAM FAC REGINAM NOSTRAM VICTORIAM PRIMAM—'O Lord, keep safe our Queen Victoria the First.'

Some material objects no longer bear the weight that they did. Before the war, gloves were an essential part of women's outdoor wear; the young Elizabeth Dalloway, who dances tentatively around the question of what it might mean to be a modern woman, cares nothing for gloves or shoes. But many endure—like the roll of tweed in the Bond Street shop where Clarissa's father bought his suits for fifty years. Their very solidity can even act as a guarantee against the changes and disruption brought about by the war. The furnishings in the lodgings where Septimus and Rezia live might seem like a parodic condensation of precisely the kind of domestic interior against which Bloomsbury taste distinguished itself. Yet they also ground the shell-shocked Septimus with their reassuring *thing*ness: even 'the sideboard;

the plate of bananas; the engraving of Queen Victoria and the Prince Consort … the mantelpiece, with the jar of roses. None of these things moved. All were still; all were real' (*MD*, 127).

## Interrogating the 'real'

Woolf continually interrogates what is meant by the 'real'. On the one hand, it consists of the visible and tangible and audible, yet as Septimus knows to his own cost, a hallucination of a dead man can seem as 'real' as anything else. This question of presence and absence, of perception and imagination, is of course one that Woolf revisits in *To the Lighthouse*, in part an homage to the lasting impact of her very Victorian father, Leslie Stephen, with his interest in the eighteenth-century philosophers, like Hume, who wrestled with these issues. In *Mrs. Dalloway*, Woolf uses the continual eruption of memory to destabilise the locations of the present. In palimpsestic fashion, characters remember the London of their childhood and write it onto the contemporary topography. Thus Clarissa recollects 'the house with the china cockatoo' (*MD*, 8)—this used to hang in the big bay window of 1 Piccadilly whenever the philanthropist Angela Burdett-Coutts was in residence; Peter harks back to the Regent's Park of his youth and 'the little house where one brought air-balls' (*MD*, 50). Indeed, he is grateful for the sense of connection the location provides: 'Regent's Park had changed very little since he was a boy, except for the squirrels' (*MD*, 58). There's a banality in that observation designed to show up Peter's own superficiality, but at the same time, in continually pointing to his sentimental side, rooted in Victorian reminiscences, Woolf is exploring another side of post-World War One male vulnerability.

For there is comfort as well as damaging stagnation to be found in continuity, Woolf recognises. The novel as a whole suggests how hard it can be to change one's mindset. 'They would solidify young' (*MD*, 159) Clarissa gloomily remarks of the younger generation at her party, believing that at their age, she and Peter would have been arguing all evening long. She fails here to acknowledge that solidification is a mental process that has overtaken many of her peers. She grounds herself, indeed, part in wonder at the passage of time, with the thought, tantamount to a refrain, that 'And once she had walked on the terrace at Bourton' (*MD*, 166). Lady Bruton, ten years older than Clarissa, her past involving political and perhaps sexual intrigue in the 1880s, a now deceased General having written, at a table in her drawing room, 'with her cognisance, perhaps advice, a telegram ordering the British troops to advance' (*MD*, 95); now committed to philanthropic schemes and enjoying friendships with powerful men, dozes off after lunch: 'Always she went back to those fields down in Devonshire, where she had jumped the brooks on Patty, her pony … there were her father and mother on the lawn under the trees, with the tea-things out, and the bed of dahlias, the hollyhocks, the pampas grass …' (*MD*, 100). The past of her childhood, so infinitely far away in some respects, is simultaneously vividly present and personally significant.

Yet Woolf clearly also references the Victorian past in order to critique it, and also to do something more nuanced: to understand the inherited limitations and expectations of her own generation and those who are just slightly older than them. Clarissa herself suffers from the insufficiencies of Victorian education, the 'few twigs of knowledge Fräulein Daniels gave them' (*MD*, 8), although Peter also remembers her, and her choice of metaphors, being formed by her enthusiasm for the scientists T.H. Huxley and John Tyndall (it is as though Woolf gives her access to her own childhood reading). Clarissa herself recalls the socialist-leaning Sally Seton giving her William Morris's writings. This provocative reading material has to be concealed from Aunt Helena by a brown paper wrapper. The girls' mild iconoclasm—Sally smoking, running down a passageway naked, inaugurating a kiss with Clarissa, the pair of them 'meant to found a society to abolish private property' (MD, 30)—has faded, as each of them age, marry, fail to fulfil whatever radical intents their young selves possessed. Even though Sally marries a self-made industrialist, a Manchester cotton mill owner, his bit part is that of another Victorian stereotype, albeit a very different one from the country sportsman Member of Parliament that is Richard Dalloway.

To be sure, Woolf underscores that there have been some advances since the 1890s. Peter recalls Sally Seton asking if it mattered that the housemaid whom a neighbouring squire had married had already had a baby: '(In those days, in mixed company, it was a bold thing to say)' (*MD*, 53); and he looks back to an argument one Sunday morning at Bourton 'about women's rights (that antediluvian topic)' (*MD*, 66). The parentheses surely incorporate Woolf's sardonic comment about anyone who is blind to the distance women still have to travel, even in terms of the franchise. For unlike Peter—proud to seem modern, to have thrown off some of the fustier aspects of English life, even if his fanciful vision of himself as some kind of 'romantic buccaneer' seems culled straight from the pages of Victorian boys' stories—some characters in *Mrs. Dalloway* seem

never to have noticed that the Victorian period had ended. At
any rate, they do not want to jettison the status and sense of self-
importance it gave them. Sir William Bradshaw, the famous physician, is testimony to Victorian ideals of hard work and self-help,
'being the son of a shop-keeper' (*MD*, 85). But more damagingly, his
'sense of proportion'—something that has stood him in good stead
with his medical practice, but is patently inadequate when it comes
to dealing with a war-traumatised mind—is linked to the 'fastidious
Goddess' of 'conversion'. This is the cruel spirit that even now is
hard at work in the Empire, in the 'heat and sands of India, the mud
and swamp of Africa'; that stalks 'through factories and parliaments',
offering help; that is equated with the will to power of a nation, of
the ruling powers and of patriarchy. This desire for dominion has,
when wielded in a more domestic sphere, subdued Lady Bradshaw.
Her outer self performs its role in society, its effigy 'in ostrich feathers hung over the mantelpiece', but the fact that there is an inner,
subjugated self manifests itself, now, in just the slightest 'nervous
twitch, fumble, stumble' in the person who 'once, long ago … had
caught salmon freely' (*MD*, 90).

There is barely an echo of another formative country childhood
here, as befits the silencing performed by a patriarchal power that
Woolf ties in with both domestic and imperial institutions. But as
one of the many minor characters in the pages of *Mrs. Dalloway*, Lady
Bradshaw stands as a good example of one of those figures who are
both distinct individuals, reminding one that the social world of a
novel can contain numerous untold stories, and who also function
as types.[1] To take two further examples who carry their Victorian
pasts with them: 'Sir Harry' arrives at Clarissa's party and stands for a
type of sub-Edwin Landseer style of painting, with Woolf's description teetering on the edge of satire as she describes this 'fine old
fellow who had produced more bad pictures than any other two
Academicians in the whole of St John's Wood (they were always of
cattle, standing in sunset pools absorbing moisture, or signifying, for
he had a certain range of gesture, by the raising of one foreleg and the
toss of the antlers, "the Approach of the Stranger"—all his activities,
dining out, racing, were founded on cattle standing absorbing moisture in sunset pools' (*MD*, 156). More gently treated, Ellie Henderson
finds herself worrying about open windows and draughts, but not
on her own account: 'it was the girls with their naked shoulders she
thought of, being trained to think of others by an old father, an inva-
lid, late vicar of Bourton, but he was dead now …' (*MD*, 150). These
personages, even if mildly mocked by Woolf, share a good deal with

the more prominent characters in the novel. They cling tenaciously to an identity formed in the previous century.

Musing on how *To the Lighthouse* would be received, Virginia Woolf wrote in her Diary 'I dont [*sic*] feel sure what the stock criticism [of the novel] will be. Sentimental? Victorian?' (*D* III, 107). It is improbable that she thought that the *style* would be considered Victorian, with its passage from one viewpoint to another; its presentation of the simultaneity of action, thought and perception ('the discrepancy—that was what she was thinking, this is what she was doing—ladling out soup' (*TL*, 69); its emphasis on the heightened quality of each moment. There is, indeed, more than an echo of Walter Pater, especially his Conclusion to *The Renaissance* (1873), in her mode of calling attention to the moment's intensity—just as there was in *Mrs. Dalloway*, when Clarissa experiences a rush of feeling: 'Then, for that moment, she had seen an illumination; a match burning in a crocus; an inner meaning almost expressed' (*MD*, 29).[2] In the lyricism of the prose, there are echoes of other aesthetic writers of the late Victorian period. As Dennis Denisoff and Talia Schaffer have both noted, in emphasising her literary break with the past, Woolf not only repudiated the kind of fiction that John Galsworthy and Arnold Bennett wrote in the early twentieth century, with—as she characterised it—their emphasis on surface materiality, but she also failed to give any significant weight to such stylistic precursors as Vernon Lee and Alice Meynell.[3] But Woolf persistently presented the formal choices that she made as a novelist as ones that set her off from a preceding generation, even as she continued to acknowledge, and uphold, the existence of continuity and the claims of the past.

The word 'sentimental', in relation to *To the Lighthouse*, is telling. This is not the sentimentality of Victorian deathbeds (Mrs. Ramsay dies in parentheses), nor of romance. Paul and Minta's marriage, much anticipated by Mrs. Ramsay as a means of weaving herself into the future, of ensuring continuity, founders in a post-war climate that she could not foresee. It is not the soft-heartedness from Mr. Ramsay, who once pointed to a hen with chicks and said '"Pretty—pretty," an odd illumination into his heart' (*TL*, 20) that William Bankes thinks of as the moment that severed his feeling of friendship with the older man. Woolf, however much she too might repudiate the fluffy maternalism that makes Bankes feel so queasy, introduces this reminiscence as a means of revealing a very human aspect that co-exists with the rigorous life of the mind that Bankes so reveres.

## Woolf, her parents and the past

Rather, for Woolf, 'sentimental' signals anxiety about how she treats a highly personal past. For the Ramsays are to a very large extent portraits of Woolf's own parents, Leslie and Julia Stephen; the house and its sea view—although transported to the Hebrides—is based on Talland House, near St Ives, Cornwall. The Stephen family spent their summers there from 1882 to 1895, the year of Julia Stephen's death, so *To the Lighthouse* functions as an 'elegy'—Woolf's own term for it—(D III, 34) not just for her father and mother, but also for some of the happiest times of her childhood. Here, recreated, is the cricket-playing on the lawn, the garden with its red-hot poker flowers and the Godrevy Lighthouse that sits on a tiny island to the east of St Ives Bay. The lighthouse, built in 1858–59, sends beams of light pulsing across the darkness in *To the Lighthouse,* and these beams are as Victorian in their source as Big Ben's leaden circles of sound.

Critics of the novel have unsurprisingly seized on Woolf's diary entry for 28 November 1928 in order to try and understand what, exactly, she was doing in giving us this portrait of her parents. 'Father's birthday', she muses.

> He would have been … 96, yes, today; & could have been 96, like other people one has known, but mercifully was not. His life would have entirely ended mine. What would have happened? No writing, no books;—inconceivable. I used to think of him & mother daily; but writing The Lighthouse, laid them in my mind. And now he comes back sometimes, but differently. (I believe this to be true—that I was obsessed by them both, unhealthily; & writing of them was a necessary act.) (D III, 208)

Superficially, this entry invites one to see the novel as finally settling family ghosts. But it also acknowledges that one cannot completely lay the past to rest by writing about it, whether that past is personal or, more broadly, that of a nation's social and cultural history. Like *Mrs. Dalloway, To the Lighthouse* is threaded through with references that make us see Mr. and Mrs. Ramsay as quintessential Victorians. Woolf underscores this when Charles Tansley waits downstairs in a 'poky little house' where Mrs. Ramsay (as Julia Stephen used to do) visited a sick woman upstairs. The room is decorated with precisely the kind of dark clutter—mats and tea-caddies and shades—that Woolf most despised, in decorative terms, and when Mrs. Ramsay re-enters, she 'stood quite motionless for a moment against a picture of Queen Victoria wearing the blue ribbon of the Garter' (*TL,* 15).

Nowhere is Mr. Ramsay aligned with such visual symmetry in relation to Victoria's reign. But he is shown to be, just like Woolf's father, very much a product of his time. The portrayal of Mr. Ramsay as a thinly disguised version of Leslie Stephen is less immediately sympathetic than that of his wife. Outwardly, Mr. Ramsay is ineffably *right*. He plays the domestic tyrant over his children, wanting them to be aware from the start that life is difficult, that facts are uncompromising. Like Leslie Stephen, he has the alarming habit of marching up and down the terrace reciting Alfred Tennyson's 'The Charge of the Light Brigade' (1854)—a poem that, ironically, attacks authoritarian generals who expect unquestioning, indeed suicidal obedience from their troops. But Woolf takes pains to show his inner vulnerability, his dependence on the praise of others, his inability to put into words his feelings for his spouse—like another man moulded by Victorian expectations of masculinity, Richard Dalloway. Inwardly, he is consumed with anxiety that he has not made good on the promise that he showed as a young philosopher. He suffers from the sense that 'he had not done the thing he might have done. It was a disguise; it was the refuge of a man afraid to own his own feelings, who could not say, This is what I like—this is what I am' (*TL*, 39). In this, he is curiously like a far less emotionally explosive scholar, George Eliot's Casaubon: both men suffer from the weight of self-imposed expectations. Woolf, in language that gently satirises the tropes of Victorian heroism, shows Mr. Ramsay as a man who (unlike his literary predecessor) is able to pull himself through these moments of self-doubt: 'Qualities that in a desolate expedition across the icy solitudes of the Polar region would have made him the leader, the guide, the counselor, whose temper, neither sanguine nor despondent, surveys with equanimity what is to be and faces it, came to his help again' (*TL*, 31). But her portrayal of Mr. Ramsay's raw vulnerability and volatility indicates how clearly she recognises that the standards of patriarchy put pressure on those who were expected to uphold them—even if they are never capable of articulating this pressure themselves.

Never was Leslie Stephen more vulnerable than when he lost his wife. The portrait that we are given of Mrs. Ramsay is of a woman with Julia Stephen's famed beauty, charisma and power to inspire reverence. This aura comes across in photographs of Woolf's mother—particularly by Julia Margaret Cameron—and in paintings, such as the ca. 1870 portrait by George Frederick Watts, and several works by Edward Burne-Jones, including his 1879 *Annunciation*. She was, in other words, an icon of the later Pre-Raphaelite taste in beauty: a style of depicting femininity that also suggests a powerful and unvoiced inner sensibility. As Jane de Gay points out, in her fictional presentation 'Woolf does not simply record her own impressions, but attempts to deal with Leslie Stephen's image of Julia'.[4] In particular, the fictional figure invites comparison with the memories offered up by Stephen in his *Mausoleum Book*, written for his family just after his wife's death as an act of memorialisation—a piece of writing that also functions as a form of autobiography. Among other qualities, he stresses her maternal powers, casting her as 'a perfect mother, a very ideal type of mother; and in her the maternal instincts were, as it seemed, but the refined essence of the love which showed its strength in every other relation of life'.[5]

As Mrs. Ramsay's son James so presciently notes in the novel, though, 'nothing was simply one thing' (*TL*, 152), and Mrs. Ramsay's maternalism is both nurturing and stifling. It spills into her general philanthropic concerns as well as into her matchmaking designs. Fundamentally she is a type of hyper-femininity, a personification of Coventry Patmore's 'Angel in the House', a figure that Woolf, in her 1931 talk 'Professions for Women', describes as something that she had to kill off before she could write:

> She was intensely sympathetic. She was immensely charming. She was utterly unselfish. She excelled in the difficult arts of family life. She sacrificed herself daily. If there was chicken, she took the leg; if there was a draught she sat in it—in short she was so constituted that she never had a mind or a wish of her own, but preferred to sympathize always with the minds and wishes of others. (*CE* II, 285)

It was a fatal thing to feel the shadow of her wing or the radiance of her halo fall across the page when she was writing; to come under the sway of her conciliatory, charming spirit. Woolf learned, she said, to throw the inkpot at her every time that she came creeping back.

That inkpot gets thrown, hard, in *To the Lighthouse*. Not only is Mrs. Ramsay literally killed off, but the broader sense of continuity about which she fantasises and from which she draws a substantial part of her identity is broken and dispersed. Woolf did not simply write the novel hoping to exorcise the shadow of her parents. She also—the two emphases are of course linked—wrote it in order to help position her literary aesthetics in relation to Victorian forms and ideas. In doing this, however, books play less of a role than visual art. To be sure, Mr. Ramsay's Tennyson recitative thunders in the background, and he and Augustus Carmichael repeat the sub-Swinburnean medievalism of Charles Elton's 'Garden Song'—redolent, for them, of their college days. But Mr. Bankes laments that the young don't read Carlyle; Minta was terrified by sitting next to Mr. Ramsay her first evening at dinner and talking about George Eliot, 'for she had left the third volume of *Middlemarch* in the train and she never knew what happened in the end' (*TL*, 80); and the volumes that are left in the holiday house for the duration of the 'Time Passes' section rot on their shelves: 'long rows of books, black as ravens once, now white-stained, breeding pale mushrooms and secreting furtive spiders' (*TL*, 114). These books are part of the shabbiness of the Victorian furnishings that have been relegated to the holiday house: 'Mats, camp beds, crazy ghosts of chairs and tables whose London life of service was done' (*TL*, 25), and the flapping wallpaper. 'Things got shabbier and shabbier summer after summer' (*TL*, 25), Mrs. Ramsay laments, and the anthropomorphic self-identification is made even more clear a little later when we learn that she herself feels 'shabby and worn out' (*TL*, 37).

## Human pieces of Victorian debris

Like old furniture, there are some human pieces of Victorian debris strewing the novel's pages. Mr. Carmichael, benignly lethargic, has washed up from India, addicted to the few drops of tincture of opium that he takes every lunchtime and that stain his beard yellow. He has been turned out of his house by his wife (rather like obsolete furnishings). Surprisingly, the poetry about death that he wrote some forty years earlier found a new audience after the war. Either this may be taken to indicate the never-changing nature of grief or the fact that, in times of enormous upheaval and loss, people take refuge in the familiar, or the cliché. Lily has never read a line of this verse, but she 'thought that she knew how it went though, slowly and sonorously. It was seasoned and mellow. It was about the desert and the camel. It was about the palm tree and the sunset' (*TL*, 159). But Mr. Carmichael's sudden success also stands for the unpredictability, for an author or artist, of being able to prophesy what will become of one's work. Lily knows that her painting may be rolled up, hung in an attic, but what matters for her is the satisfaction of completing it, perfect, in aesthetic terms, for one moment.

This painting—or rather, these paintings, for Lily makes two attempts at capturing her garden surroundings and the maternal triangle formed by Mrs. Ramsay and James, one before and one after the war—differs radically from the styles that they succeeded. Although in the novel's first section she can feel her way towards compositional resolution, only the older Lily—missing Mrs. Ramsay, her surrogate mother, but no longer feeling obliged to do her bidding—can complete the canvas, throw the metaphorical inkpot. Her painting, one deduces, in its blocks of colour, its appeal to form, was highly similar to the work that Vanessa Bell, Woolf's sister, was producing in the 1910s and early 1920s. This is certainly not the bland landscape that Mr. Bankes has in his drawing room, 'of the cherry trees in blossom on the banks of the Kennet' (*TL*, 45), nor even the more experimental late Impressionist work of, say, Philip Wilson Steer, that seems to be referenced by Mrs. Ramsay when she contrasts the new style of painting, all green and grey with lemon-coloured sailing boats, with that of her grandmother's friends, who 'took the greatest pains; first they mixed their own colours, and then they ground them, and then they put damp cloths on them to keep them moist' (*TL*, 15). Lily's final painting, in other words, is as much of a rupture with a range of earlier forms as is Woolf's own novel.

The presentism of Lily's pictorial vision, even as it is, immediately slips into the past tense, concludes *To the Lighthouse*. Structurally, this personal and aesthetic moment of triumph parallels the fragile family unity-in-separateness as Mr. Ramsay and his two youngest children land at the lighthouse. *Mrs. Dalloway* similarly ends on a revelatory instant, as Peter notes how the presence of Clarissa at the end of her party fills him with terror, excitement, ecstasy. But these two instances of achievement are quite different, in ways that point very tellingly to how each novel understands the Victorian past. For Peter Walsh, it is as though the passion that he felt as a young man is very much alive: passion for Clarissa, to be sure, but it is also as though he is consoled that he is still the same person; that neither thirty years of life, nor the First World War and the social shifts that it brought with it made any real difference to his true self.

*Mrs. Dalloway* is a novel about the pains of aging, and about the continual backward-looking process that aging can induce. By giving so much space to characters in their fifties, Woolf ensures that we recognise the sway that the Victorian period still has over those who wield power within the early 1920s. By contrast, the later novel, far less steeped in nostalgia, puts forward the period as tired and spent. Mrs. Ramsay, before her dinner party stirs to life, 'had a sense of being past everything, through everything, out of everything' (*TL*, 68); Mr. Ramsay in the boat is an old man reading a book with a mottled cover. Even as its echoes continue to reverberate—and even as

Woolf was to return again and again to the nineteenth century in subsequent novels—*To the Lighthouse* presents the Victorian period as being firmly over.

## Notes

1 See Rachel Bowlby, 'Introduction: Two interventions on realism. Untold stories in *Mrs. Dalloway* and versions of realism in George Eliot's *Adam Bede*', *Textual Practice* 25.3 (2011), 395–436.
2 For Pater's influence on Woolf, and how it combined with that of her father, Leslie Stephen, see Perry Meisel, *The Absent Father: Virginia Woolf and Walter Pater* (New Haven: Yale University Press, 1980).
3 See Dennis Denisoff, 'The Forest Beyond the Frame: Picturing Women's Desires in Vernon Lee and Virginia Woolf', in *Women and British Aestheticism*, eds. Talia Schaffer and Kathy Alexis Psomiades (Charlottesville: University Press of Virginia, 1999), pp. 251–69; and Talia Schaffer, 'The Angel in Hyde Park: Alice Meynell's "Unstable Equilibrium"', Chapter 5 of *The Forgotten Female Aesthetes: Literary Culture in Late-Victorian England* (Charlottesville: University Press of Virginia, 2000), pp. 159–96.
4 Jane de Gay, *Virginia Woolf's Novels and the Literary Past* (Edinburgh: Edinburgh University Press, 2006), p. 100.
5 *Sir Leslie Stephen's Mausoleum Book*, intro. Alan Bell (Oxford: Clarendon Press, 1977), p. 83.

# 4

# Modernism and Bloomsbury Aesthetics

Gabrielle McIntire

## Introduction: The formation and aims of the Bloomsbury Group

In 1904, following the death of their father, Sir Leslie Stephen, Virginia and her three siblings, Vanessa, Thoby and Adrian, chose to rent a house in the then-unfashionable Bloomsbury district of London. Once established there, Thoby sought to continue the stimulating discussions he had had at Cambridge University with members of the Apostles, a student society dating back to 1820 and boasting an impressive list of current and former members.[1] His Apostle friends included Leonard Woolf (later to be Virginia's husband as well as an author, critic and co-founder of the precursor to the United Nations, the League of Nations), John Maynard Keynes (who would become one of the most important economists of the twentieth century), Lytton Strachey (later to become an influential writer), Roger Fry (soon to become a ground-breaking art critic and a well-received painter) and E.M. Forster (soon to be recognised as a major novelist). The group met on a weekly basis, and Thoby's siblings were included amongst those in attendance: Virginia Stephen (later Woolf, who became one of the most celebrated novelists of the century), Vanessa Stephen (later Bell, who would become a respected Post-Impressionist painter) and Adrian Stephen (who became an important early psychoanalyst). Over the years several others would become associated with this close-knit group, including Duncan Grant, Saxon Sydney-Turner, David Garnett and Desmond and Mary MacCarthy.[2] T.S. Eliot, though not a member of the Bloomsbury Group, was a frequent visitor, and read *The Waste Land* for the first time in public at one of its gatherings.[3] Later he was to say of Virginia Woolf that she 'was the centre, not merely of an esoteric group, but of the literary life of London'.[4]

The initial conversations at 46 Gordon Square, the Stephens' house, centred on the work of Cambridge philosopher, G.E. Moore, and on questions of 'the good' in relation to Moore's 1903 book, *Principia Ethica* (*Ethical Principles*). Part of what was so intriguing and even thrilling about Moore's treatment of age-old Aristotelian and Platonic ethical questions was his insistence that 'the good' is radically indeterminate; it is a problematic category which we *must* and *should* query, but one whose answers—like so much of emerging modernist art and literature—can only ever remain partial, undecidable and even fragmented. At various points in *Principia Ethica*, Moore's discussion makes its way into aesthetics: towards the end of the book he asserts, for instance, that we ought not 'assume that the truth of any subject-matter will display such symmetry as we desire to see—or (to use the common vague phrase) that it will possess any particular form of "unity"'.[5] Under this rubric, 'truth' itself has proportions and dimensions—an aesthetics—that we long to 'see', even when these might evade our enquiries. In much of her fiction Woolf explores precisely these kinds of correspondences between truth, indeterminacy and personal and aesthetic insight, both metacritically—*within* her fiction as a self-reflexive commentary on the meaning of her characters' dilemmas—and extra-critically, for herself as a writer.

This interest in ethics forms a central tenet for the 'Bloomsberries', as they called themselves, for although they later became associated with sexual experimentation and avant-garde art, ethics was never displaced, and the group's *raison d'être* remained fundamentally engaged with questions of how best to live and contribute to the society around them. Several Bloomsbury figures took their ethical values into the realm of politics, with Duncan Grant, David Garnett and Lytton Strachey granted exemption from military service as conscientious objectors and pacifists during World War One. The philosopher Bertrand Russell, often associated with the group, was jailed for six months for his objections to the prospect of the United States entering the war. Both Clive Bell and Adrian Stephen belonged to the 'No Conscription Fellowship',[6] and Leonard Woolf's experiences as a colonial officer in Ceylon were part of what inspired him to help found the League of Nations. Virginia Woolf includes feminist critiques in virtually all of her novels, while her long essay, *A Room of One's Own* (1929), addresses the social and economic plight of women who might aspire to be writers and remains widely read today; she followed this a decade later with a

brilliant anti-war polemic, *Three Guineas* (1939), that linked the patriarchal sexism of the times with fascism and a desire for war.

A major change in focus for the group's discussions occurred
around 1910, when as Vanessa Bell remarked, 'we stopped talking
about "the good" and started talking about Cézanne'.[7] Quentin Bell
traces the impetus for this shift to the influence of Roger Fry, who
organised the first Post-Impressionist Exhibition that year. The significance of this event for art and aesthetic sensibilities, awareness
and taste in Britain cannot be overstated. Reflecting on the dramatic
changes to the English art world stimulated by the exhibition, Woolf
writes in the last book published before her suicide, *Roger Fry: A
Biography* (1940), that the 'public in 1910 was thrown into paroxysms
of rage and laughter',[8] while Fry 'became the most read and the most
admired, if also the most abused, of all living art critics (*RF,* 160).
The exhibition brought together in Britain for the first time, somewhat belatedly, a collection of experimental European artists, including Paul Cézanne, Vincent Van Gogh, Paul Gaugin, Georges Seurat,
Pablo Picasso and Henri Matisse. Like the Impressionists, these artists
had moved away from traditional depictions of human form and
natural landscapes; they had also moved closer to abstraction, pushing
the limits of the quasi-photographic paintings produced a generation
earlier further away from realism, privileging instead emotionally
inflected expression. As Roger Fry writes in 1912, 'it is not the object
of these artists to exhibit their skill or proclaim their knowledge, but
only to attempt to express by pictorial and plastic form certain spiritual experiences'.[9] We will find some of these same preoccupations
in both Virginia Woolf's own practice as a writer and in her renditions
of art, aesthetic experience and meaning in *Mrs. Dalloway* and *To the
Lighthouse*. In these two novels Woolf engages in a version of Post-
Impressionist literary expressionism, with attention to fluctuations
in mood and experience as intensely noted as the Impressionists had
rendered fluctuations in light and shadow.

At nearly the same time as the talk at Bloomsbury moved from
being centred on ethics to being concerned with the most modern of
art, the group also began to talk more openly about the body and sexuality. These were conversations that had not been possible in a society still circumscribed by Victorian values and prohibitions. Virginia
Woolf writes of a single word that changed the field of conversation
around 1909: Lytton Strachey came into a room where Virginia and
Vanessa Stephen were waiting for Clive Bell, and, 'Suddenly the
door opened and the long and sinister figure of Mr. Lytton Strachey
stood on the threshold. He pointed his finger at a stain on Vanessa's

white dress. 'Semen?' he said.'[10] Virginia's initial shock was that such a word could be uttered at all; what came next was that 'Sex permeated our conversation. The word bugger was never far from our lips. We discussed copulation with the same excitement and openness that we had discussed the nature of good. It is strange to think how reticent, how reserved we had been and for how long.'[11] Part of the Bloomsbury renaissance, then, was to make what was unspeakable about sexuality and bodily functions not only speakable, but *de rigueur*. A mere fifteen years after Oscar Wilde was publicly condemned to imprisonment and hard labour under the Criminal Law Amendment Act that made 'gross indecency' (in Wilde's case, homosexual activity) severely punishable, the Bloomsbury group began to de-pathologise sexual diversities within its own microcosm, which had important links to broader English and European communities.

Even before 'sex' entered Bloomsbury discourse—before it was something that could be spoken about frankly—it had permeated the group in a mix of traditional and unorthodox ways, and it would continue to do so. Though most of the men were homosexual, some were heterosexual. Vanessa Stephen married Clive Bell in 1907, and Virginia Stephen married Leonard Woolf in 1912. In 1942, in an especially complicated union, David Garnett married Angelica Bell, the biological daughter of Vanessa Bell and her former male lover, Duncan Grant. Both Vanessa and Virginia also developed extra-marital affairs that were known about and basically sanctioned by their husbands. Virginia Woolf fell in love with Vita Sackville-West in the 1920s while remaining married to Leonard, and her sister Vanessa Bell had a long-term affair with the painter Duncan Grant while she remained amicably married to Clive Bell. We might say that Bloomsbury practised versions of 'free love' long before this became part of the cultural vocabulary of the 1960s.

Importantly, then, Bloomsbury is also known for the ways in which its extraordinarily talented members flouted conventions of all kinds and practised new freedoms of desire and sexuality, new freedoms of artistic expression, new freedoms of social and familial mores, and even new political and legal freedoms. Bloomsbury was thus not only a group but a way of life.

### *To the Lighthouse*: Vision and light

The passionate determinations and experiments of Bloomsbury, and its attention to the intersections of ethics, aesthetics and the workings of desire, found their way into Woolf's novels, both as self-evident surface effects and as layers woven into her characters' motivations and into the fabric of her narration. While Woolf often shied away from making absolute pronouncements about 'art'—tending, like other modernists, to suggest its indefinable qualities[12]—she ardently sought to create new formal and thematic experiments that would depart significantly from the literary efforts of her Victorian and Edwardian predecessors. Woolf notably describes her writerly goals by detailing elaborately—and with an element of good-humoured jest—what her writing aspires *not* to be, since 'life is not a series of gig lamps symmetrically arranged; life is a luminous halo, a semi-transparent envelope surrounding us', she insists in 'Modern Fiction' (1925).[13] She also believed in the necessity of breaking away from the failings of novelists such as Arnold Bennett, nearly a generation older than Woolf, who precipitated the disastrous 'age when character disappeared or was mysteriously engulfed'.[14] Hers is thus an aesthetics of departure from the status quo in favour of a new *via negativa* of sorts in which her aims would *not* be like who and what had come before, but would allow her to forge a revolutionary path into the future of fiction. Many of her techniques of psychological realism, detailed and highly introspective stream of consciousness, a de-privileging of life's 'major' events—such as birth, marriage, death—in favour of minute attention to the intensities of everyday life, are intrinsic to the values of modernist art and literature and are still relied upon by postmodern writers today.

Virginia Woolf closes *To the Lighthouse* with Lily Briscoe's triumphant, epiphanic words about the painting she had been working at over a ten-year period: 'It was done; it was finished. Yes, she thought, laying down her brush in extreme fatigue, I have had my vision' (*TL*, 170). Lily's words render in shorthand some key aspects of the aesthetic philosophy of the modernist Bloomsbury Group. At the core of Bloomsbury's values was striving for 'vision', and for art to be centrally meaningful, both within one's own life and within the larger cultural, social and political milieu of early twentieth-century British society. Roger Fry, an influential Bloomsbury art critic and painter, uses this very word when he argues in 'The Artist's Vision', an essay that came out just one year after Woolf published *To the Lighthouse*, that 'creative vision' is crucial to making art that matters. Fry conjoins aesthetics with the socio-historical, the political and the ethical, suggesting that even simple 'ornaments' are 'not merely curious for the eye, but [are] stimulating to our socio-historical imagination' (*VD*, 48). Art is all the more so, and he draws a further link between *passion* and 'vision', proposing that the artist must see things with a 'detached and impassioned vision, and, as he contemplates the particular field of vision, the (aesthetically) chaotic and accidental conjunction of forms and colours begins to crystallize into a harmony' (*VD*, 51). Fry's passage echoes many of Woolf's own aims in writing *To the Lighthouse*, and after the novel was published Woolf explained in a letter to Fry that for her the lighthouse was less a symbol than a structural, aesthetic unifier: 'One has to have a central line down the middle of the book to hold the design together.'[15] Fry's emphasis on 'vision' and 'harmony' also sheds light on Lily Briscoe's painterly and personal struggles with colour, shade and composition, as well as on Mrs. Ramsay's creative efforts at achieving harmony among her family and friends.

As if to echo Roger Fry's emphasis on the centrality of 'vision' to modernist art, *To the Lighthouse* is preoccupied with ways of seeing throughout. We recall the early mention of James's 'fierce blue eyes' (*TL*, 7) and his desire to go to the beacon of light offshore; the repeated (perhaps ironic) indications of Mrs. Ramsay's 'short-sighted' eyes (*TL*, 13, 28, 59) in contrast to Mr. Ramsay's 'long-sighted eyes' (*TL*, 168); Lily Briscoe's 'Chinese eyes' (*TL*, 17); the rhythmic punctuation of the narrative flow by the 'light' of the lighthouse beam, and Mrs. Ramsay's belief that every third stroke of the lighthouse beam is hers; the narrator's complaints that the novel's anti-hero, Mr. Ramsay, 'luxuriated in no vision' (*TL*, 38) and 'never looked at things' (*TL*, 59); the climactic dinner party, exactly at the centre of the novel, where 'looking together united them' (*TL*, 79); Prue's desire for others to 'look' at her mother, whom she considers 'the thing itself' (*TL*, 94); the exchange of 'gaz[es]' in the boat as Mr. Ramsay and the children voyage out, with Cam realising at a distance that she had lost sight of the family house—'She could not see it' (*TL*, 137); the sheer, ongoing repetition of the word 'light' within the novel; and the innumerable ways that Woolf makes ways of seeing crucial to the book's message. As we read, then, we discover, as if on our own voyage, that this is a story about light, love, family and art: about *going to the lighthouse*, and about the dream-deferred of this emotionally laden voyage.

Lily Briscoe labours at her canvas during two brief periods spanning the ten-year gap the novel covers—just prior to World War One and just after. She is an unmarried, female experimental painter in a world still dominated by male artists, and she is seeking to render a contemporary, Post-Impressionist, abstract, secularised not-quite-Madonna-and-child portrait of her beloved Mrs. Ramsay and her young son James. Lily's 'vision' is as hard to come by as James's own quest to go to the lighthouse, and it initially eludes her as broken, fragmented and vulnerable: she struggles in the early part of the novel to find the 'courage' even to speak of what she 'see[s]', and tries to 'clasp some miserable remnant of her vision to her breast' (*TL*, 19). She then must suffer both the critical gaze of William Bankes as he intrusively taps her canvas with his bone-handled pen-knife—a phallic, violent symbol—and Charles Tansley's repeated admonitions, 'Women can't write, women can't paint', that haunt Lily's consciousness like a painful refrain (*TL*, 42, 71, 74, 132). When she finally achieves her 'vision' it is an intensely private experience—a feminist triumph attained on her own, without any help from men, and despite the male prejudices that have plagued her. Lily's labour is also distinctly *physical* as well as emotional and aesthetic: we recall her 'extreme fatigue' as she lays down her brush; we remember her moving the salt shaker to a position on the table so that it might function as a version of T.S. Eliot's 'objective correlative' to remind her of an insight about her composition; and we think of her visceral appeals to the ghost of Mrs. Ramsay in the last section.[16] Her 'vision' is an especially powerful way to close the novel because it is all at once a revelation with supremely personal and private significance—a spiritually inflected illumination that takes place precisely as Mr. Ramsay, James and Cam reach the 'light'-house and take steps towards healing primal family wounds—and the end of Lily's prolonged labour at a quintessentially modern(ist) painting.

Invited, as a friend of the family, to Mr. and Mrs. Ramsay's remote summer home on the Isle of Skye, Lily works in an isolated mini-society that bears some resemblances to the Bloomsbury Group: upper-middle class with the leisure to consider questions relating to art and philosophy; geographically situated in such a way as to make social encounters especially intense; and linked by decades-long bonds of family and friendship. Indeed, the book as a whole is highly autobiographical, with Woolf's sister, Vanessa Bell, serving, for example, as a model for Lily Briscoe. Bell herself commented on how poignantly and powerfully Woolf had brought both of their parents to life again, decades after their deaths. She borrows the language of visual art to describe Woolf's literary work as a 'portrait': 'you have given a portrait of mother which is more like her to me than anything I could ever have conceived of as possible. ... You have given father too as clearly but perhaps, I may be wrong, that isn't quite so difficult. There is more to catch hold of' (*L* III, 572). In her unfinished autobiography, 'A Sketch of the Past', Woolf recalls that in composing the book she helped lay to rest the ghost of her parents, and she marvels at this fact in terms of 'vision': 'Why, because I described [my mother] and my feeling for her in [*To the Lighthouse*], should my vision of her and my feeling for her become so much dimmer and weaker?' (*MB*, 81). She speculates that she had participated in a kind of Freudian writing cure, whereby 'expressing' herself 'deeply' (*MB*, 81) had allowed her to elegise them and let them go.

While Lily Briscoe is the text's explicit artist, Woolf also renders the novel's primary heroine, Mrs. Ramsay, as a creative figure who wrestles with trying to achieve her own vision(s). She is the creative force behind the entire gathering on the Isle of Skye, she reads to her boy, attends to her husband and guests, and inspires with 'the torch of her beauty' (*TL*, 36). Woolf also repeatedly links her with the 'light' of the mysterious and potently charged lighthouse (signifying the object of James's desire, the *telos* of the text, a partial, symbolic domestication of 'light' itself on a distant sea rock, and possibly a substitute for something divine—a light that one perpetually seeks), as if to suggest that Mrs. Ramsay herself is *like* the light—radiant, compelling and essential to both vision and anything visionary. Further, she draws the house, the family and the guests together through intense artistic labour: 'she *created* drawing-room and kitchen, set them all aglow' (*TL*, 33–34; italics mine), and in 'exquisite abandonment to exhaustion' (*TL*, 34)—much like Lily's 'extreme fatigue'—Mrs. Ramsay delights in 'the rapture of successful *creation*' (*TL*, 34; italics mine) when she knows that she has 'restored' and 'renewed' both James and Mr. Ramsay. At the dinner party—the central climax of the novel, replete with images of light, and the farewell to Mrs. Ramsay and the book's only moment of a total group connection, in echo of Christ's Last Supper—Mrs. Ramsay is the one who manages to 'unite' the disparate, alienated guests by bringing them together through light, pronouncing 'Light the candles' (*TL*, 78) as if echoing the biblical 'Let there be light'. As we will see in the case of Mrs. Dalloway, Woolf renders Mrs. Ramsay as a great, though under-recognised, artist of life, a housewife and mother whose endless giving to her family and guests ultimately depletes her and leads to her premature death.

### *Mrs. Dalloway*: Ways of seeing

In *Mrs. Dalloway* we do not find the same clear analogy and meta-critical commentary on early twentieth-century Bloomsbury-inflected artistic labour that we do in *To the Lighthouse*, but we still find several characters for whom aesthetics are central to defining their identity. For Mrs. Dalloway, Septimus Warren Smith and Peter Walsh—the characters whose interior states of mind we have most access to—questions about how to 'see' the world and how to attain a meaningful and possibly even spiritual vision of life are inseparable from other existential and ethical issues. None of the three possesses the capacity to translate his or her vision of the world into art, although each lives a passionate life of the mind as each tries to draw together the contrary memories and desires of the past with the facts of the present, suggesting that adulthood means still learning how to see. Mrs. Dalloway, another great artist of life, plans her evening party with a life-affirming drive that will bring together old friends and loved ones as if she is orchestrating a re-kindling of the past within the new frame of the present. Peter Walsh wanders in and out of the narrative like a *flâneur*, just as he wanders through London's streets, and while he revels in the richness of past memories that flood him through the day he anticipates and theorises about the 'beauty' he will discover at Clarissa's party in terms that remind us of Roger Fry: 'Not the crude beauty of the eye', but 'straightness and emptiness ... symmetry' (*MD*, 146). For these two characters, returning to the past in memory is a pleasant, if mixed, experience; for Septimus Warren Smith, on the other hand, it is distinctly unpleasant, with his inability to reconcile haunting war-time visions of loss and trauma with life in post-war England leading to 'madness' and suicide. Woolf had hoped the reader would understand Mrs. Dalloway and Septimus Smith as 'doubles' or 'foils' for each other, with the news of Septimus's suicide permeating Mrs. Dalloway's party as an inverse but intrinsic side to Mrs. Dalloway's revelry: Woolf writes in her diary while composing the novel, 'I adumbrate here a study of insanity & suicide: the world seen by the sane & the insane side by side ...' (*D* II, 207). And in their doubling we understand that Septimus's suicidal pathology mirrors and complements Mrs. Dalloway's alternating life and death wishes that culminate in an affirmative will to live. All three suffer because they cannot reconcile their visions of how life *should* be with the realities of how it is; each suffers because of acute, artistic sensitivities.

Even from the second page of *Mrs. Dalloway* we learn that Mrs. Dalloway sees herself as a creative agent in her life's experience. After observing the 'musical' sound of Big Ben that soars over London as it marks the hours, and after noting the synaesthetic quality of the *sound* of the tolling bells that simultaneously takes on weight and geometric shape—'the leaden circles dissolved in the air' (*MD*, 4)—she reflects. 'For Heaven only knows why one loves [life] so, how one *sees* it so, *making it up, building it* round one, tumbling it, *creating* it every moment afresh' (*MD*, 4; italics mine). On the next page, the narrator reports, she 'was going that very night to kindle and illuminate; to give her party' (*MD*, 5). For the remainder of the book the *telos* of the story involves preparing for her party as she contemplates re-encounters with friends from the past and present, juxtaposing their current relations with those from years ago, moving freely through streams of memory and time. Like Mrs. Ramsay in *To the Lighthouse,* who also 'creates' by drawing people together in community at a party, Mrs. Dalloway's primary role and social signification is as a wife and mother who is called to soothe and subdue feelings of isolation by labouring to generate a meaningful coming-together (we note that both characters are known mainly through their married surnames; indeed, we never once learn Mrs. Ramsay's first name). Lacking formal education or training, neither woman can step into the role of the 'New Woman', but each can still create her vision of life, relations and an aesthetically inflected social milieu which they order as if 'all the world's a stage'.

Peter Walsh, too, sees life with an artist's feeling and passion that Woolf imbues with quasi-mystical experience. After noting that Peter is 'By conviction an atheist perhaps', the narrator tells us that 'he is [nevertheless] taken by surprise with moments of extraordinary exaltation' (*MD*, 51). There follow three paragraphs that each begin, anaphorically, with the phrase, 'Such are the visions' (*MD*, 51–52); in the second one he reflects on his desire for 'peace', 'merg[ing] in one thing' (*MD*, 52). Later we learn of his 'blinding' 'revelation' that Clarissa would marry Dalloway (*MD*, 55)—a loss of a possible love that haunts him for decades. Still, he believes that with age and maturity he has become better able to see: 'The compensation of growing old' is 'that the passions remain as strong as ever, but one has gained— at last!—the power which adds the supreme flavour to existence—the power of taking hold of experience, of turning it round, slowly, in the light' (*MD*, 71). At the party Mrs. Dalloway does just that, even while never ceasing to see the whole event through the lens of the past, yet realising as it drew to a close that 'She felt more deeply, more passionately, every year' (*MD*,173). What both Peter Walsh and Clarissa Dalloway have learned to do, in other words, is to *see* life as it occurs; they have gained the 'power' of framing experience through an almost visionary 'light' that reminds us of Fry's insistence that the Post-Impressionists desired to express 'certain spiritual experiences'.

In creating the shell-shocked character of Septimus Smith, then, Woolf weaves together a pacifist critique of the fall-out from World War One with a condemnation of the tragic limitations of early twentieth-century psychiatry. And she does so precisely while other members of Bloomsbury such as Leonard Woolf and John Maynard

Keynes were engaged in analysing the disastrous consequences of the world's first global war. Septimus is a war veteran, an everyman (the novel self-consciously notes the banality of his surname, 'Smith') and a failed visionary. Like Lily Briscoe he exists on the margins of community, and experiences life with exquisite sensitivities to the 'unimaginable beauty' within the everyday (*MD*, 20); he wrote poetry before the war and was likened to Keats. Septimus, though, remains emotionally frozen in a post-war, post-traumatic hell. Like Lily's distress over her painting being looked at while she works, Septimus is self-consciously preoccupied with anxieties that he is being 'looked at and pointed at' (*MD*, 14); his wife also worries about his strange behaviour in public—'People must notice; people must see' (*MD*, 14)—while she experiences her own discomfort at being 'exposed' (*MD*, 59). At the same time, his doctor has advised him to 'take an interest in things outside himself' (*MD*, 19), and his wife seizes upon this advice to try to insist that he *see* the scenes they walk through as they meander through London: 'Look, look, Septimus!' she calls (*MD*, 19). Septimus does look—in this case it is at the aeroplane spelling out an advertisement for Kreemo toffee—but the looking causes a series of thoughts that 'would have sent him mad', and so he decides he 'would shut his eyes; he would see no more' (*MD*, 20). He cannot help but see, however, and he focuses not on the spectacle of the aeroplane that enthrals others, but on a monistic sense of immanence, with his body feeling 'connected by millions of fibres' to the vitality in 'leaves' and 'trees' (*MD*, 20). This leads Septimus to contemplate 'the birth of a new religion—' (*MD*, 20), establishing Septimus as a modern-day seer who is all at once afraid of being looked at and yet, when he himself *looks* he sees *too* potently into the life of things. These visions then shift to hallucinations of his beloved friend, Evans, killed shortly before the Armistice. Living still in the past, and dwelling on fragments stimulated by memory as if they were real—as if Evans were still with him—Septimus, unlike Lily Briscoe or Mrs. Dalloway, is unable to exist meaningfully in the present, and suffers partly because of his post-war inability to experience life with the same aesthetic intensity he possessed before he went to the front. After the war 'he could not feel', Woolf writes repeatedly, and 'beauty', while still visible, becomes unbearably remote and untouchable: 'behind a pane of glass' (*MD*, 79).

Septimus's melancholic attachment to his lost comrade suggests not only the emotional loss of a friend, but also the loss of the chance to see where a love between men might have taken them. Post-war London with a wife who speaks broken English and who does not seem to understand him—he is relieved when he momentarily believes their marriage is over—is bleak by comparison. In his revisitations of a lost (same-sex) love, we find another parallel with Mrs. Dalloway, who also compulsively revisits memories of her early youth when she loved—and was able to express this love—Sally Seton with a physical intensity that she has never again achieved. Still, Mrs. Dalloway has been able to cherish her memories of Sally's kiss that had been a 'sudden revelation ... an illumination; a match burning in a crocus; an inner meaning almost expressed' (MD, 29) while continuing to embrace an evolving present that celebrates its now-ness: on the day of the party, decades after her kiss with Sally, she feels vitally alive, and she 'plunged into the very heart of the moment, transfixed it, there' (MD, 33). Septimus, on the other hand, is tortured by being unable to separate the past from the present; he has fallen out of time just as he will fall—jump—to his death, and his hallucinations of the deceased Evans paradoxically occur immediately after he sings aloud 'an ode to Time' (MD, 63). Evans' apparition is initially terrifying to Septimus, and he tries to ward it off, but when he sees Evans with 'no wounds' and 'not changed' (MD, 63) the image takes on a revelatory quality, filling him with a momentary 'relief' and 'joy' (MD, 63). His visions have become detached from reality, though, and instead of being able to revel in achieving insight and 'vision', Septimus exists as a failed, 'mad' visionary who is doomed to experience psychosis rather than illumination.

Importantly, both books place the question of meaning at their centre. In a review of To the Lighthouse in The Times shortly after the novel appeared, one critic proposes that 'this question of the meaning of things' that dominates the book 'is not only the essence but the real protagonist in the story'.[17] Not much actually 'happens' within the Aristotelian-influenced single day's drama of Mrs. Dalloway, but its thematic focus is to explore personal ruminations on meaning, time, memory, friendship, love and desire. Bloomsbury had aspired to yoke together meaning, art, pleasure, intellectualism, various forms of politics (from feminism to pacifism and critiques of colonialism) and avant-garde experimentation, and we discover all of these concerns elaborated in Woolf's fiction. Indeed, one of the great recurring preoccupations of modernist writing is the problem of finding personal meaning when faced with the isolation and alienation of a modern society that is focused increasingly on the individual subject rather than on the community. Joseph Conrad's first-person narrator, Marlow, laments in Heart of Darkness, 'we live, as we dream—alone'.[18] The principal characters in both To the Lighthouse and Mrs. Dalloway struggle anxiously, too, with the fact of their ultimate isolation which they feel acutely even while in company, among family and friends. Still, Bloomsbury itself was structured like an extended family, with most of its members involved through some kind of family bond or an otherwise long-term sexual or emotional connection, and in the closing scenes of both books the narrative frame draws together the most disparate figures for the reader, retrieving them from isolation. At the end of *To the Lighthouse* and *Mrs. Dalloway* Woolf doubles two characters of different social positions and genders: Lily achieves her 'vision' exactly as Mr. Ramsay and his children complete their voyage 'to the lighthouse', and Septimus's suicide punctuates Mrs. Dalloway's party, representing a triumph of the death instinct even while the party-goers celebrate life. Both of these doublings bridge a gulf between radical otherness, insisting that despite the fracturing, fragmentation and isolation so central to the ethos of modernist literature, we are ultimately, if not 'one', then bound together in time and linked by simultaneity in ways that we may not always perceive. Woolf's closing message in each story is thus not to underscore alienation and isolation, but to revel in shared experience and mutual passionate efforts at finding meaning, even when these efforts fail.

## Notes

1   The Apostles continue to thrive at Cambridge today, and the principal subjects under discussion remain strikingly close to what later Bloomsbury members experienced around the turn of the twentieth century. A current webpage at King's College, Cambridge, notes, 'The Apostles is a secret society of Cambridge University members that meets to discuss and debate such topics as truth, God, and ethics'. See: http://www.kings.cam.ac.uk/archive-centre/archive-month/january-2011.html.

2   The parameters of the Bloomsbury Group are famously loose, but I include here figures given particular mention by two people who were central to the group, Leonard Woolf and Quentin Bell. See Woolf's *Downhill All the Way: An Autobiography of the Years 1919 to 1939* (London: Harcourt Brace Jovanovich, 1967), and Bell's *Bloomsbury Recalled* (New York: Columbia University Press, 1995). See also S.P. Rosenbaum's *A Bloomsbury Group Reader* (Oxford: Blackwell, 1993), and *The Bloomsbury Group: A Collection of Memoirs and Commentary*. Revised edition (Toronto: University of Toronto Press, 1995).

3   T.S. Eliot gave his first-ever reading of *The Waste Land* to an audience of several members of the Bloomsbury Group at Virginia and Leonard Woolf's country house in Sussex in June 1922. Woolf writes in her diary,

'He sang it & chanted it rhythmed it. It has great beauty & force of phrase: symmetry; & tensity. What connects it together, I'm not so sure. ... One was left, however, with some strong emotion. The Waste Land, it is called ...' [*sic*] (*D* II, p. 178). She and her husband, Leonard Woolf, would publish *The Waste Land* with their Hogarth Press in 1923.

4    'Virginia Woolf and Bloomsbury', in *The Bloomsbury Group: A Collection of Memoirs and Commentary*, ed. S.P. Rosenbaum, p. 416.

5    G. E. Moore, *Principia Ethica* (1903; rev. ed. Cambridge: Cambridge University Press, 1993), p. 270.

6    For an excellent discussion of the Bloomsbury Group in relation to World War One, see Christine Froula, *Virginia Woolf and the Bloomsbury Avant-Garde: War, Civilization, Modernity* (New York: Columbia University Press, 2005).

7    Quoted in Quentin Bell's *Bloomsbury Recalled*, p. 52.

8    Virginia Woolf, *Roger Fry: A Biography* (1940; rpt. New York: Harcourt, 1968), p. 153. Hereafter I will cite passages in text with the abbreviation *RF*.

9    Roger Fry, 'The French Post-Impressionists' (1912), in *Vision and Design* (1920; rpt. London: Chatto & Windus, 1928), p. 237. All quotations from *Vision and Design* are from this edition; hereafter, page numbers will be given in the text, preceded by *VD*.

10    Virginia Woolf, 'Old Bloomsbury', in *The Bloomsbury Group: A Collection of Memoirs and Commentary*, ed. S.P. Rosenbaum, p. 54.

11    Ibid.

12    Woolf gives a fascinating discussion of art's ineffability in 'Hours in a Library,' originally published in the *Times Literary Supplement* in 1916. Rpt. in *Granite and Rainbow* (London: Hogarth Press, 1960), p. 30.

13    Woolf, 'Modern Fiction', 1925, (*E* IV, p. 160).

14    Woolf, 'Mr. Bennett and Mrs. Brown', 1923 (*E* III, 385).

15    Virginia Woolf to Roger Fry, 27 May 1927 (*L* III, 385).

16    In Eliot's 1920 essay, 'Hamlet and His Problems', he proposes that 'The only way of expressing emotion in the form of art is by finding an "objective correlative"; in other words, a set of objects, a situation, a chain of events which shall be the formula of that *particular* emotion'. *The Sacred Wood: Essays on Poetry and Criticism* (1920; rpt. London: Methuen, 1960), p. 100.

17    A.S. McDowall, 'Mrs. Woolf's New Novel', *TLS*, 5 May 1927, quoted in *The Modern Movement: A TLS Companion*, ed. John Gross (Chicago: University of Chicago Press, 1993), p. 117.

18    Joseph Conrad, *Heart of Darkness* (1899; rpt. New York: Norton, 2006), p. 27.

# 5

# 'Women Can't Write, Women Can't Paint': Art and the Artist in *To the Lighthouse*

Bonnie Kime Scott

## Introduction: The painter Lily Briscoe

Artists appear in several of Woolf's novels, but nowhere else in her writings are the painter's formal choices, and the special challenges faced by women artists, more fully and sensitively viewed than in *To the Lighthouse*. The painter Lily Briscoe is an important contributor to the opening and closing parts of this novel. Having joined the Ramsay family on summer holiday on the Isle of Skye, she serves as an interpreter of the physical setting and its personal dynamics, while demonstrating her own struggles with her painting. In Part I, she sets about painting a view looking toward the house, where Mrs. Ramsay sits in the dining room window with her youngest child, James. Through Lily's perceptions and recent recollections, we become aware of the children's vigorous activities, the imposing figure of Mr. Ramsay, and the viewpoints of other guests. Lily thinks intently about her intimate friendship with Mrs. Ramsay, who both holds valuable secrets for this younger woman, and advocates less appealing, traditional ideals of marriage and maternal devotion, while failing to take Lily's painting seriously.

Woolf gives Lily's perceptions and goals time to mature by continuing her story ten years later, when Lily offers the primary perspective in the novel's concluding segment. She completes a second painting that satisfies her memory of the Ramsays and their guests, and gives expression to her artistic vision. Lily not only paints, she colludes in the narrative and, in doing so, is very useful to Woolf. While this essay concerns itself with Lily as a woman negotiating the problems of being an artist, it is equally concerned with Woolf's use of her character to explore options in representation more generally, as women become players in modernist art.

## A matter of confidence

The dismissive, sexist quotation that appears in my title, 'Women can't paint; women can't write', is delivered to Lily early in the novel by Mr. Charles Tansley, an aspiring philosopher, one of Mr. Ramsay's most admiring disciples, and another visitor to the Ramsays' summer cottage. As various feminist critics of the novel have noted, it was partly to counter male pontifications of this sort that Woolf wrote her fictionalised essay, *A Room of One's Own*, published two years after *To the Lighthouse*.[1] It is significant to Woolf's own sense of her vocation that Tansley insults women's abilities as both writers and painters in one glib pronouncement. The thoughts of Mrs. Ramsay and Lily concerning Tansley anticipate Woolf's later comments about judgemental males in *A Room*. Lily senses 'his desire to impress himself' (*TL*, 74). Similarly, Mrs. Ramsay infers that 'he wanted to assert himself, and so it would always be with him till he got his Professorship or married his wife, and so need not be always saying "I—I—I"' (*TL*, 86). However, Mrs. Ramsay's solution is to coerce Lily into helping him join the dinner conversation. Mrs. Ramsay is in effect the 'magnifying mirror' that the narrator finds men expecting in *A Room of One's Own*. That bemused narrator might as well be offering the perfect explanation for Mr. Tansley's statement on women as painters and writers: 'Possibly when the Professor insisted a little too emphatically upon the inferiority of women, he was concerned not with their inferiority, but with his own superiority' (*R/TG*, 44).

As we look at the place of the woman artist in the twenty-first century, we have the added perspective of decades of feminist activism and scholarship that have challenged former hierarchies, criteria, subjects, forms of patronage, intended audience(s) and display spaces in the arts. Starting in 1985, Guerrilla Girls—women artists costumed and masked in ape apparel and bearing as pseudonyms the names of noted women artists—have been challenging the cultural establishment through demonstrations, performances, books and posters. Among their most memorable works is *The Guerrilla Girls Bedside Companion to the History of Western Art*, a zine-style compendium that both satirises the politics of the art establishment and supplements usual male-centered histories with biographies of women artists. Also memorable is the poster, 'Do Women have to be Naked to get into the Met Museum?' It depicts a classic female nude with a fierce gorilla head and presents the discouraging statistics on women artists in the New York Metropolitan Museum of Art versus its number of female nudes.[2] The figure on the poster grimaces back at the tradition that made women the objects, rather than the subjects of representation. Laura Mulvey introduced via film criticism the further observation that women have been represented, not just as objects, but as the objects of a controlling male gaze. Feminist art scholars have sought not just to bring recognition to women artists, i.e., to get them into the Met; they encourage us to interrogate the very system, originating with and focused upon white male Europeans, who set standards of achievement and norms of exclusion. Though an alternate culture for women artists and writers began to emerge, particularly in Paris at the turn to the twentieth century, and modernist art broke with many of the stylistic assumptions of the past, women artists of the period had very few female artists or art critics to mentor them.[3] The traditional system also assigned women to the practice of less privileged genres (e.g. embroidery, floral illustration or portraiture), or associated them with the productions of mass culture. No wonder that many an English woman painter in the early twentieth century was lacking in self-assurance.

In Lily, Woolf offers us a character in the process of developing and sustaining conviction, purpose and satisfaction, somewhat apart from male-dominated and -dictated standards and venues. Lily is not the most confident of artists, and so it is understandable that Mr. Tansley's statement plagues her repeatedly throughout the novel, and that no retort to it is recorded. Instead of standing firm on her painterly vocation, she wavers in her thinking, not only about women as artists, but more generally about women's roles, particularly as she faces the model and expectations of Mrs. Ramsay. She repeatedly refers to herself, pejoratively, as an 'old maid', a term that was routinely used in the early twentieth century. She also thinks of herself is as a homemaker for her father—a common expectation for unmarried daughters of the period. We are not told whether Lily has ever studied painting, or would have been encouraged or financed to do so. Nor do we know whether she has a circle of artist friends to discuss and support her work, or if she has exhibited publicly— advantages Woolf's artist sister, Vanessa Bell, availed herself of. Lily has travelled a bit on the continent, but has not been able to look at many works of art. Her one trip to Paris is in service of an aunt.

While a more confident artist might have preferred working without undue influence, Lily puts it less positively: 'perhaps it was better not to see pictures; they only made one hopelessly discontented with one's own work' (*TL*, 60). Lily makes pessimistic predictions about the paintings she works on in both the first and final segments of the novel, thinking that, if hung at all, they will be consigned to the attic. Unlike a local male artist who has ten boys clustering around his work, Lily is very self-conscious about having anyone take a look at her work in progress.

Mrs. Ramsay has let Lily know that 'an unmarried woman has missed the best of life', to which Lily registers mental protest, 'gathering a desperate courage she would urge her own exemption from the universal law; plead for it; she liked to be alone; she liked to be herself' (*TL*, 43). Indeed, Woolf may have denied Mrs. Ramsay a first name to suggest that she has suppressed aspects of herself after marriage. We find later that Mrs. Ramsay does respect Lily's originality, musing that 'there was in Lily a thread of something, a flare of something, something of her own which Mrs. Ramsay liked very much indeed' (*TL*, 85). But she goes on to imagine what sort of man could like what Lily has to offer, settling on Mr. Bankes and hatching a plan to bring Lily together with him.

Lily does have sufficient confidence to let Mr. Bankes look at and discuss her work in progress. She holds up her end in a conversation that shows awareness of idealised maternal figures in Renaissance art, as well as her own Post-Impressionist goals. She senses that, as a scientist, he will respond to a discussion of form and balance. This perhaps calculated explanation resonates with the doctrine of 'significant form' advanced by Roger Fry and Clive Bell, while slighting the importance Vanessa Bell placed upon colour, when in fact Lily constantly thinks of colour as she works.[4] Lily's independence of mind comes out in other ways. She does not bear Renaissance masters in mind as she paints. She is aware of local artistic trends, such as the vogue for pale colours and semitransparency. Instead, she asserts her need to paint things as she sees them, in more vibrant colours, as did the Post-Impressionists. Even as she is satisfying Mrs. Ramsay's desire that she draw out Mr. Tansley during the dinner discussion, she is mentally rearranging her painting, using a salt cellar on the leaf pattern of the tablecloth to imagine the effect of relocating a tree more to the centre of her work. By the final segment of the novel, Lily's dedication to her painting shows in her determination to solve the problems posed by her earlier attempt in this setting.

## Artists in Woolf's life and fiction

Woolf's family on her mother's side had taken an interest in the arts since her grandmother's generation. Interestingly, Woolf's mother, Julia Prinsep Stephen, frequently served as a model for this earlier generation of visual artists, just as she also served as the model for Mrs. Ramsay in *To the Lighthouse*. Little Holland House, the home of Woolf's great-aunt Sarah Prinsep, served as a residence for the Victorian painter and sculptor George Frederic Watts, who decorated its walls and would eventually paint portraits of both of Woolf's parents. Frances Spalding's biography of Vanessa Bell opens with Vanessa's respectful though curious impressions of a 1903 visit to this elderly advocate of allegorical high art. Among the opinions he shared with her was his scorn for Impressionist painting. Sara Prinsep also welcomed younger Pre-Raphaelite painters to her Sunday at-homes: Dante Gabriel Rossetti, Edward Burne-Jones, John Everett Millais and Frederic Leighton. Woolf's mother virtually grew up at Little Holland House. Burne-Jones painted Julia as the Virgin of the Annunciation. Another of Woolf's great aunts, Julia Margaret Cameron, was a noted Victorian photographer, specialising in staged historical scenes and also soft portraits of famous Victorian writers, scientists and painters. Again, Julia was a favorite subject. Though Cameron got mixed reviews as a photographer during her lifetime and died three years before Virginia's Woolf's birth, her work interested her grandniece. As owners of the Hogarth Press, the Woolfs published a collection of her photography, with Virginia's introduction, while Virginia was working on *To the Lighthouse*. Jane de Gay deftly draws attention to the Burne-Jones and Cameron images of Julia, as well as paintings from Renaissance art and family photographs that Woolf had access to, as sources for the maternal triangle in Lily's first painting in *To the Lighthouse*.[5]

As Diane Gillespie has argued in her book, *The Sisters' Arts,* Woolf's most immediate influence in the arts was Vanessa, as she made her way in the artistic world and developed into a noted Post-Impressionist/Fauvist painter.[6] Leslie Stephen supported his daughter's talent for painting, even though he had little interest in the genre. Stephen arranged for Vanessa to have drawing lessons with Ebenezer Cook, who brought to her John Ruskin's influence. By 1896, Vanessa was attending a small art school three days a week, and in 1901 she qualified for the Royal Academy Schools. Among their visiting instructors was one that impressed Vanessa for a time—John Singer Sargent, whose technique involves a thick style of painting to achieve desired tones.[7]

The death of Leslie Stephen in 1904 released his children to travel. That first summer took them to Italy and France, where they could experience a variety of artistic styles and meet artists influenced by Whistler and Van Gogh. With the exception of a few weeks' study at the Slade School, Vanessa's formal training was over. Her portrait of Lady Robert Cecil, done in 1905, was the first that she exhibited to the public. Also in 1905, Vanessa founded the Friday Club, which offered lectures and discussions by artists and critics, as well as occasional exhibitions. Participants included acquaintances made at the Royal Academy Schools and the Slade School, as well as her family and friends. She invited Roger Fry to give a lecture in 1910, when he was re-establishing himself in England after years abroad working for the New York Museum of Art. Duncan Grant, Vanessa's final partner in life, emerged as one of the top Friday Club exhibitors. One eager early participant was her brother Thoby's university friend, Clive Bell, who had cultivated his taste for modern art over many years, knew many Parisian artists, and was very capable of expressing artistic principles. Their marriage in 1907 preserved and enhanced her connection to the artistic scene.

As girls Virginia and Vanessa worked side by side in a conservatory at the back of their house at Hyde Park Gate. As Vanessa painted, Virginia read aloud or did her writing.[8] They corresponded with each other about their respective arts throughout their lifetimes, rivals in some ways, but fully appreciative of each other's talents. Vanessa provided illustrations for her sister's works and furnished her house with paintings, textile designs and decorative elements. Many of Vanessa's techniques and preferences may be detected in Lily Briscoe's paintings. If not a consultant in Woolf's writing of *To the Lighthouse*, Vanessa's opinion was important in artistic as well as personal ways. Virginia was pleased to find that her depiction of Mrs. Ramsay captured their mother so effectively in Vanessa's opinion; indeed, Vanessa used a painterly analogy: 'so far as portrait painting goes you seem to me to be a supreme artist'.[9] Concerned about whether her description of Lily's technique was convincing, Woolf was pleased to hear that Vanessa and Duncan 'didn't laugh about the bits about painting' and 'surely Lily Briscoe must have been a very good painter—before her time perhaps—but with great gifts, really?'.[10] Vanessa deliberately leaves the face blank in a number of her portraits, including one of Virginia. One effect of this is to liberate the human, and particularly the female subject from the observer's gaze, or to suggest depths of contemplation not readily available to the observer—effects Lily brings to her abstract representation of Mrs. Ramsay.

Hermione Lee has suggested that 'Lily Briscoe's thoughts about her work owe more to Vanessa Bell than to anyone. But without Roger Fry, the thoughts would not have taken the shape they did.'[11] Fry encouraged Woolf's sense of her craft, including her ability to work comparatively between the arts of the writer and the painter— a topic they repeatedly discussed. By planning and executing two major Post-Impressionist exhibitions, Fry at first shocked the British artistic establishment with examples of contemporary French art; gradually he facilitated its formal understanding, acceptance and influence, in Woolf as well as a more general audience. The first of these exhibitions, 'Manet and the Post-Impressionists', ran from 8 November 1910 to 15 January 1911, featuring Cézanne, Matisse, Picasso, Van Gogh and Gauguin. It is widely seen as one of the events that led Woolf to proclaim in her 1924 essay, 'Character in Fiction': 'on or about December 1910, human character changed'.[12] The second Post-Impressionist Exhibition in 1912, which included British and Russian, as well as French artists, became more of a family venture. Leonard Woolf, who had married Virginia earlier that year, served as the exhibition's secretary, and Vanessa was among the exhibitors. Woolf attended and commented upon both exhibitions. Indeed, over a lifetime, she made many comparisons of the arts of painting and writing, not all of them consistent, or designed for the same purpose. Initially she was more impressed by the furor caused by the first Post-Impressionist exhibit than the paintings themselves. In 1910, she states a preference for books over pictures. She was, however, drawn to social commentary on the Exhibition, wondering 'why all the Duchesses are insulted by the Post-Impressionists, a modest sample set of painters, innocent of indecency' (*L* I, 440). Woolf would describe critical and popular reactions in considerable detail in her biography of Fry, published in 1940, long after the Post-Impressionists had become accepted.[13]

Through her essays and letters, we can see Woolf gradually developing interest and respect for the newer art, which had the strongest relation to her own modernist work. Christopher Reed has noted that Fry and Woolf had more to discuss as Fry's artistic theories adjusted to his increasing interest in literature.[14] It is significant to this study that Fry and Woolf exchanged ideas on form, emotion and symbolic representation, both in person and in reading each other's writing—exchanges so significant that she wished she had dedicated the novel to him. In a much-quoted letter to Fry written soon after the publication of *To the Lighthouse*, Woolf resists making a symbol of the lighthouse, but does place a value on 'a central line down the middle of the book to hold the design together' (*L* III, 385). Both Woolf and Lily unify their work with a central line—Woolf's being the central 'Time Passes' section of her triptych novel; Lily drawing a final line in the centre of her painting. As Mark Hussey notes, in 'An Essay on Aesthetics', Fry advocated 'the balancing of the attractions of the eye about the central line' of a picture to achieve unity.[15]

Woolf also followed the painting of Walter Sickert, whose Camden Town group was emerging at the same time as the Post-Impressionist exhibitions. Though written in 1934, well after the publication of *To the Lighthouse*, her essay, 'Walter Sickert: a Conversation', exemplifies the sorts of exchanges she had with both Vanessa Bell and Roger Fry. Woolf blurs the distinction between painter and writer and demonstrates formal appreciation, as well as personal reaction to Sickert's Post-Impressionist style. She declares, 'painting and writing have much to say to each other' and goes on to demonstrate ways that the novelist tries to make us see by producing pictures. She finds Sickert operating in several literary genres: biographer, novelist and poet. Particularly impressive to her is his Post-Impressionist use of colours, which 'went spirally through my body lighting a flare as if a rocket fell through the night and lit up greens and browns grass and trees, and there in the grass a white bird' (*E* VI, 37).

Her essay, 'Pictures', published in 1925, is less reverent in its consideration of the relationship between the writer and the painter. She suggests that, even if modern art were destroyed, a future critic would be able to deduce from the works of Proust 'the existence of Matisse, Cézanne, Derain, and Picasso' (*E* IV, 243). But it is not sufficient for the writer to put on the eye of the painter, to give pictures without creating emotions and thoughts. More self-servingly, she suggests that the writers go through galleries like pilferers, picking and choosing what 'may be helpful to themselves' (*E* IV, 244), rather than seeking to understand the problems encountered by another sort of artist.

Artists have had a presence in Woolf's writing from the very beginning, their styles occasionally detectable in her depiction of landscapes, or artists are cast in minor, peripheral roles, many of them women, clearly amateurs. There is gentle satire as Woolf describes the commanding Mr. Flushing selecting scenes for his wife to paint during an expedition upriver into the jungle in *The Voyage Out*. Aunt Helen sets about representing the landscape, complete with savages, in some equally questionable embroidery. The presence of Cézanne can be felt in descriptive passages of *The Voyage Out,* as for example this view of land, when their ship is pulling into its South American port: behind the 'white crescent of sand' on the beach was 'a deep green valley, with distinct hills on either side. On the slope of the right-hand hill white houses with brown roofs were settled, like nesting sea birds, and at intervals cypresses striped the hill with black bars' (*VO*, 81). As if to show that she is aware that her written subjects can be simultaneously approached by artists, Woolf' opens *Jacob's Room* from the perspective of an artist attempting to get Betty Flanders down in paint, just as Woolf is getting her into print. The central character in this novel, Jacob, visits artists' communities in London and Paris and has a relationship with an artist's model. When evoking her earliest memories in 'A Sketch of the Past', Woolf thinks largely in terms of painting: 'If I were a painter I should paint these first impressions in pale yellow, silver, and green'. Hers is 'a picture of curved petals; of shells; of things that were semi-transparent: I should make curved shapes, showing the light though, but not giving a clear outline. Everything would be large and dim' (*MB*, 66). This painterly vision is supplemented, however, with sound. In Woolf's final novel, *Between the Acts*, we are invited to read much into two paintings that contribute to the décor of Pointz Hall. In this work, Woolf blends numerous arts, including drama, music and painting, and makes room for popular artistic genres as well.

In *To the Lighthouse*, Mrs. Ramsay recalls that artists have been coming to the Isle of Skye, where the family spends their summers, since her grandmother's day. There was a similar, enduring tradition in St Ives, Cornwall, the locus for many summers of the Stephen family as Virginia and Vanessa were growing up. While Lily is the featured artist of *To the Lighthouse*, old Mrs. Beckwith composes a collection of sketches in the same setting. Mrs. Ramsay encourages the artistic side of her daughter Rose, whose arrangement of fruit resembles classical artworks.[16] Mrs. Ramsay herself displays what might be described as a painter's imagination, as for example when she feels briefly 'suspended' from those she has brought together for dinner, achieving a momentary sense of balance and coherence:

> It could not last, she knew, but at the moment her eyes were so clear that they seemed to go round the table unveiling each of these people, and their thoughts and their feelings, without effort like a light stealing under water so that the ripples and the reeds in it and the minnows balancing themselves and the sudden silent trout are all lit up hanging, trembling. So she saw them; she heard them; but whatever they said had also this quality as if what they said was like the movement of a trout when, at the same time, one can see the ripple and the gravel, something to the right, something to the left, and the whole is held together ... (*TL*, 86–87)

Habitually she composes herself by associating with the third stroke of the nearby lighthouse, which resonates with Lily's association of triangles in representing Mrs. Ramsay in her painting, and the overall triptych design of the novel. (TL, 17)

## Approaches to representation

Lily Briscoe sets up her easel on the lawn of the Ramsay's vacation home, facing the house, rather than the ocean view that had attracted previous painters to the area. Mrs. Ramsay is aware that she is to be an element in the picture. Even though she doesn't take Lily's painting 'very seriously', she follows Lily's instructions to keep her head 'as much in the same position as possible.' Lily is trying to 'look at the mass, at the line, at the colour, at Mrs. Ramsay sitting in the window with James'. She works 'with all her senses quickened … looking, straining, till the colour of the wall and the jacmanna beyond burnt into her eyes' (TL, 18). Phrased along with these artistic considerations is the constant worry that someone will come and look at her work. The youngest daughter, Cam, is careening about. More ominous is Mr. Ramsay, who nearly knocks over her easel as he storms by, waving and shouting verses of Tennyson's 'The Charge of the Light Brigade'. William Bankes is the one spectator she can respond to, though with some reluctance: 'it was with difficulty that she took her eyes off her picture'. She wants to be honest about the 'bright violet' of the jacmanna and the 'wall staring white' and 'beneath the colour was the shape'. It is a huge challenge to get the 'vision' she can see clearly onto the canvas (TL, 19) and clearly she does not think she has achieved this. We get an idea of what she is after later in the sequence: 'She saw the colour burning on a framework of steel; the light of a butterfly's wing lying upon the arches of a cathedral' (TL, 42).

Her discussion of the painting with Bankes provides a significant detail. He notes a purple triangle, which she identifies as Mrs. Ramsay and James. Asked why mother and son had been introduced, she suggests that brightness in one corner is balanced with the darkness of this element. He brings to this his interpretation: 'Mother and child— objects of universal veneration' that resonate with his experience of sacred Renaissance paintings of the Virgin and Child. Lily tries to move him away from the idea that the picture is of Mrs. Ramsay and James, and issues of 'irreverence' and whether or not a picture need be a 'tribute' (TL, 45). Indeed, Lily's palette features the suffrage colours of white, purple and (in later passages) green, as Jane Goldman has remarked.[17] Though she may not be a card-carrying suffragist,

Lily does exhibit a rebellious attitude toward traditional womanhood, which is reinforced in Woolf's novel by the complaints of the Ramsay daughters regarding their mother's expectations.

Woolf's play with sequence in her novel allows her to introduce a number of relationships that have a bearing on the role of art in her novel. In the brief time between William Bankes' approaching Lily and their departing together, we tunnel back into earlier experiences and attitudes. Overlooking the bay on a previous walk with William, Lily notes, 'First, the pulse of colour flooded the bay with blue, and the heart expanded with it and the body swam, only the next instant to be checked and chilled by the prickly blackness on the ruffled waves' (*TL,* 20). Lily has a tendency to triangulate relationships as she observes interactions, queering traditional male/female dyads. Her stroll through the orchard with William reveals how each of them thinks about Mr. Ramsay. Memorable here is Lily's image of Ramsay's mind as a 'phantom table' lodged in a pear tree. She has to resist tuning her mind into 'silver-bossed bark of the tree, or upon its fish-shaped leaves' in order to approach the 'angular essences' of his (*TL,* 22). In another triangulation, Lily detects the rapturous effect Mrs. Ramsay has for a time on Bankes, as his gaze settles upon her.

Lily strives to represent the precious intimacy she felt for Mrs. Ramsay as she leaned her head against her knee, offering a sequence of images—the space beside the moon when briefly uncovered by clouds; 'perceptions, half-way to truth … tangled in a golden mesh'; and more sensuous images of secret chambers or dome-shaped hives (*TL,* 43). Earlier Lily has rejected flinging herself at Mrs. Ramsay and saying, 'I'm in love with you'. She substitutes as closer to the truth '"I'm in love with this all"', waving her hand at the hedge, at the house, at the children' (*TL,* 19). If not a picture of Mrs. Ramsay, Lily's painting at least balances her as an element in the larger design. As Lily leaves the scene with Mr. Bankes, she is feeling thankful to both Mr. and Mrs. Ramsay. At this point a narrator constructs momentary unity in a scene that incorporates both art work and novel: 'she nicked the catch of her paint box to, more firmly than was necessary, and the nick seemed to surround in a circle forever the paint-box, the lawn, Mr. Bankes, and that wild villain, Cam, dashing past' (*TL,* 46). The paint box is left in storage.

Lily Briscoe plays a central role in Part 3 of the novel. Not only does she complete a new painting in the same setting, but importantly she allows Woolf to leverage the narrative through her. With the lapse of ten years and the deaths of Mrs. Ramsay, Prue and

Andrew, blankness of feeling at first dominates Lily's mind. Already that morning, she has been the detached observer of a chaotic family drama, as a still needy Mr. Ramsay prepares finally to sail with Cam and James to the lighthouse. The 'unreality' of the scene also poses the excitement of finding out how to bring parts of the scene together: the proposed sailing, the symbolic words 'perished' and 'alone' from lines of poetry shouted by Mr. Ramsay, and the 'grey-green light' on the kitchen wall. She recalls the picture she never completed, a problem with the foreground, and the idea of repositioning a tree. 'It had been knocking about in her mind all these years' (*TL*, 122).

She sets up her easel in roughly the same place as before and reviews the elements: 'the wall; the hedge; the tree' (*TL* 123) and the question of how to relate the masses, which she thinks she now can solve. But Lily still has cautions, insecurities and even resentments. Pacing back and forth as he did years ago, Mr. Ramsay emanates chaos and distracts her from beginning her task. She has trouble seeing her work as anything more than 'playing at painting' (*TL*, 124). His appeal for sympathy, previously visited on Mrs. Ramsay, falls upon Lily, and she is at first unable to respond. Fortuitously, she glimpses another symbol of the angular essence of his mind—his fine boots, working much as the kitchen table had earlier. She spontaneously praises the boots, revitalising him and moving him forward, though not totally relieving herself of the sense that the sympathy she now feels might have been expressed in a final phrase.

Part of Lily's attention remains with the expedition to the lighthouse, even as she turns to the blank canvas, which stands usefully apart from the emotions of the morning. Her memory of the elements in the picture includes details not previously recorded: relations of 'lines cutting across, slicing down, and in the mass of the hedge with its green cave of blues and browns' (*TL*, 130). The jacmanna blossoms are missing, or perhaps not so bright in morning, as opposed to evening light.[18] In the description of her process, there is a new insistence on rhythm and a seemingly related metaphor of a swimmer negotiating waves. She applies first one running mark in brown, and then rhythmically strikes other 'brown running nervous lines'. As if situated in the hollow of a wave, she glimpses the space as the next one looms above her. It is a crisis point that pulls her away from human society and reminds her of Tansley's denial of the woman painter. But she meets it, rhythmically building up blues and umbers, as if following a current. Her mind becomes less conscious of her surroundings. She is able to draw from its depths scenes and memories 'like a fountain spurting over that glaring, hideously difficult white space' (*TL*, 132). Among these memories, each of which encourages brush strokes, is a new triangle, a scene in which Lily and Mr. Tansley are briefly in accord as they sit on a beach with Mrs. Ramsay; Lily cherishes a 'fertile' moment of silence beside Mrs. Ramsay, symbolically ramming a round hole in the sand to bury it (*TL*, 141). Other scenes feature former visitors and her amiable relationship with William Bankes, which notably has not resulted in marriage. Memories of her visions of Mrs. Ramsay accompany her desolation at the emptiness of the step where she formerly sat. Several sections later, Lily gets help from an unexpected source, when someone sits down inside the house, casting 'an odd-shaped triangular shadow over the step' (*TL*, 164). This alters the composition in a potentially helpful way.

Throughout the morning, Lily follows the progress of the sailboat, frequently providing Woolf with a segue to chapter segments set in the boat with Ramsay and his two children. She feels a need to balance Mr. Ramsay with her picture, and, it would seem, her emotions for Mrs. Ramsay—another triangulation. This seems to come after she has an illusion of Mrs. Ramsay on the step, exciting unsatisfied desire. It is replaced by an everyday sense of her as part of the scene.[19] Lily is able to make the final stroke on her canvas as she, together with Mr. Carmichael, realises that Mr. Ramsay has reached the lighthouse. Just as important, she no longer doubts herself as an artist, or bows to established measures of success set by male-dominated traditions and institutions. It does not matter to her if or where her picture will be hung. She is satisfied with her own subject matter— a version of Post-Impressionism comparable to that of Vanessa Bell. Her vision, set to canvas, unites as it organises her experiences of human relationships and emotions. Like her creator in writing, she has negotiated her own integrity, and like her, she offers confidence to future women in her field.

## Notes

1   Mark Hussey, 'Introduction', *To the Lighthouse*. Annotated and with an introduction by Mark Hussey (Orlando: Harcourt, 2005), p. 1.

2   In 1989 5% of the artists were women; 85% of the nudes were women. The news for women artists as of 2012 was not an improvement. By then the figures were 4% women artists, 76% women nudes.

3   See Diane Gillespie, 'The Gender of Modern/ist Painting', in *Gender in Modernism: New Geographies, Complex Intersections*, ed. Bonnie Kime Scott (Urbana: University of Illinois Press, 2007), pp. 765–808. Gillespie

not only gives a fine summary of recent feminist contributions to the history of modernist art; she anthologises rare criticism by modernist women painters, including Vanessa Bell, and notes Bell's challenge to traditions of the female nude and the gaze, pp. 773–74.

4   See Jane Goldman, *The Feminist Aesthetics of Virginia Woolf* (Cambridge: Cambridge University Press, 1998), p. 167.

5   Jane de Gay, 'Behind the Purple Triangle: Art and Iconography in *To the Lighthouse*', *Woolf Studies Annual*, 5 (1999), pp. 1–23.

6   Goldman furthers this argument, focusing on Vanessa Bell especially as a colourist—an element of Post-Impressionism that she sees dissipating in the statements of Fry and Clive Bell after 1912. See Goldman, p. 130.

7   Frances Spalding, *Vanessa Bell* (London: Weidenfeld and Nicolson, 1983), pp. 37, 38.

8   Spalding, *Vanessa Bell*, p. 13.

9   Vanessa Bell, 'Letter to Virginia Woolf,' in *Selected Letters of Vanessa Bell*, ed. Regina Marler (New York: Pantheon, 1993), p. 317. Vanessa was equally moved by *The Waves*, and compares the novel's meaning to a painting she had been working on for years, p. 367.

10  Ibid., p. 318. The letters exchanged between the sisters present good sense of their give and take over their respective arts. The recent novel by Priya Parmar, *Vanessa and her Sister* (New York: Ballantine Books, 2014), constructs a fictional journal for Vanessa in which she is not much concerned with her painting techniques, or the more positive sides of her relationship with Virginia.

11  Hermione Lee, *Virginia Woolf* (New York: Knopf, 1997), p. 283.

12  Virginia Woolf, 'Character in Fiction', *The Collected Essays of Virginia Woolf, Vol. 3: 1919–1924*, ed. Andrew McNeillie (San Diego: Harcourt Brace Jovanovich, 1988), p. 421. This is a later version of the essay, 'Mr. Bennett and Mrs. Brown'.

13  Virginia Woolf, *Roger Fry: A Biography* (New York: Harcourt, 1940), pp. 154–58.

14  Christopher Reed, 'Through Formalism: Feminism and VW's Relation to Bloomsbury Aesthetics', in *The Multiple Muses of Virginia Woolf*, ed. Diane Gillespie (Columbus: University of Missouri Press, 1993), pp. 11–35.

15  Hussey, 'Introduction', p. lxi.

16  In his annotation, Hussey cites works associated with the Roman god Bacchus by Sir Lawrence Alma-Tadema and Caravaggio, p. 225.

17  See Goldman, p. 112.

18  For one artist's rendition of Lily's paintings, see Suzanne Bellamy's 'Lily Briscoe Series'. Bellamy offers a triptych, the central panel representing the dark middle interval of the novel and an eclipse that Woolf saw at the time of its composition. All of her paintings extend to the harbour and the lighthouse. The final panel offers a set of flying purple and black

triangles, resembling sails, seeming to depart the step. See 'Painting the Words: A version of Lily Briscoe's Paintings from *To the Lighthouse*', in *Virginia Woolf Turning the Centuries*, eds. Ann Ardis and Bonnie Kime Scott (New York: Pace University Press, 200), pp. 244–50.

19  DeGay sees Woolf's balancing as a sort of compromise. Accordingly Lily's sympathy for Mr. Ramsay shows the enduring power of Mrs. Ramsay's influence. I would argue that Mrs. Ramsay has assumed a place in Lily's design, which is her own.

# 6

# On the Death of the Soul: a Jungian Reading of *Mrs. Dalloway*

Katherine Tarbox

## Introduction: Virginia Woolf and Carl Jung

Carl Jung was a Swiss psychiatrist who for six years collaborated with Sigmund Freud to develop the new science of psychoanalysis. In 1912 they parted ways after a somewhat acrimonious disagreement about the nature of the unconscious. Freud believed that the unconscious is the repository of repressed desires and wishes, and Jung thought that view too narrow. Jung proposed that in addition to the personal unconscious, we have a deeper stratum called the collective unconscious, an inherited trove of archetypes, or drives—towards feeling, reasoning, spirituality, maternity, paternity, power and so on—that comprise all the potentials, capacities and energies that define what it is to be human. Jung went on to draw from many fields—anthropology, folklore, comparative religion, alchemy—to develop an extensive picture of the archetypes and their influence on the psyche. Contemporary neuroscience, with its imaging capabilities, is continually verifying Jung's findings.

Though Woolf and Jung knew very little about each other, they were contemporaries who shared the same *Zeitgeist*, the same unique pressures and conditions of late- and post-Victorian European culture. Both spent much of their creative energies analysing and writing about the ways that culture adversely affects an individual's psyche. Woolf's view, as expressed in *Moments of Being*, that 'all human beings … are connected to a "pattern" that underlies our daily reality' (*MB*, 72) is remarkably similar to Jung's concept of the collective unconscious. Both Jung and Woolf realised that psychological trouble arises when, to participate in culture and gain its rewards, one must thwart

any number of one's natural drives, and thereby destroy one's wholeness. Woolf spoke of culture 'impinging on [us]', and urged us to
consider what 'immense forces society brings to play on each of us'
(*MB*, 80). Jung filled more than twenty volumes analysing the devas-
tating consequences of deviating from 'the truths of the blood', and
developing the 'soul-sickness' that defined their age.[1] Jung's science
sheds a new light on Woolf's work and illuminates in new ways her
characters, who seem so baffled by themselves and by each other.

*Mrs. Dalloway* presents us with the story of the ongoing battle between the inner world of the mind and the outer world that
impinges on it. In the outer world, immense cultural power fields
create society, gender roles, empire, war and the sublimation of war,
capitalism. 'Conversion' is the mechanism the State uses both to gain
colonial holdings and to colonise the minds of its people. It subdues
people to the 'true belief' by using an 'impress' (*MD*, 90) to brand, dis-
figure and homogenise surfaces, to 'stamp indelibly in the sanctuaries
of others the image of [it]self' (*MD*, 91). Lady Bradshaw exemplifies
the cost to individuals of culture's tampering, because she has had to
be 'cramped, squeezed, pared, pruned' (*MD*, 90) to be what society
expects of her, illustrating Jung's observation that the citizens of his
and Woolf's day seemed to be 'walking in shoes too small for them'.[2]
Eventually she has 'gone under' (*MD*, 90), conceding so much of her
wholeness to accommodate the impress that she becomes an effect
of the State, a phenomenon Jung describes in much the same way as
Woolf: '[the individual is] ... morally and spiritually crushed [by the
State] ... Everything [that does not conform to the needs of the State]
goes under.'[3]

## Anima and animus

The State splits individuals' native wholeness, allowing or disallowing
whatever energies suit its agenda, but the most traumatic mutila-
tion is the split of the syzygy—one's inborn imperative to unify and
express both the masculine and feminine archetypes that lie within.
In *A Room of One's Own* Woolf says that 'in each of us two powers preside, one male, one female' (*R/TG*, 128), adding that '[s]ome
marriage of opposites has to be consummated' (*R/TG*, 136). Jung
calls the feminine archetype in men the 'anima' (or soul), and says
that this archetype offers the gifts of feeling, compassion, irrationality,
empathy, Eros, intuition and connectedness to nature. Its counterpart
in women is the animus (which he again refers to as the soul), the

masculine archetype that provides power, intellect, discrimination, initiative, courage and agency in the world. The State Woolf portrays is a male entity run amok, indulging its power, aggression and privilege, and operating with impunity in the absence of feminine feeling and empathy. Sir William Bradshaw insists that all men be like him, a powerful guardian of the *status quo,* and that all women be like his wife, psychologically hobbled. This 'true belief' (*MD,* 90) in the importance of playing strict roles ensures that men lose their feeling and women their power. In effect, men and women both lose their souls. Bradshaw is rewarded with a 'wall of gold' (*MD,* 85) for seeing to it that individuals conform to a pre-established norm, and for locking misfits away, making it impossible for them to be heard. For Septimus he prescribes the rest cure, a horrific parody of re-birthing, where the patient is infantilised and subjected to the remedial reparenting of the State in the attempt to produce a born-again 'man'.

The beggar woman defines the psychosexual injury and the staggering archetypal loss both men and women suffer. She is keening for the 'man' from whom she has been separated, and she sings in a frail voice a song that is unintelligible, filled with all the vowels except the agential 'I'. Three of the images that describe her—a funnel, a rusty pump, and a barren, wind-beaten tree—voice her soul-loss and her inability to carry the water of life. The funnel has no agency, the pump is disempowered, and the tree, symbol of the amalgamation of all life forces, is blighted.[4] She speaks for the dis-animated feminine in this culture, and the splitting of her psychological hermaphroditism causes not only her ruin, but the male's freedom to wage war, to convert, to wield 'death's enormous sickle' across the world until the earth is a 'cinder of ice' (*MD,* 73). She implores passing men to look into her eyes, to give her presence, to see her, but they either ignore or patronise her.

These psychologically maimed citizens join to create a collective *consciousness,* moving as one mind, one body, with a vacant stare, as if drugged. Because huge swathes of their psyches are unrealised and unconscious, and because whatever is unconscious is projected, they collude to create a subjective reality, a world viewed through a tapestry of projections and fantasies. This is evident in their many interpretations of the plane and the motor car, a reality Jung calls the 'infantile dream state' of 'mass man'.[5] As in a dream, the people to whom they relate represent their own unconscious part-selves. As Peter Walsh realises, 'Nothing exists outside of us except a state of mind' (*MD,* 51).

## The State and the privacy of the soul

Clarissa laments that the State makes a relentless assault on the privacy of the soul, replacing private speech with State speech, which gives voice to the State's ideals. Miss Kilman condemns herself ruthlessly for her perceived flaws—her awkward body, broad forehead, plainness, clumsiness and bad hair. It is a testament to the State's power that it can so easily introject such self-lacerating, self-annihilating thoughts, and that it replaces natural self-acceptance with its own ideas of what is valuable. Thinking as the State does is at odds with inner impulses, and especially with the mandate of what Jung calls the Self, the central archetype whose drive is to draw together and centre the welter of human archetypes into an undivided whole. As Jung often said, this imperative to be and express one's wholeness in the world is the goal of all psychological functioning. In *Mrs. Dalloway* the State hijacks individuals' archetypal energies through symbols and uses these energies for its own purposes. The motor car 'grazes something very profound' (*MD*, 16), the archetype for spirituality, and the crowd becomes rapt with religious spirit, a spell that will lead them unquestioningly 'to the cannon's mouth' (*MD*, 17). When Elizabeth feels the deep, enlivening flush of animus energy, she can only imagine using it to create the brilliant career that, as Bradshaw insists, will assure her belonging in the *status quo*.

Woolf knew that what is 'convenient to call reality' (*MB*, 142) is institutionalised unconsciousness, but she also knew that 'some real thing' (*MB*, 72) often made itself known. When the bewildered, colonised psyche can no longer tolerate its enslavement, spontaneous archetypal self-healing mechanisms spring to life, seeking the demise of faulty adaptations, causing internal restructuring, renewal and transformation. Self, once a hidden text but now clamouring for wholeness, begins to speak its language of image, symbol and fantasy; synchronicities abound, and what has been lost re-appears. On the day *Mrs. Dalloway* takes place, Clarissa, Peter and Septimus struggle to accommodate this harrowing process, to bear the burden of Self as it tries to assert its power against the State.

In her youth Clarissa possessed the expansive energy that 'filled the room' (*MD*, 27), but through time and enculturation she becomes diminished and contracted, 'never showing a sign of all the other sides of her' (*MD*, 33). She imagines herself driven into place, an erect pole or stake, a limb or branch, once alive, but now lopped from its life-source, the tree. When we meet her she is experiencing the appearance of fantasy and strange moods, the liminality, depression and loss of balance that herald the spontaneous and autonomic process of self-renewal.

## Liminal fantasies

Throughout the day that the novel presents she has liminal fantasies that place her neither here nor there, now nor then, a place of stasis-disrupting possibilities. In the morning the doors come off their hinges, and she remembers her plunge into 'open air' (*MD*, 3) at Bourton. Despite her protestations that she loves the present moment, she feels the strong undertow of the unconscious as it keeps drawing her back to the past, the lost, especially to that liminal terrace, the mediating space between inside and outside. Her energy introverts even in her present perceptions, as when she describes a street scene with lively present-progressive verbs—galloping, whirling, laughing, bouncing—but ends with the thud of infinitives: 'To dance, to ride, she had adored all that' (*MD*, 6). The fate of her vitality is found in the movement from active and alive to indefinite and inactive, her youthful energy buried in a compound past.

She has a sense of being 'far out to sea and alone' (*MD*, 8), feels 'invisible; unseen; unknown; ... not even Clarissa any more' (*MD*, 9–10), a terrifying but fecund image of her Self's lack of presence, the dissolution of the artifact called Clarissa, and the salutary benefits of invisibility, of being simultaneously alive in this world and the other. She suffers sudden, baffling depressions, and when she becomes desperately unhappy after Richard leaves, she feels she has 'dropped some ... pearl or diamond into the grass' (*MD*, 108). Both pearl and diamond are symbols of Self's coming into being, as base matter—the defective self—is transformed into something infinitely precious.[6] The image of her lost treasure conjures the thought of why she gives parties, and she finds she feels the presence of disparate people scattered all about London; 'she [wishes that] they could be brought together' (*MD*, 109). The party is an intra-psychic impulse to unite into one whole her scattered part-selves, whom she projects onto the party guests. These fantasies portray a unified Self, a being who does not fall apart when Richard leaves.

The preoccupation with death is a symbolic wish for rebirth, and Clarissa's unconscious desire for re-expansion finds voice when she imagines her (old) self dying and becoming a 'mist' (*MD*, 8), a liminal, indeterminate state between water and air, symbol of primal fertility, as in Genesis, where mist impregnates the new Earth. The amorphousness of mist returns her to her youthful transcendental theory where 'the unseen part of us ... spreads wide' (*MD*, 137). Her fantasy ends with her realization that an autonomic process is working in her, and she wonders, 'what was she dreaming ... What was she trying to recover?' (*MD*, 8). 'Recover' suggests getting something back as well as coming back to health and waking from unconsciousness.

In her need to be genteel and well-liked, she has buried other vital aspects of Self, all that is ordinary, or low, coarse, base and animal. In her fantasy her mist spreads to become part of even an old, ugly, ramshackle house, but awake she clings to hauteur, miffed that the 'Queen' in the car is impeded by the 'ridiculous' (*MD*, 15) masses. She loathes Peter's 'vulgar, trivial, commonplace' (*MD*, 114) women, but she loathes them for qualities she cannot tolerate in herself. We witness the moment she cuts herself off from all that culture deems inappropriate in its women when she condemns the marriage between her neighbour and his maidservant who has had a baby. She decrees, 'I shall never be able to speak to *her* again' (*MD*, 53; italics mine). 'Her' is the image of her own animal, sexual, transgressive qualities, now psychically ex-communicated, condemned and dis-integrated.

Clarissa's fiery, bestial energies find their symbol in Miss Kilman, whom she perceives as low, grubby and unrefined. Most of all she resists the intolerable rage Miss Kilman provokes, which 'rasp[s]' her, feels like the physical pain of a 'brutal monster ... planted down in the depths of ... the soul' (*MD*, 11), and makes a shambles of her beautiful, orderly life. She feels the corrosive effects of a confrontation with the lost, its efforts to dissolve the edifice she builds to maintain the fantasy of the genteel lady she believes herself to be. Her rage flares in the flower shop, kindling a fantasy of a flowerbed at liminal dusk, when each flower 'glows, ... seems to burn by itself ... in the misty beds' (*MD*, 12). Each flower, symbol of the fruition of Self's destiny, like the Buddhists' thousand-petaled lotus, separates itself from the mass to become only itself. Her movement from rage to flower is a journey from what needs to be seen to what that seeing might bring.

## Clarissa Dalloway's loss of animus

Clarissa's greatest loss, though, is the loss of animus, and her story is the contemporary iteration of the beggar woman's ancient plight. She wishes she could have an interest in worldly things 'like a man' (*MD*, 9), but she cannot differentiate Albania from Armenia. Without animus she lives through Richard, a prosthetic animus, sees the world through his eyes, largely thinks what he thinks, and knows he is at his committee settling 'her difficulties' (*MD*, 108). Discovering that he is lunching with Lady Bruton, she feels annihilated by the loss of her man: 'He has left me; I am alone forever' (*MD*, 42). She had been singing a paean to her happy life, of which Richard is the 'foundation' (*MD*, 26), when she takes up the offending pad with its terrible message. Immediately she feels the shocks, pangs and shivers that mark the moment when something lost in the unconscious is touched. She feels 'as a plant on the river-bed feels the shock of a passing oar' (*MD*, 27), a revelatory image of herself as an unconscious, underwater vegetable being, stuck, without agency, rooted, vulnerable to shocks, while the air denizens have power and movement. Weak, unworldly and abandoned, she fears she has no place in the world of the amusing people who have power.

In *A Room of One's Own* Woolf describes a woman's integration of animus in sexual terms:'[A] woman must ... have intercourse with the man in her ... It is when this fusion takes place that the mind is fully fertilized (*R/TG*, 128). Clarissa has a virginal psyche, unpenetrated by the masculine, a fact that explains her 'virginity preserved through childbirth' (*MD*, 28). Young Clarissa knew that 'one must seek out the people who completed them' (*MD*, 136); it was Peter who drew out her animus when she was younger and Peter with whom she has unfinished business. He is the image of the insistent animus, pressing his suit, interrupting her, intruding upon her; he haunts her thoughts through the years. The contrasexual complex always presents a mighty challenge to the ego, the conscious part of the mind that adapts to outer reality and orients itself to success in the world. The ego, however, is occupied territory and will judge even one's own archetypal energies, when they arise, by acquired cultural norms. The ego feels contrasexual power to be dangerous: men have historically devalued the feminine, even—or perhaps especially—in themselves, and women have learned that owning male power is taboo. Peter dares her to be an individual rather than the perfect hostess. He tutors her understanding of the world, begs her to use her intellect seriously, not to talk 'nonsense, ... blunting the edge of her mind, losing her discrimination' (*MD*, 70). He chides her and calls her out for insincerity, coldness and timidity, and when she finally chooses Richard and conventionality, her new 'impenetrability' (*MD*, 55) devastates him. She comes to find Peter's challenge intolerable and knows that Richard will support her slide into normative womanhood and be oblivious to her splinteredness.

On this day they instantly resume their inter-psychic drama and Peter barges in, saying, 'She will see me' (*MD*, 36). '[L]ike a virgin protecting chastity' (*MD*, 36), Clarissa tries to hide what to Peter is her mermaid dress: a mermaid is the underwater female who must remain without a soul until she 'marries' a man. Their meeting crackles with archetypal energy, is a war, and she clings to her familiar, established life—her husband, her daughter, her house—to hold her ground and 'beat off the enemy' (*MD*, 40). Still, she feels 'the pressure of an emotion' (*MD*, 38), and buried things are about to burst to the surface without her permission. She blurts out, 'Do you remember the lake?' (*MD*, 38), and her body reacts with pains and spasms, as the lake is a symbol of the source of life's power, as well as a mirror for the Self. She remembers being a child at the lake with all her Self's potentials intact, then feels the failures and concessions of the life she has actually lived. A new fantasy follows as she sees herself as a queen bewitched to sleep surrounded by defenses—brambles and guards—which have failed and left her vulnerable to Peter's intrusion, open to the Prince's dangerous kiss. She takes her rightful place in the Sleeping Beauty myth, archetypal tale of the female awakened by the animus who holds her power. Though she fights this awakening, she realises that if she had married Peter she would have 'gaiety' (*MD*, 42), the feeling of soul. The desire for symbolic marriage to the animus appears earlier in her mist fantasy, as she and Peter finally 'lived in each other' (*MD*, 8), mingled at the molecular level. Troubled by these disruptive fantasies, she decides her relationship to Peter has been like a play, and now she wants to leave the theatre. Ironically, her actual life is histrionic, while this drama with Peter provides a stage for her authenticity's presence.

If Peter draws out the animus's worldly energy for Clarissa, it is Sally, who also returns synchronously this day, who holds for her its more soul-like spiritual energy. Sally's 'power was amazing' (*MD*, 30), her 'charm was overpowering' (*MD*, 31), and Clarissa 'could not take her eyes off' (*MD*, 29) her, a bewitchment marking the highly emotional and 'numinous character' of an awakened archetype that 'draws the subject under its spell'.[7] Sally has *spirit* that expresses itself as freedom, abandonment, sexuality, swagger and sedition—the same kind of pirate energy Elizabeth finds on the Strand. Clarissa recognises in Sally her own 'sheltered' (*MD*, 30) spirit and feels the 'ecstasy' (*MD*, 31) of love when she meets its symbol. The animus spirit thus evoked blooms as a love with masculine nuances, such as 'chivalry' (*MD*, 31), and it is Othello's words ('if it were now to die …') that speak her feelings. Sally's kiss overwhelms her with the 'religious feeling' (*MD*, 32), because it brings to life her spirit, her soul, a revelation that always carries with it the deep feeling of the sacred.

A flicker of this fire survives in Clarissa, and she continues to be drawn to transgressive women who are 'confessing … some scrape, some folly' (*MD*, 28–29), and who revivify her memory of spirit. In those moments she comes to 'feel what men felt' (*MD*, 29), the presence of soul as a male orgasm flooding her psyche. She feels 'expansion, … swollen with some astonishing significance, … which … gushed … with an extraordinary alleviation' (*MD*, 29), an epiphanic consummation that remains infertile because she cannot find the courage to integrate it with her outward adaptations, cannot live and express spirit in the world as the young Sally had.

## The party

At her party Clarissa feels strongly the fire of the deconstructive process that has been smouldering all day. She tries to swell with pride at the Prime Minister's presence, but feels only hollowness, knowing her pretensions to be an 'intoxication' (*MD*, 156), a poisoning. She fills her rooms with guests who support her persona, but soon realises they are merely 'semblances' (*MD*, 156). Like her psyche, her party is defended against unwanted intruders, but it seems that nature herself has destined that she be confronted, *en masse*, by what she has excluded. When she admits that her party 'satisfied her no longer' (*MD*, 156), the unconscious opens and thoughts of Miss Kilman rush at her. That loathed part-self comes intensely alive, and she has a brief but extraordinary insight, feels love for Miss Kilman, and realises 'it was enemies one wanted' (*MD*, 156), because enemies give rise to self-awareness. She has no such insight about Ellie Henderson, who represents all that is ordinary, meek and dull in herself, knows only that she seeks 'pinnacles' (*MD*, 150) with these parties to hold herself above the rabble. With her brittle charm she defends herself against being 'some Ellie Henderson' (*MD*, 150). Peter enters her house and proffers his critique, distressing Clarissa because '[h]e made her see herself' (*MD*, 150). Sally's presence still has the power to accuse Clarissa of abandoning her. All night Clarissa avoids the interlopers.

Clarissa is clearly rattled by these disruptions. Part of her fears her party is a failure, yet another part wishes for an explosion, a burst of anarchic power and heat. Her familiar hostess role now chafes, makes her feel 'something not herself, … unreal' (*MD*, 152). She panics when the bird-of-paradise curtains blow into the room like 'a flight of wings' (*MD*, 150). As Joseph Henderson points out, a flight of birds is an archetypal symbol of the need to fly, 'to break all ties with … containment, … to live … in a new way'.[8] Here nature becomes another intruder, frightening Clarissa with the images of spirit, freedom, instinct and aleatory flight, because to her they augur the nothingness left in the wake of her safe world's crumbling.

Ultimately death makes its trespass, and she confronts the void she so fears. She realises at once what Septimus has thrown away: 'a thing … that mattered; a thing wreathed about with chatter, defaced … in her

own life, ... the centre' (*MD*, 165). The centre is a circle, symbol of the
Self, about which she lays a wreath to memorialise what is buried, and
Clarissa's circle is defaced with the impress of conversion. She knows
instinctively that Septimus plunged to preserve his 'treasure' (*MD*, 165),
while she has 'lost herself in the process of living' (*MD*, 166), recoiled
from life in terror and squandered her treasure—her individuality. This
realisation is the climax of her process, and for a moment she wants
to forsake 'all this' (*MD*, 166), to 'go back, ... [to] find Sally and Peter'
(*MD*, 167). As quickly as this monumental epiphany arises, however, it
dissolves, as she decides to reassemble her hostess persona and go back
to the party. In this culture it appears to be dangerous to flower, and
we last see her as someone who 'was'.

## Peter Walsh's unintegrated anima

Peter Walsh clearly has a 'woman problem'; in psychological terms,
he has an unconscious, unintegrated anima who, because he indulges
himself by projecting this inner feminine element on every desirable
woman, has taken possession of his faculties. As Jung warns, when
the anima takes possession of her host, 'she causes bewitchment, ...
playing all kinds of tricks, ... causing ... delusions, depressions and
ecstasies, outbursts of affect'.[9] Marie-Louise von Franz adds that the
host 'becomes effeminate, unable to cope with the hardships of life'
and is forever falling in love.[10] Peter certainly recognises that 'he [is]
not altogether manly' (*MD*, 139) and is 'dependent on women' (*MD*,
141). The process he undergoes this day confronts him with these
facts and move him toward taking ownership of his anima and her
powers rather than vampirising the powers of the women in his life;
it is a telos that speaks in his decisive and impressive—to the other
diners—ordering of Bartlett pears, symbol of a femininity he needs
to metabolise.

    In his youth a radical, Peter still feels 'the future of England
lies ... in the hands of young men [such as he was]' (*MD*, 46). In
the present he is a henchman for the empire, supervising coolies
in India, his radicalism gone under. When the young Peter meets
Clarissa she receives the full projection of his ravenous anima, and
he sees Clarissa in mythic terms, arising out of nature, on a hill in a
wind-blown cloak, in a wood at an open fire, walking miles through
stubbled fields. She 'pilot[ed]' (*MD*, 138) him, 'made him look with
her' (*MD*, 138), and he believes that 'they would change the world if
*she* married him' (*MD*, 139; italics mine). Had he been able to own
the ecstasies she evoked in him rather than needing to own Clarissa

herself, had he made that symbolic marriage, his radicalism might have been potent and effective, since a man-with-integrated anima would present a prodigious challenge to his culture.

In his morning meeting with Clarissa, he still projects his anima, believing that he is speaking to someone 'raised up in the dark' (*MD*, 40), at whose feet one must lay garlands. Together they are a case of psychological reciprocity, and she offers him the same withering challenges he offered to her. 'Those uncontrollable forces' (*MD*, 42), the archetypal energies, affect him as they affected her, and 'she drew up to the surface something which positively hurt him' (*MD*, 39). Eventually he breaks down and submits to the emotional intemperance that 'had been his undoing' (*MD*, 64).

When Clarissa ends their relationship he plunges into a depression consistent with soul-loss, and he spends the intervening years searching for her surrogate. In choosing Daisy, a married woman with children, he chooses someone 'with no sense of discretion' (*MD*, 140)—an image of the transgressive part of Clarissa that went under at that terrible dinner. It is as if in Daisy he is trying to get the whole Clarissa back, and he harbours the fantasy of getting Clarissa to accept 'her', be 'nice to Daisy', and help find her a 'lodging' (*MD*, 141). In the end Daisy fails to evoke the same numinosity as Clarissa: Peter realises that she would look very 'ordinary beside Clarissa' (*MD*, 39), and he knows he has made another mess with these magically complicated relationships.

His synchronous return to Clarissa heralds the beginning of his own deconstruction, and, drawn inward by depression, he feels 'hollowed out, … empty' (*MD*, 44). Like Clarissa, he becomes emotionally labile and intuits the workings of the autonomous process where 'the soul' (anima) who inhabits 'deep seas … suddenly … shoots to the surface … to kindle herself' (*MD*, 144). Alone in Trafalgar Square, he feels 'another hand' pulling his strings, while he has 'nothing to do with it'. His mind goes 'flat as a marsh' (*MD*, 47), a liminal image of earth that is neither land nor water, and he feels 'utterly free' from 'being … what he was' (*MD*, 47). He disarticulates himself from his roles, his history, his affairs, the ego–accretions called Peter, to become blank. At this moment the necessary fantasy erupts: a woman on the street becomes 'the very woman he had always had in mind'. She is a mythic figure, 'enchanting' (*MD*, 47), a totality that embraces both youthfulness and *gravitas*, merriment and discretion, and, sensing she is a symbol, Peter calls her 'it' (*MD*, 49). She brings out latent energies in him as he stalks her, and he becomes a buccaneer, no longer Peter, but what he might have been, the radical pirate who metaphorically sails on unbounded seas, outside laws and norms. In his mind she speaks to him as 'you', 'his private name for himself' (*MD*, 48), and he and she are finally one voice.

Dismissing this definitive fantasy, he moves on; but his anima turns trickster and commandeers his dreams. He is the solitary traveller, a man travelling alone, trampling nature, when an accusatory feminine figure arises from the 'troubled sea' (*MD*, 52) of his restless unconscious. Under her influence he realises he wants something other than quotidian life among 'craven men and women' (*MD*, 51), whereas moments before his sleep he thought the crowd 'admirable, good fellows' (*MD*, 50). The dream is compensatory, and his anima again connects him to his native subversive nature. The majestic figure heals, nourishes, offers cornucopias full of ripe fruit, but she is also dangerous, as Ulysses learned, because her seduction can be overpowering. The 'siren' (*MD*, 51–52) ungrounds him, causing him, in a contrasexual version of Clarissa's Sleeping Beauty fantasy, to wish eternal enchantment. His dream, as a statement of inner fact, elaborates his problem: his anima will 'ceaselessly float up' from the depths of his psyche and Peter will ever put her face 'in front of the actual thing' (*MD*, 52); that is, he will continue to confuse actual women with that haunting feminine power within. When he wakes he knows he is dreaming of losing Clarissa, and the rest of the dream reveals the personal cost of his parasitising women. The traveller returns to an ordinary world, a village over which hangs a sense of annihilation, a world deconsecrated, demystified, disenchanted. The magical, resplendent world of wild, endless carousing, copious ripe fruit and the never-ending siren song gives way to the landlady, mistress of tame domesticity, while the image of luscious living fruit contracts to marmalade, dead, jarred fruit she shuts away in a cupboard. The siren song comes to an end.

His waking utterance, 'the death of the soul' (*MD*, 53) acknowledges that Clarissa's going under was his going under, but it is a tragic misperception. In both his and Clarissa's fantasies, soul is profoundly alive, active and clamouring. Failing, as Clarissa failed, to embrace these insights, he remains bewitched to the end, imagines her as the mermaid of his dream. His final vision of her is filled with the 'extraordinary excitement' of both 'terror' and 'ecstasy' (*MD*, 174), raptures evoked by the contemplation of the divine, the extreme emotional jolt created in an encounter with an archetype. He has failed to grasp the hidden hand's meaning, remains unconscious, and when he says, 'there she was' (*MD*, 174), he continues to confound Clarissa with the archetypal 'She', his anima.

## Septimus Warren Smith

Septimus Warren Smith endures a process that is different, not in kind but in degree, from that of the others, and his destiny reveals why it is so dangerous for individuals to surrender to the archetypal drive to be whole. It is in Bradshaw's interest to call his affliction shell-shock, because to pathologise is to abet hegemony; those who resist the impress challenge the impress, and to call them sick puts them in his power and makes them available for remediation. Jung, like Septimus, had a similar 'creative illness', as he called it, commenting that 'I consciously submitted myself to the impulses of the unconscious'.[11] This declaration mirrors Septimus's decision, made with 'complete consciousness' (*MD*, 81), to surrender to the process of confronting what lay buried in his unconscious. Conscious submission reveals the presence of an ego that can survive and differentiate itself from the onslaught of the unconscious, while psychosis swamps and overtakes the conscious mind. He undergoes the complete psychological deconstruction that Mircea Eliade calls 'initiatory sickness',[12] what in other cultures would be called 'shamanic initiation'. Eliade describes the initiate as one who exhibits bizarre behaviour; alternates between bliss and terror; loses space–time boundaries; talks to the dead; receives sacred wisdom; and feels torn apart, dismembered and skeletonised.[13] Eliade stresses that the initiate's self-cure and return to the world are what differentiate this illness from psychosis: Shamans are shamans *precisely because they had succeeded in becoming cured* (his italics).[14]

Septimus insists he is falling into flames, an image of purifying dissolution, as is his skeletonisation, his extreme weight loss, revealed when he offers Rezia his arm, and we learn that it is only 'a piece of bone' (*MD*, 14). He feels his body is 'macerated until only the nerve fibres were left … spread like a veil on a rock' (*MD*, 61). When ego melts he becomes a veil, symbol of the transparent tissue that both conceals and reveals great powers and truths. In an imaginal sea he is the drowned sailor who has 'been dead, and yet now [is] alive' (*MD*, 62), a fantastic expression of his boundary-destroying descent to the world of the other, where he will find his lost soul, his ability to feel. Like other mythic heroes who have taken this journey, he finds flowers growing through his flesh and becomes consanguineous with nature. In this psychological hinterland sound becomes visible, roses grow through the snow, and the dead walk among us. Because linear time is meaningless, he sees the dead of all wars and becomes their 'giant mourner' (*MD*, 63). If Peter and Clarissa cling to their ego-identities as the hidden hand attempts to dismantle them, Septimus releases his, causing Rezia to lament, 'he was not Septimus now' (*MD*, 21).

The agenda of initiatory sickness seeks not only the individual's healing, but also the healing of the culture that has gone awry, and, according to the pattern, Septimus would return from his ordeal to correct the imbalances in this clearly depressed culture. In Jung's analysis conversion transforms humans into 'depotentiated social units',[15] and, unaware of what ails them and living a charade of wellness, citizens, mere avatars of their whole Selves, inhabit abysses of private suffering and fragmented Selfhood. In the bookshop window a volume of Shakespeare lies open at *Cymbeline's* dirge, a paean to comforting death, as if all who pass will relate to it. Clarissa reads it and thinks, 'This late age of the world's experience had bred in them all … a well of tears' (*MD*, 9). Big Ben is an omnipresent disciplinary voice which forces people to move at his call, upholds 'authority' and counsels 'submission' (*MD*, 92). Big Ben casts leaden circles, gathering the populace under a toxic sky of dissolving lead, the basest element, symbol of the depression that heralds the beginning of a transformative alchemical process. The heat wave that smothers the city puts the collective in the alembic, making them feel as if the world is about to burst into flames. Septimus, through no choice of his own, is elect, the 'scapegoat' (*MD*, 37) who 'had come to 'renew society', and must undergo this ordeal for a society that can neither understand nor support it; 'he did not want it' (*MD*, 37).

He begins this journey in his youth, when, from the mixed seeds of 'vanity, ambition, idealism, passion, loneliness, courage, laziness'—his archetypal potentials—he 'flowered' (*MD*, 76). He blooms when he is pollinated by Miss Pole, the teacher who brings his anima to life. Unlike Peter, he owns 'her' power and uses it to individuate, to disentangle himself from the cultural script, to eschew the edicts of Big Ben and pace the streets in the middle of the night or write at 3 am. He fasts one day, drinks another. He unifies masculine and feminine energies, writing masterpieces—becoming master of Logos—while submitting to the wild passion and caprice of Eros. His flower is crushed and torn apart in the war, where, to kill strangers for a putative cause, he must achieve 'manliness' (*MD*, 77), the absence of feminine feeling. With his history of flowering and its subsequent ruination, he becomes the perfect scapegoat, the rare being who has tasted wholeness and cannot tolerate its fracturing.

Bradshaw's agenda is to repatriate Septimus to consensual reality, but Septimus cannot communicate with him, has abandoned the signifying systems of this world for those of the other, and sees with the other's eyes, an optic that gives him a remarkable discernment of what is real and what is not. He observes people on the street 'making up lies as they passed' (*MD*, 60), knowing that in their unconsciousness they can only project their fantasies onto the world. Sitting in the park he sees the world as charade, theatre, where the grass is 'green stuff' (fabric) and the sky a 'ceiling cloth of blue' (*MD*, 22). Conversely, he knows the difference between objective reality and his delusions about it. When he hears grand music in the hills, he knows it is only a car horn; he knows that a shepherd boy's piping is only someone playing a penny whistle; he knows that the roses growing in the snow are inspired by his bedroom wallpaper. His acuity contrasts sharply with the delusional mentality of the crowd who see a motor car and actually believe there is greatness within. The dissolution of his ego allows him to see the world naked, to see that the world 'made out of ordinary things as it was, was the truth now' (*MD*, 62–63). He ridicules the doctors who believe the world is as they see it, and who, unlike Septimus, 'mixed the vision and the sideboard; saw nothing clear' (*MD*, 127).

These doctors will never be able to hear the corrective message Septimus is to bring back from his journey. He is desperate to tell them about 'human cruelty—how they tear each other to pieces' (*MD*, 126)—a bold acknowledgement of Britain's conduct in the First World War, its colonial adventure and its program of psychological colonisation at home. He needs to tell them that the 'whole world was clamouring: Kill yourself' (*MD*, 83), knowing that for its survival the hegemony requires subjects to dismantle their whole Selves. As he sits on a park bench mumbling in his shabby overcoat, he appears to be a ruined man; but inside that mind he is formulating 'the birth of a new religion' (*MD*, 20), one which disentangles archetypal spirituality from its co-option by the State and allows individuals to reconnect to nature within and without. He, like all initiates, comes to understand the mystery of the Tree, symbol of the connectedness of all life forces with the physical laws of the universe, and insists trees must not be cut down. His ritual mission requires that he 'make it known' (*MD*, 22) that this religion will 'change the world' (*MD*, 22). His illness and its agenda are political, and he clamours for his message to be 'told to the Cabinet' (*MD*, 61), told eventually to the Prime Minister himself.

Just as Septimus consciously surrendered to his role as scapegoat, so he also consciously decides to be 'mad' (*MD*, 127) no more. He has seen what he has needed to see, he 'knew the truth! He knew everything' (*MD*, 125), and his agonies, his trembling and sobbing are over, 'burnt out' (*MD*, 128). He makes his return to still air and happiness,

able to 'become himself' (*MD,* 129) in a second flowering. His feeling returns because his anima returns, reveals her presence as he takes
up hat-making, an activity he once left to Rezia, his surrogate anima.
He creates an odd, one-of-a-kind hat that stands as the final testimony
to his individuation, his Self's survival, and when he is done, he beams
that '[it] was so real' (*MD,* 129). He finds his spine as well, the masculine power to stand up to the doctor's 'must' (*MD,* 134). He knows,
though, that the snuffling beast of conversion will pursue him forever,
that he cannot live in this world with his treasure intact. Septimus
sees that the only way to save his Self is to kill himself. The plot of
this novel is the futile attempt of desire itself to move towards its end,
and at the end, as in a Shakespearean tragedy, the stage is littered with
the dead; the catharsis is for the reader. Jung might say that Woolf, in
a shamanic gesture of her own, was speaking for her age and that the
age's errors 'come to light in … the visions of artists … thus restoring
the psychic equilibrium of the epoch'.[16] Its restoration is central to
*Mrs. Dalloway.*[17]

## Notes

1   What I have quoted here is from C. G. Jung, *The Structure and Dynamics
of the Psyche*, trans. R. F. C. Hull (Princeton: Princeton University Press,
1960), p. 415. The title of one of Jung's books in particular, *Modern Man
in Search of a Soul*, is indicative of the subject of his lifelong inquiry. See
*Modern Man in Search of a Soul*, trans. W. S. Dell and Cary F. Baynes (New
York: Harcourt, Brace and World, 1933).
2   Ibid., p. 381.
3   C. G. Jung, *Two Essays on Analytical Psychology*, trans. R. F. C. Hull
(Princeton: Princeton University Press, 1953), p. 150.
4   When I use the term 'symbol', I refer to the *archetypal* symbol: an object
from the phenomenal world that, through all time and in all cultures,
represents a particular archetype. For example, the moon universally
symbolises feminine power.
5   C. G. Jung, *The Undiscovered Self*, trans. R. F. C. Hull (Boston: Little
Brown, 1957), p. 59.
6   Woolf parallels Jung's comments on the unifying Self elsewhere, when
Clarissa reflects that 'her self … drew the parts [of her mind] together
… into one centre, one diamond' (*MD*, 33).
7   *The Structure and Dynamics of the Psyche*, pp. 205–206.
8   Joseph L. Henderson, 'Ancient Myths and Modern Man', in *Man and
His Symbols*, ed. C. G. Jung (New York: Doubleday, 1964), p. 152.
9   C. G. Jung, *The Archetypes and the Collective Unconscious*, trans. R. F. C.
Hull (Princeton: Princeton University Press, 1959), p. 26.

10  Marie-Louise von Franz, 'The Process of Individuation', in *Man and His Symbols*, p. 179.

11  C. G. Jung, *Memories, Dreams, Reflections*, trans. Richard and Clara Winston (New York: Vintage, 1989), p. 173.

12  Mircea Eliade, *Rites and Symbols of Initiation*, trans. Willard R. Trask (Woodstock: Spring, 1958), p. 89.

13  *Rites and Symbols of Initiation*, pp. 87–95.

14  Ibid., p. 88.

15  C. G. Jung, *The Undiscovered Self*, p. 105.

16  *Modern Man in Search of a Soul*, p. 171.

17  This essay is dedicated to Dr William Frank in recognition of his generosity of spirit.

# 7

# On Not Being Able to Paint: *To the Lighthouse* via Psychoanalysis

Maud Ellmann

## Introduction: Virginia Woolf among the psychoanalysts

In an essay called 'Freudian Fiction' (1920), Woolf objects to psychoanalysis for imposing a doctrinal 'key' on literature:

> Our complaint is ... that the new key is a patent key that opens every door. It simplifies rather than complicates, detracts rather than enriches. The door swings open briskly enough, but the apartment to which we are admitted is a bare little room with no outlook whatever. (*E* III, 197)

In this well-known denunciation, Woolf is attacking reductive Freudians rather than Freud himself, whose work she claimed not to have read until 1939. This avoidance must have cost her some effort, given that her husband Leonard Woolf was an early champion of Freud, her brother Adrian Stephen and his wife Karin were practising psychoanalysts, and James Strachey, brother of her close friend Lytton, had travelled to Vienna with his wife Alix to be analysed by Freud, and the couple had returned as Freud's official English translators.[1] Their translations, moreover, were published by the Woolfs' Hogarth Press, along with nearly seventy volumes of the International Psycho-Analytical Library. As Matt ffytche has pointed out, psychoanalysis was 'woven into the daily life' of Woolf's Bloomsbury.[2]

Yet Woolf had many reasons for steering clear of Freud, not least because they shared such deep affinities. Possibly she found his work too close for comfort.[3] Besides, her painful experience of mental illness had taught her to distrust mind–doctors, as caricatured in the egregious figure of Sir William Bradshaw in *Mrs. Dalloway*. Alix Strachey thought Woolf avoided psychoanalytic treatment for her mental breakdowns for fear of inhibiting her creativity. 'Virginia Woolf's imagination, apart from her artistic creativity, was so interwoven with fantasies—and indeed with her madness—that if you stopped the madness you might have stopped the creativeness too.'[4] By 1939, however, Woolf by her own admission was 'gulping up Freud' (*D* V, 249). In the same year she recalled that writing *To the Lighthouse* in the previous decade had freed her from the haunting presence of her mother, Julia Stephen, who had died in 1895. 'I ceased to be obsessed with my mother', Woolf writes in her memoir, *A Sketch of the Past*:

> I no longer hear her voice; I do not see her.
>      I suppose that I did for myself what psycho-analysts do for their patients. I expressed some very long felt and deeply felt emotion. And in expressing it I explained it and then laid it to rest. (*MB*, 81)

This statement marks a dramatic turnaround in Woolf's attitude to psychoanalysis. Following Woolf's lead, many critics have enlisted Freud, Melanie Klein and their successors to examine the psychobiographical implications of *To the Lighthouse*.[5] In this chapter I offer a prismatic view of *To the Lighthouse* from several psychoanalytic perspectives. I begin by sketching in broad outlines the implications of Freudian and Kleinian theory for this novel. Illuminating as they are, neither of these theories offers a sufficient account of the art of painting, which looms so large in Woolf's *Künstlerroman*. To explore this dimension of the novel I turn to the British psychoanalyst Marion Milner, specifically her autobiography study *On Not Being Able to Paint*, a title remarkably germane to the theme of artistic inhibition in *To the Lighthouse*. By comparing these texts, I do not mean to suggest that Milner's theories can explain Woolf's novel, but to challenge the dichotomy between the analytic and the fictional. Milner's theories, which owe as much to art and fiction as to psychoanalytic doctrine, bring to light the theoretical dimension of *To the Lighthouse*, which contains its own implicit psychoanalysis of creativity.

## Freudian perspectives

Many of Freud's theories map so neatly onto *To the Lighthouse* that the critic's task becomes almost too easy. The Freudian concepts of the Oedipus complex, screen memories, the primal scene, castration anxiety, deferred action and compulsive repetition—not to mention the looming phallic symbol of the Lighthouse—announce themselves on every page, making the novel something of a primer in psychoanalysis. Indeed these motifs are so blatant, so knowing, that one wonders if they represent a smokescreen, concealing secrets that resist translation into textbook Freud.

Portrayed as the Be that as it may, the novel opens with an Oedipal crisis, when James's idyll with his mother is interrupted by Mr. Ramsay, who demands the undivided attention of his wife. Portrayed as the castrating father—'lean as a knife, narrow as the blade of one'— Mr. Ramsay shatters the 'heavenly bliss' (*TL,* 7) of mother and son, those 'objects of universal veneration' (*TL,* 45) enshrined in the image of the Madonna.

> Mrs. Ramsay, who had been sitting loosely, folding her son in her arm, braced herself, and, half turning, seemed to raise herself with an effort, and at once to pour erect into the air a rain of energy, a column of spray, looking at the same time animated and alive as if all her energies were being fused into force, burning and illuminating (quietly though she sat, taking up her stocking again), and into this delicious fecundity, this fountain and spray of life, the fatal sterility of the male plunged itself, like a beak of brass, barren and bare. He wanted sympathy.... Standing between her knees, very stiff, James felt all her strength flaring up to be drunk and quenched by the beak of brass, the arid scimitar of the male, which smote mercilessly, again and again, demanding sympathy (*TL,* 33–34).

James, whose character was based on Adrian Stephen, the future psychoanalyst, reacts to his father's intrusion with parricidal fury: 'his son hated him', Woolf writes (*TL,* 33). 'Had there been an axe handy, a poker, or any weapon that would have gashed a hole in his father's breast and killed him, there and then, James would have seized it' (*TL,* 7). Love for the mother, murderous resentment of the father: this is the classic Oedipal predicament. But Woolf's imagery also foreshadows the imminent dissolution of Oedipus complex, when the little boy will renounce the mother and identify with the father. Perceiving his father as a scimitar, James himself is armed with scissors and cutting out pictures of knives from an Army and Navy Stores' catalogue (*TL,* 7). His fantasies of axes and pokers also align him with his father's phallic weaponry, prefiguring the rite of passage to the Lighthouse when the son accedes to the paternal role of 'lawgiver' (*TL,* 138).

That the Lighthouse stands for the paternal phallus seems embarrassingly obvious: 'There it loomed up, stark and straight ...' (*TL,* 165). But Woolf subverts this Freudian correspondence by associating Mrs. Ramsay, rather than her husband, with the Lighthouse, specifically with the third stroke of its pulsating beam (*TL,* 53). Mrs. Ramsay evidently thinks in threes: when she listens to a watch she counts 'one, two, three' (*TL,* 69), whereas it is customary to count tick-tock as two, as William Empson observes in an early discussion of the novel.[6] Freud also thinks in threes, such as the Oedipal triangle, or the triadic psychic agencies of id, ego and superego. In religious terms, three is the number of the Holy Family and the Christian Trinity; it is also the number of panels in a triptych, a structure emulated in the tripartite structure of this novel, its three parts corresponding to Mrs. Ramsay's life, death and resurrection in the form of Lily's painting. This painting pays further homage to the number three by depicting Mrs. Ramsay as a purple triangle, the traditional geometry of the Madonna.[7]

As Bonnie Kime Scott points out in her chapter in this volume, Lily has 'a tendency to triangulate relationships'. But instead of sta-bilising gender roles, as in the normative outcome of the Oedipal triangle, Lily's threesomes have the effect of 'queering' traditional male/female dyads. Lily, of course, is not a Ramsay but the motherless daughter of a father who never appears. Her position at the sidelines of the family evokes the child's feeling of exclusion from the parents' intimacy, but also a desire to escape their stranglehold.

This ambivalent relation to the parents could be compared to a photograph (Figure 7.1) in Leslie Stephen's family album, compiled as a memorial to his dead wife, which Woolf consulted when writing *To the Lighthouse.* The photograph in question, a favourite of Leslie Stephen's, shows him reading on a sofa with his wife, scrutinised by a young Virginia in the background.[8] Although the parents are not embracing, the picture conveys a powerful impression of their conju-gal intimacy and their daughter's fascination with 'the extreme obscu-rity of human relationships' (*TL,* 141). Incidentally the photograph abounds in triplets: three persons, three paintings, three walls, three verticals framing the arches on the door and a triptych screen, which probably portrays three birds.

In *To the Lighthouse* Woolf places Lily Briscoe in much the same position occupied by her young self in the Oedipal configuration of this photograph. 'Standing on the edge of the lawn' (*TL,* 140), unable either to become a Ramsay or to break free of their magnetic field, Lily gazes at the family from the distance of her canvas, both inside and outside the spectacle that she beholds. This spectacle recalls the Freudian 'primal scene', in which the infant supposedly witnesses the parents' sexual intercourse,[9] interpreting this act as a paternal assault. This scene, which is vigorously repressed, can only be reconstructed through its memory-traces, which are invested with new meaning in

Figure 7.1

the course of sexual development. Freud uses the term *Nachträglichkeit*, (mis)translated by the Stracheys as 'deferred action', to describe this retroactive revision of the past.[10] Due to this revision, the reality of the original event can never be established; Freud admits that the primal scene may be a primal fantasy, or even a 'construction in analysis' designed to account for the patient's symptoms.[11]

A comparable process of revision takes place in the third section of *To the Lighthouse*, when a tickling sensation on James's leg triggers his recollection of his earlier battle with his father. In 'The Window', as we have seen, Mr. Ramsay interrupts James's rapturous intimacy with his mother while debarring the journey to the Lighthouse. At the same time his father flicks a 'tickling spray' (*TL,* 29) at James's bare leg, leaving a sensory scar that acts as a repository of the past. In

James's fantasy this spray is magnified into a harpy's beak: 'he could feel the beak on his bare legs, where it had struck when he was a child' (*TL*, 151). Evidently this portion of James's body has become 'hystericized': Freud argues that '*hysterics suffer mainly from reminiscences*', which are written on the body in the form of psychosomatic symptoms (*SE* 2:7). Similarly James's body remembers the original event before his mind retrieves its images; like Proust's madeleine, this ghostly tickle opens the floodgates to the past. The scene that James recalls, however, could be interpreted as a Freudian 'screen memory' that serves to conceal the primal scene.[12] In James's case, the image of the harpy's beak plunging into the maternal fountain, 'again and again' (*TL* 12–13), both marks and masks the repressed scene of parental intercourse.

## Kleinian perspectives

While the phallic imagery associated with father and son belongs to a classic Freudian repertoire, other details complicate this reading. For one thing, the harpy is traditionally female, rather than male: a 'fabulous monster, rapacious and filthy, having a woman's face and body and a bird's wings and claws, and supposed to act as a minister of divine vengeance', according to the *Oxford English Dictionary*. Furthermore, James directs his anger at his father's 'breast', rather than his phallic attributes. 'Had there been an axe handy, a poker, or any weapon that would have gashed a hole in his father's breast and killed him, there and then, James would have seized it' (*TL*, 7). If Mrs. Ramsay is depicted as a phallic mother in this scene, pouring 'erect into the air a rain of energy, a column of spray' (*TL*, 33), Mr. Ramsay is depicted as a breasted father.

For this reason Perry Meisel argues that Mr. Ramsay has assumed the role of the 'bad breast' in James's imaginary. The bad breast is defined by Melanie Klein as a vengeful part-object derived from the infant's frustration with its mother's absences.[13] The infant attributes its hunger and despair to the attacks of a sadistic breast, which is itself a projection of the infant's oral rage, its 'beak of brass': an image in which James projects his own voracious mouth onto his father. While demonising the bad breast, the infant idealises the good breast, epitomised in James's view of Mrs. Ramsay as 'this delicious fecundity, this fountain and spray of life' (*TL*, 33). Indeed this mammary goodness is exaggerated to the point of parody in Mrs. Ramsay's obsession with 'real butter and clean milk', along with her habitual invectives against 'the iniquity of the English dairy system' (*TL*, 84).

This opposition between good breast and bad breast characterises what Klein calls the 'paranoid–schizoid position', associated with the early months of life when the infant apprehends the mother only in the form of part-objects. These are split into 'good objects' and 'bad objects', whose prototypes are the good, responsive breast and its fickle, persecutory antithesis. The infant's destructive fantasies, in which the breast is bitten, torn to pieces and eviscerated, lead to fears of retaliation in kind, provoking fantasies of being annihilated by a poisonous, voracious or exploding breast.

This schizoid–paranoid position is succeeded by the 'depressive position', in which the infant comes to recognise the mother as a whole object, rather than a battlefield of body parts. Through this integration the bad breast is defanged, but only through the loss of its idealised counterpart. In the depressive position, 'nothing [is] simply one thing', as James acknowledges in *To the Lighthouse* (*TL,* 152). Bad breast and good breast are reunited in a mother who is neither all-giving nor all-murdering. A period of mourning ensues in which reparative fantasies strive to compensate for the infant's previous assaults against the breast. According to Klein, these fantasies provide the wellspring of art and culture, which arise from the impulse to make reparation to the mother.[14]

Lily's painting, in which the mother killed off in 'Time Passes' is resurrected in the form of art, seems to endorse this Kleinian hypothesis. As Abel points out, Woolf added Lily to the novel as a supplement to Cam, who seems to languish in a Freudian narrative whereas Lily triumphs in a Kleinian alternative.[15] In the third section of the novel, Cam bears mute witness to the drama of inheritance in which Mr. Ramsay symbolically delivers 'the tablets of eternal wisdom' to his son, so that James can become the 'lawgiver' and accede to the position of the father (*TL,* 138). In contrast to Cam's effacement in this Freudian scenario, Lily's reparative impulse comes to fruition in a painting that restores the mother in symbolic form. In general, a Kleinian perspective on *To the Lighthouse* shifts attention from the father and the son to the mother and her daughters, while also bringing creativity into the foreground.

### Marion Milner: To paint or not to paint

Lily's completion of her painting coincides with the Ramsays' arrival at the lighthouse, both enterprises having been impeded for ten years. For this reason Woolf's novel could be seen as a study of inhibition, of not being able to travel to the lighthouse, and of 'not being able to paint'. In her book bearing this title, Marion Milner (née Blackett, 1900–1998) interprets her own paintings as expressions of unconscious processes, especially the dialectic of fusion with and separation from the mother. As Abel observes, 'Milner meticulously parallels the compositional tasks of painting with the psychological tasks of drawing boundaries' (Abel, 70).

Milner read and alluded to Woolf's works, although Woolf did not return the compliment. Nonetheless there are striking similarities between these authors. Both wrote diaries and essays; in Milner's case, the essays analyse the diaries, producing a 'double-time sense'[16] comparable to the *nachträglich* or revisionary effects of *To the Lighthouse*. Both Woolf's novel and Milner's *On Not Being Able to Paint* are forays into autobiography, and both reveal that the sources of creativity reach back into what Freud describes as the 'oceanic' world of infancy (*SE* 21:68), a state of fusion with the mother prior to the intervention of the father's arid scimitar.

It is more than possible that Woolf and Milner were acquainted with each other, given that their homes in London were only two miles apart and their social and intellectual circles overlapped. Milner's brother, Patrick Blackett (1897–1974), a scientist who won the Nobel Prize for physics in 1948, knew Woolf's brother Adrian at Cambridge, that male bastion where Woolf is excluded from the library in *A Room of One's Own* (1929). Marion Milner, by contrast, took a first-class degree in psychology at a more enlightened institution, University College London, which had been admitting women on the same terms as men since 1878. After leaving university, Milner was commissioned by the Girls' Public Day School Trust (GPDST) to study the psychology of learning, the findings of which were later published as *The Human Problem in Schools* (1938).

Meanwhile Milner had embarked on a pseudonymous career as a writer of idiosyncratic works of reverie and self-exploration. The title of the first, *A Life of One's Own* (1934), pays homage to Woolf's *A Room of One's Own* (1929). Milner published this book under the *nom de plume* Joanna Field, lest her employers at the GPDST should be alarmed by this unorthodox experiment. She retained this pseudonym for the next two books of the series, concluding with *On Not Being Able to Paint* (1950), which she began writing on the first day of World War Two, 3 September 1939.[17] By this time Milner had embarked on psychoanalytic training at the London Institute of Psychoanalysis. On the first night of the V1 ('doodlebug') bombings, 13 June 1944, Milner delivered her qualifying paper in the basement where the assembled company had taken shelter.

Although the early works of 'Joanna Field' rarely refer to psychoanalysis, this reticence—like Woolf's professed ignorance of Freud—seems somewhat disingenuous. In fact Milner had been reading Freud since her twenties when her brother had given her a copy of the Stracheys' translation of Freud's *Introductory Lectures on Psychoanalysis*. Patrick Blackett also gave her Montaigne's *Essais*, which inspired Milner's open-ended explorations of her inner life: 'I study myself more than any other subject', Montaigne declares in his essay 'On Experience'.[18] In *A Life of One's Own*, Milner quotes Woolf's essay on Montaigne in *The Common Reader*, which argues that the 'soul, or life within us by no means agrees with the life outside us'.

> If one has the courage to ask her what she thinks, she is always saying the very opposite of what other people say ... Really she is the strangest creature in the world, far from heroic, variable as a weathercock, 'bashful, insolent; chaste, lustful; prating, silent; laborious, delicate; ingenious, heavy; melancholic, pleasant; lying, true; knowing, ignorant; liberal, covetous and prodigal'—in short so complex, so indefinite, corresponding so little to the version which does duty for her in public that a man might spend his life in merely trying to run her to earth.[19]

Milner agrees that what Montaigne calls the soul 'is totally different from all that one expects it to be, often being the very opposite'.[20] In *A Life of One's Own*, as in her subsequent autobiographical works, she discovers that the only way to achieve a life of one's own is to acknowledge 'the force by which one is lived', and to submit the ego to the otherness within.[21] 'Je est un autre' ('I is someone else'), as Rimbaud famously asserted.[22] This other within has purposes drastically at odds with the orderly intentions of the ego.

In particular, Milner insists that the unconscious yearns to dissolve the boundaries imposed upon the world by the logical, discriminating intellect. As she puts it in her 1956 paper, 'Psychoanalysis and Art':

> The unconscious mind, by the very fact of its not clinging to the distinction between self and other, seer and seen, can do things that the conscious mind cannot do. By being more sensitive to the samenesses rather than the differences between things ... it provides the source for all renewal and rebirth.[23]

Arguably idealising the unconscious, Milner attributes its creative power to its tolerance for merger and indistinction. This hypothesis recurs as a keynote of her work, both before and after she became a psychoanalyst.

Woolf expresses similar impatience with boundaries in her manifesto, 'Modern Fiction' (1925), with its famous declaration: 'Life is not a series of gig lamps symmetrically arranged; life is a luminous halo, a semi-transparent envelope surrounding us from the beginning of consciousness to the end' (*E* IV, 160). For Woolf as for Milner, life is not a neat symmetrical succession of events, in which subjects and objects 'keep themselves to themselves'.[24] Instead life is a halo in which past and present, self and other, feeling and perception interpenetrate. To do justice to this halo, the explorer must dispense with the linear development of argument or narrative and cultivate what Keats calls 'Negative Capability': 'when a man is capable of being in uncertainties, mysteries, doubts, without any irritable reaching after fact and reason'.[25] This state of reverie, as Milner understands it, corresponds to the Freudian technique of free association, which in turn resembles surrealist experiments in automatic writing, as well as modernist experiments in stream of consciousness.

While Milner's first two books examine her own diaries as clues to unconscious processes, her third book, *On Not Being Able to Paint*, makes use of her 'free drawings' for this purpose, doodles in which she suspended 'any conscious intention to draw "something"' (*Paint*, 4). Instead of copying objects 'out there', which seemed to deprive her drawings of independent life, she begins to seek out 'some kind of relation to objects in which one was much more mixed up in them than that' (*Paint*, 12). What she discovers is that objects are neither discrete nor self-contained, but belong to 'a world of change, of continual development and process, one in which there [is] no sharp line between one state and the next, as there is no fixed boundary between twilight and darkness but only a gradual merging of the one into the other' (*Paint*, 29).

Such visions of fusion, however, are always overshadowed by the threat of madness, because they hark back to 'a primary "madness" which all of us have lived through …' (*Paint*, 33). This is the madness of early infancy, when there is no boundary between the baby and the breast, but merely a 'luminous halo' encompassing the inner and the outer worlds. This fear of madness, Milner speculates, lies behind the 'fierce opposition and anger' to new experiments in painting that challenge customary ways of seeing (*Paint*, 20), such as Roger Fry's famous exhibition, 'Manet and the Post-Impressionists', of 1910–1911. In her later biography of Fry, Woolf remembers the furore provoked by this exhibition: 'The works of Cézanne, Matisse, Picasso, Van Gogh and Gauguin possessed what now seems an astonishing power to enrage the public …'[26]

In *To the Lighthouse*, Lily Briscoe is portrayed as a Post-Impressionist, verging on abstractionism, who is making 'no attempt at likeness' but trying to capture 'that very jar on the nerves' (*TL*, 45, 158). This attention to the body and the nervous system chimes with Milner, who is fond of quoting Nietzsche's aphorism that 'the body is a big sagacity'.[27] It is this sagacity, she argues, that painting brings to light: the 'life of a body, with all its complexities of rhythms, tensions, releases, movement, balance, and taking up room in space' (*Paint*, 186). Similarly, Woolf stresses the bodily rhythm of Lily's brushstrokes: 'And so pausing and so flickering, she attained a dancing rhythmical movement, as if the pauses were one part of the rhythm and the strokes another, and all were related ...' (*TL*, 130).

In Milner's terms, Lily is constructing a 'symbol for feeling', for symbols are the means by which the artist makes the inner life of psychophysical experience available to consciousness (*Paint*, 173). One of the feelings that painting symbolises is absorption, in which the perceiving self is absorbed *by* the objects absorbed *into* its gaze. As Milner points out, absorption can be cannibalistic: 'looking intently at an object, devouring it with one's eyes, can seem ... a potentially destructive act' (*Paint*, 72). Unlike the mouth that destroys what it ingests, however, the eye can eat the object and have it too, which is perhaps the prototype of aesthetic experience. Nonetheless the analogy between these organs elicits fantasies about the evil eye, the eye that mortifies the objects it beholds.

As if to underline this analogy between seeing and eating, Woolf juxtaposes Lily's art of painting to Mrs. Ramsay's art of nourishing her household, the masterpiece of which is her orchestration of the dinner table: 'They all sat separate. And the whole of the effort of merging and flowing and creating rested on her' (*TL*, 69). This commensal ritual also bears comparison to the cannibalistic Feast of Communion in which the blood and body of the Saviour are consumed. Lily, however, resists commensality, taking in nothing of the meal—at least as far as the narrative records—although she takes in a strong draught of the emotional undercurrents of the dinner table. Instead of partaking of the *boeuf en daube,* Lily toys with the salt cellar, a salty affront to her hostess's 'real butter and clean milk' (although Mrs. Ramsay co-opts Lily as an ally in her rant against the British dairy system: 'Lily anyhow agrees with me' [*TL*, 84]). Lily's anorexia may explain why Mr. Ramsay finds her 'skimpy', while his wife concurs that 'everything about her was so small' (*TL*, 81, 85). It is as if Lily were refusing to be suckled for fear of destroying the good breast. Only by consenting

to destructiveness as part of the creative process does Lily ultimately
overcome her painter's block. According to Milner, space is 'the main preoccupation of the
painter.' From a psychoanalytic perspective, space is 'the primary
reality to be manipulated for the satisfaction of all one's basic needs,
beginning with the babyhood problem of reaching for one's mother's
arms, leading through all the separation from what one loves that the
business of living brings ... .' [28] Similarly Woolf presents painting as
a dialectic of proximity and separation; for Lily, painting is a way of
reaching out to Mrs. Ramsay but also of keeping her at bay. 'So much
depends', Lily muses, 'upon distance' (*TL*, 156). Her easel creates a
barrier between the artist and the figures that she paints—a flimsy
barrier, for Cam and Mr. Ramsay nearly knock it over (*TL*, 46). By
contrast, Mrs. Ramsay abhors any form of separation, from single
women to disgruntled guests, and Lily, an artist and a spinster, finds
this maternal compulsion to connect as oppressive as Mr. Ramsay's
compulsion to divide and conquer. While the father separates, the
mother knits, as if to repair the paternal lesions in the family web.
In her painting Lily strives to achieve a 'razor edge of balance' (*TL*,
158) between these forces of fusion and severance, forces embodied
in the two parental figures of the novel.

   For Lily as for Milner, the frame is essential to the art of painting.
For the frame creates an oasis in the outer world in which the inner
world of fantasy may find expression; it 'marks off an area within
which what is perceived has to be taken symbolically, while what is
outside the frame is taken literally'.[29] This framed space functions as
a holding environment for objects, providing the necessary ground
on which a figure may emerge. Without this blank space nothing can
take shape; indeed, Milner treated a psychotic patient who suffered
from a sense of having lost her background, which precluded the for-
mation of a bounded self.[30] Commenting on Milner's theory of framing, the art critic Adrian Stokes proposes that in art 'an all-embracing
element, the stage, silence, the blank canvas, can serve as the sleep of
which dreams, though wakeful and rapid, are the guardians'.[31] The
physiological purpose of dreams, according to Freud, is to maintain
the state of sleep; by analogy, Stokes suggests that the surface agitation
of the painting serves to protect the space enclosed within the frame.

   But the blank canvas may also be experienced as emptiness and
desolation, a vacuum in which objects are annihilated: 'that glaring,
hideously difficult white space', as Lily perceives it (*TL*, 132). This
blankness mocks the artist with a mirror of her own vacuity. In *An
Experiment in Leisure*, Milner links this experience of inner blankness

to the myth of the dying god.[32] Meditating on the Christian crucifixion story, Milner interprets Christ's terrible cry—'my God, my God, why have you forsaken me?'—as an admission of powerlessness and futility. In the Gospels of Matthew and Mark, Christ's death is followed by earthquakes, a trope that Milner associates with the resurgence of creativity. The psychic destitution expressed in Christ's despair, the collapse of the imperious ego, unleashes the hidden powers of the unconscious. The artist must therefore try to 'accept this futility … just sit still and feel [one]self to be no good—then the crystallisation begins—after the corruption, blackness, despair'.[33] Milner concludes that the 'inescapable condition of true expression [is] the plunge into the abyss, the willingness to recognise that the moment of blankness [is] the moment of incipient fruitfulness, the moment without which the invisible forces within could not do their work'.[34] Thus painting depends on not being able to paint; only through the loss of power, the surrender of the bossy purposive ego, can the artist regain what Yeats calls 'the old nonchalance of the hand' ('Ego Dominus Tuus').

In *To the Lighthouse*, Lily undergoes a similar cycle of despair, followed by the renewal of creative force. Whenever she begins to paint, 'her own inadequacy, her insignificance' force themselves on her, 'in that chill and windy way' (*TL* 19). Her self-doubts are reinforced by those around her, especially by Charles Tansley's withering refrain, 'Women can't paint, women can't write' (*TL,* 42, etc.). Lily herself predicts that her painting, should it ever be completed, will be 'rolled up and stuffed under a sofa' (*TL* 131). Her ultimate success, however, suggests that her abjection has brought about a release of inhibition. Apparently she has undergone the process that Milner likens to the death of Christ, the breakdown of the ego that precedes the earthquakes of renewal.

So far I have been comparing Milner's meditations on creativity to the psychodynamics of Lily's painting. But Milner's insights also pertain to the structure of *To the Lighthouse*, which exemplifies the cycle of disintegration and restoration that Milner identifies with the creative process. Echoing and possibly alluding to the Gospels' darkness at noon, 'Time Passes' describes 'a downpouring of immense darkness' (*TL,* 103) in which the 'walls of partition' melt away: 'Not only was furniture confounded; there was scarcely anything left of body or mind by which one could say "This is he" or "This is she"' (*TL,* 92, 103). Gender and identity dissolve, as in the oceanic state of infancy; indeed the darkness is described as oceanic, a downpouring comparable to Noah's flood.

In 'Time Passes' Mrs. Ramsay's death is reported in a curt paren-
thesis, as if this tragedy were less important than the weather that
invades the crumbling house: 'The nights now are full of wind and
destruction ...' (*TL*, 105). When Mr. Ramsay stretches out his arms
for Mrs. Ramsay they remain empty, much as Lily stretches out her
arm towards the emptiness framed within her canvas. The parallel
between these gestures supports Milner's intuition, quoted earlier, that
the art of painting harks back to 'the babyhood problem of reaching
for one's mother's arms', and reenacts 'all the separation from what
one loves that the business of living brings ...' Painful though it is,
this separation is essential to establishing an independent self. Only
through the mother's absence, which elicits the infantile fantasy of
the bad breast, does the subject learn to distinguish the 'me' from the
'not-me', as well as to acknowledge the independence of the outside
world. The alternative is the primeval chaos evoked in 'Time Passes'.

Milner argues that painting is 'deeply concerned with ideas of
distance and separation and having and losing' (*Paint*, 152–53).
The same could be said of 'Time Passes', which Woolf described as
the 'corridor' connecting the first 'block' of the novel to the last.[35] In
an obvious sense, 'Time Passes' is concerned with losing the mother,
but it also suggests a fantasy of 'having' her in the form of a return to
the womb. In this reading, the downpouring of darkness alludes not
only to the Flood but to the primal bath of amniotic fluid, where the
infant can be 'one with the object one adored', 'like waters poured
into one jar, inextricably the same' (*TL*, 44). In this uterine world,
circulating energies take the place of solid objects: 'those stray airs,
advance guards of great armies, blustered in, brushed bare boards,
nibbled and fanned ...' (*TL*, 105).

Without 'some cleavage of the dark', however, there can be no
individuation. This 'cleavage', a ray of light introduced by Mrs.
McNab, enables this aged servant to recognise her face framed in
the mirror, thus re-establishing a framework for identity (*TL*,107).
In 'Time Passes', Mrs. McNab is portrayed as an ark in the storm,
albeit a dilapidated vessel, groaning, creaking, lurching, rolling, leer-
ing on the floodwaters: 'she lurched (for she rolled like a ship at
sea) and leered'; she 'rolled from room to room ...' (*TL*, 107). The
same goes for her crony Mrs. Bast: 'Mrs. McNab groaned; Mrs. Bast
creaked' (*TL*, 114). In all this creaking and groaning there is little to distinguish flesh from furniture; the servants are portrayed as
swollen wood and rusty metal. Even their names evoke rigging and
hardware: an obsolete meaning of 'nab', according to the *OED*, is
'the keeper in a door jamb, into which the bolt fits'; while 'bast' is a

woven fibre used in ropes. As the servants and the woodwork groan in labour, the house is reborn out of the wreckage: 'with the creaking of hinges and the screeching of bolts, the slamming and banging of damp-swollen woodwork, some rusty laborious birth seemed to be taking place ...' (*TL,* 114). In this way the servants perform the same kind of renewal that Milner attributes to unconscious forces. It is when the master is away (in *To the Lighthouse*), or the ego is off-duty (in Milner's psychomachia), that these forces bring about their miracle.

Meanwhile the laborious birth of Lily's painting necessitates the release of infantile aggression:

> With a curious physical sensation, as if she were urged forward and at the same time must hold herself back, she made her first quick decisive stroke ...; and so, lightly and swiftly striking, she scored her canvas with brown running nervous lines which had no sooner settled there than they enclosed (she felt it looming out at her) a space. (*TL,* 130–31)

Here painting is portrayed as anal sadism, striking, scoring, cutting, slicing, squirting, smearing and otherwise assaulting the maternal space enclosed within the frame. In addition to their excremental associations, Lily's 'brown running nervous lines' mark a new attention to the line, whereas colour predominates in earlier descriptions of her technique. Associated with violent division—'lines cutting across, slicing down' (*TL,* 130)—the line also testifies to Lily's rejection of verisimilitude, for there are no outlines to be found in nature. As Milner quotes from an instruction manual on painting, 'The outline is the one fundamentally unrealistic nonimitative thing in this whole job of painting' (*Paint,* 16). In colour, on the contrary, one shape blends into another in a luminous halo.

At the end of the novel, Lily 'looked at her canvas; it was blurred. With a sudden intensity, as if she saw it clear for a second, she drew a line there, in the centre' (*TL,* 170). As many critics have noted, this line corresponds to Woolf's description of the Lighthouse as 'the central line' that holds the novel's design together.[36] If the central line unites the composition, however, it also splits the canvas into two halves, just as the central 'corridor' of 'Time Passes' both bridges and divides the two 'blocks' of the novel. These central seams in the novel and the painting mark the absence of the mother, but they also hold together what they tear asunder, creating a razor-edge of balance between 'having and losing' the object of desire (*Paint,* pp. 152–53).

'I have had my vision.' With these words Lily falls away from her painting like a contented child from the breast, 'laying down her brush in extreme fatigue' (*TL*, 170). In this moment both painting and artist are reborn, but each embarks on a separate future after ten years of mutual enmeshment. Woolf's *Künstlerroman* suggests that every work of art reenacts this struggle between fusion and separation. While Klein emphasises the reparative dimension of the work of art, Woolf reminds us of its origins in violence. For Lily Briscoe, art provides a space to murder and create, to get rid of the haunting mother and to resurrect her as a vision.

## Making Scenes

This chapter has tried to show how *To the Lighthouse* both invites and resists psychoanalytic theorisation. As I have suggested, there is something knowing, even tongue-in-cheek, about Woolf's presentation of James Ramsay, a portrait of Adrian Stephen—the future Freudian—as an infant Oedipus. The same could be said of the Kleinian portrayal of Mrs. Ramsay and her comical anxiety about clean milk. By exaggerating these psychoanalytic trademarks, Woolf seems to be poking fun at mind-doctors. In her depiction of Lily's artistic labour, however, Woolf leaves Freudian and Kleinian clichés behind to explore the psychodynamics of painting, an art that harks back to preverbal bodily experience. In this respect Woolf's enterprise corresponds to Marion Milner's exploration of creativity in *On Not Being Able to Paint*.

To say preverbal, however, is to posit a before that can be accessed only through its after-effects. For this reason, it is worth considering that Woolf is using painting to envision a *post*-verbal, rather than pre-verbal world, or more specifically a post-narrative condition. It is well-known that Woolf resented the 'appalling narrative business of the realist: getting on from lunch to dinner' (*D* III, 209), and declared a preference for scene making over chronological sequence: 'in all the writing I have done, I have almost always had to make a scene' (*MB*, 122). Painting provides a way of making scenes that dispenses with the 'waste, deadness, superfluity' of linear time (*D* III, 209). This does not mean that painting does away with history, but that it circumvents the narrative principle of sequence: hence Lily goes on 'tunnelling her way into her picture, into the past' (*TL*, 142) moving 'backwards & forwards' (*D* III, 209). For Lily, the past is not over. And it is Woolf's sense of the persistence of the past that shows her deepest affinity to psychoanalysis.[37]

## Notes

1   Alix Strachey was analysed by Karl Abraham in Berlin; see Elizabeth Abel, *Virginia Woolf and the Fictions of Psychoanalysis* (Chicago and London: University of Chicago Press, 1989), p. 9.

2   Matt ffytche, 'The Modernist Road to the Unconscious', in *The Oxford Handbook of Modernisms*, ed. Peter Brooker et al. (Oxford and New York: Oxford University Press, 2010), p. 415.

3   On this point see Lyndsey Stonebridge, *The Destructive Element: British Psychoanalysis and Modernism* (London and New York: Routledge, 1998), pp. 62–63; Sanja Bahun, 'Woolf and Psychoanalytic Theory', in *Virginia Woolf in Context*, eds. Bryony Mandell and Jane Goldman (Cambridge: Cambridge University Press, 2012), p. 97.

4   *Bloomsbury/Freud: The Letters of James and Alix Strachey 1924–1925*, eds. Perry Meisel and Walter Kendrick (London: Chatto and Windus, 1986), p. 309.

5   See, *inter alia*, Elizabeth Abel, *Virginia Woolf and the Fictions of Psychoanalysis*; Daniel Ferrer, *Virginia Woolf and the Madness of Language*, trans. Geoffrey Bennington and Rachel Bowlby (London: Routledge, 1990); Mary Jacobus, '"The Third Stroke": Reading Woolf with Freud', in *Virginia Woolf*, ed. Rachel Bowlby (London and New York: Longman, 1992), pp. 102–20; Makiko Minow-Pinkney, *Virginia Woolf and the Problem of the Subject: Feminine Writing in the Major Novels* (Edinburgh: Edinburgh University Press, 2010); Maud Ellmann, *The Nets of Modernism: Henry James, Virginia Woolf, James Joyce, and Sigmund Freud* (Cambridge: Cambridge University Press, 2010), and 'A Passage to the Lighthouse', in *The Blackwell Companion to Virginia Woolf*, ed. Jessica Berman (Oxford: Blackwell, 2015, forthcoming). 'A Passage to the Lighthouse' differs from the present chapter by focusing on the work of Ella Freeman Sharpe (1875–1947), who was Adrian Stephen's analyst.

6   William Empson, 'Virginia Woolf', *Scrutinies*, vol. 2, ed. E. Rickward (London: Washart and Co., 1931), p. 205.

7   See Jane de Gay, 'Behind the purple triangle: Art and iconography in *To the Lighthouse*', *Woolf Studies Annual* 5:1 (1991), 1–23; and Rebecca Zorach, *The Passionate Triangle* (Chicago: University of Chicago Press, 2011).

8   Plate 38h of Leslie Stephen's photograph album, housed at Smith College, http://www.smith.edu/libraries/libs/rarebook/exhibitions/stephen/38h.html.

9   The theory of the primal scene makes its most dramatic appearance in Freud's case history of the Wolf Man; see Freud, *From the History of an Infantile Neurosis* (1918) in *The Complete Psychological Works of Sigmund Freud*, Standard Edition, trans. James and Alix Strachey, 24 vols (London: Hogarth, 1953–74), Vol. 17, esp. pp. 29–60; henceforth cited as SE.

10  For a fuller definition of 'deferred action' see J. Laplanche and J. B. Pontalis, *The Language of Psycho-Analysis*, trans. Donald Nicholson-Smith (London: Hogarth Press, 1973), pp. 111–14.

11  See Freud, 'Constructions in Analysis' (1937), SE 23: 255–70.

12  See Freud, 'Screen Memories' (1899), SE 3: 299–322.

13  See Perry Meisel, 'Woolf and Freud: The Kleinian Turn', in *Virginia Woolf in Context*, eds. Bryony Mandell and Jane Goldman (Cambridge: Cambridge University Press, 2012), pp. 332–41. For a succinct account of Kleinian theory see Juliet Mitchell's introduction to her edition of *The Selected Melanie Klein* (London: Penguin, 1991), pp. 9–32.

14  See Abel, p. 11.

15  Ibid., pp. 68, 151n2.

16  See Hugh Haughton, 'The Milner Experiment: Psychoanalysis and the Diary,' *British Journal of Psychotherapy* 30.3 (August 2014), 351.

17  Marion Milner, *A Life of One's Own*, intro. Rachel Bowlby (1934; rpt. London: Routledge, 2010), p. xxxv.

18  Michel de Montaigne, *The Complete Works*, trans. Donald Frame (New York: Everyman, 2003), pp. 1000–1.

19  Quoted by Milner, *A Life of One's Own*, pp. 9–10; the passage, slightly misquoted, comes from Virginia Woolf's 'Montaigne' (1925), in *E* IV, 72–73.

20  Milner, *A Life of One's Own*, p. 173.

21  Milner, *An Experiment in Leisure*, intro. Maud Ellmann (London: Routledge, 2011), p. 196.

22  Arthur Rimbaud, *Complete Works, Selected Letters*, trans. Wallace Fowlie, ed. Seth Widden (Chicago: University of Chicago Press, 2005), p. 370.

23  Milner, *The Suppressed Madness of Sane Men: Forty-Four Years of Exploring Psychoanalysis* (London: Tavistock, 1987), p. 214.

24  Milner, *On Not Being Able to Paint*, intro. Janet Sayers (1950; rpt. London: Routledge, 2010), p. 19. Henceforth cited as *Paint*.

25  John Keats, *Selected Letters*, ed. Robert Gittings (Oxford: Oxford University Press, 2009), pp. 41–42.

26  Virginia Woolf, *Roger Fry* (1940; rpt. Harmondsworth: Penguin, 1979), p. 157.

27  For example, Milner, *Bothered by Alligators*, intro. Margaret Walters (London: Routledge, 2012), p. 29.

28  Ibid., pp. 12–13.

29  Milner, *A Life of One's Own*, p. 184.

30  Milner, *The Hands of the Living God*, intro. Adam Phillips (1969; rpt. London: Routledge, 2011).

31  Adrian Stokes, 'Form in Art', in *New Directions in Psycho-Analysis: The Significance of Infant Conflict in the Pattern of Adult Behaviour*, ed. Melanie Klein, Paula Heimann, R. E. Money-Kyrle (London: Tavistock, 1955), p. 408.

32  See Milner, *An Experiment in Leisure*, pp. 100–102.

33 Ibid., pp. 118–19.
34 Ibid., pp. 152–53.
35 Virginia Woolf, *To the Lighthouse: The Original Holograph Draft*, ed. Susan Dick (London: Hogarth Press 1983), p. 48.
36 Virginia Woolf, *Collected Letters*, ed. Nigel Nicholson, 6 vols (London: Hogarth Press, 1975–80), vol. 3, p. 283.
37 I would like to thank the Humanities Visiting Committee at the University of Chicago for their generous support of my research. I also thank Heather Glen and David Hillman for their careful reading and helpful suggestions.

# 8

# *Mrs. Dalloway* and the War that Wouldn't End

Brian Finney

## Introduction: The Great War (1914–1918)

The Great War scarred Virginia Woolf for life. Her friend, the poet Rupert Brooke, died in action, as well as two of her cousins and a brother-in-law, Cecil Woolf, who was killed by the same shell that left his brother Philip severely wounded. In addition she experienced a number of German air raids first-hand, during which she and the servants took refuge in the coal cellar of her London home. The closest she came to being killed in a raid was in January 1918, as she wrote to her sister Vanessa: 'Well, you almost lost me. Nine bombs on Kew; seven people killed in one house, a hotel crushed' (*L* II, 214). The War haunts her third novel, *Jacob's Room* (1922), mainly by its absence; her fourth novel, *Mrs. Dalloway* (1925), by its refusal to go away; and her next novel, *To The Lighthouse* (1927), by the poignancy of the death of Andrew Ramsay as a young man. Her opposition to war grew steadily over the years. In an extended essay, *Three Guineas* (1938), she proclaimed that 'War ... is an abomination; a barbarity; war must be stopped at whatever cost' (*R/TG*, 165). How to express this view satisfactorily in her writing is a challenge that she faced in each of her novels in succession.

At the time of writing this, the world is commemorating the centenary of the start of the Great War. According to the *New York Times*, 8.5 million soldiers on both sides of the conflict died, and 20 million were severely wounded.[1] The War also accounted for the death of 7 million civilians. When, in 1916, the number of dead among the 2.4 million volunteers enlisting for the British army grew too high for replacement by more volunteers, the government introduced

125

conscription. That summer witnessed the Battle of the Somme, on the first day of which 20,000 British soldiers died and another 40,000 were wounded. The poet Siegfried Sassoon called the war 'a treacherous, blundering tragic-comedy'.[2] The British generals were slow to adapt to change, and continued to retain three cavalry regiments, despite the introduction of tanks, until the end of the War.[3] This was the first war in which there was aerial bombardment of civilians. Through the use of airships, then fixed-wing bombers, the Germans killed a total of 1,413 civilians and wounded another 3,409.[4] There quickly developed an absolute divide between those fighting at the Front and the civilian population back in Britain. As Siegfried Sassoon wrote in his *Memoirs*, 'the man who had really endured the War at its worst was everlastingly differentiated from everyone except his fellow soldiers'.[5] Initially attracted by Lord Kitchener's recruitment campaign for volunteer troops ('Your Country Needs YOU'), or shamed by women handing out white feathers to those not wearing a military uniform, soldiers at the Front were soon alienated from their civilian fellow countrymen by the disparity between their experience and the jingoistic rhetoric employed by newspapers and political leaders and swallowed whole by most of the public. Representative is the way the *Daily Mail* transformed the slaughter of the opening day of the battle of the Somme (which Siegfried Sassoon called in his *Diary* 'a sunlit picture of Hell')[6] to a glowing account of a 'great battle' in which 'we have beaten the Germans'.[7] Censorship prevented reporters and troops from reporting the truth. In 1914 a secret War Propaganda Bureau recruited such famous writers as Thomas Hardy, H.G. Wells, Arthur Conan Doyle, Arnold Bennett, John Galsworthy and others to write pamphlets and books that would justify the war being waged.[8] By 1917 Parliament felt it necessary to establish a National War Aims Committee to counter civilian war weariness and rekindle public patriotism through a massive propaganda campaign. As late as July 1919 the *Times* was invoking 'the immortal dead who gave youth, and manhood, and all the good things of life to save England from the pollution and the blight of German supremacy'.[9]

Not everyone was taken in by the barrage of propaganda and waves of patriotism. By January 1915 Woolf herself was writing of attending 'a Queen's Hall concert where the patriotic sentiment was so revolting that I was nearly sick' (*L* II, 57). She dismissed the pro-war stance of the Northcliffe newspapers (including the *Daily Mail* and the *Times*), writing that they 'do all they can to insist upon the indispensability & delight of war' (*D* I, 200). Woolf was surrounded by members of the Bloomsbury Group, who belonged to the small but vociferous number of British citizens opposed to the War. Some opponents of the War published works expressing their views, such as Bernard Shaw's *Common Sense About the War* (1914), Francis Meynell's 'War's a Crime' (1914) and Clive Bell's *Peace at Once* (1915). After conscription was introduced Clive Bell, Duncan Grant and David Garnett avoided military service by working on the land, and Keynes by working for the Treasury. Lytton Strachey and Leonard Woolf were exempted on medical grounds. As Samuel Hynes observes, 'Bloomsbury ... from the war's very beginning, was a continuing demonstration of the fact that opposition to the war—continuous, principled opposition—was a possible attitude for intelligent English men and women.'[10] 'We were all [Conscientious Objectors] in the Great War,' Woolf wrote.[11] From 1916–1920 she organised and chaired monthly meetings of the Richmond branch of the Women's Cooperative Guild, a pacifist organisation. In her eyes the War was nothing but a 'preposterous masculine fiction' (*L* II, 76).

### New historicism

So Woolf's writings were part of a discourse dominant during and for a long time after the Great War that addressed issues of militarism and imperialism, its cause in the eyes of many historians. The four novels she wrote in which the Great War featured can all be read as contributions to this discourse, as well as texts controlled by its parameters. In other words I am making some small use of New Historicism. This is an approach to historical literary interpretation that emerged in the field of Renaissance studies in the 1980s. Unlike earlier literary historians, new historicists do not accept that history is a monolithic background that is necessarily reflected in literary works of the period. New historicism textualises history just as it historicises texts. Its practitioners see history as a series of cultural contentions between dominant and subversive forces or social practices. In Woolf's case she enters a discourse about imperialism and militarism that pits the dominant force that favours military solutions against the subversive force of pacifist resistance.

The same year in which *Mrs. Dalloway* is set (1923) Mahatma Gandhi was in prison (put there by the occupying British power) for his campaign of mass civil disobedience, an essentially pacifist response to the dominant imperial force in India. Four years previously the British General Reginald Dyer, fearing a repetition of the Indian Mutiny of 1857–1858, was responsible for the massacre of over 1,000 Indian civilians in Amritsar. He was greeted on his return to Britain as the Saviour of the Punjab and presented with a purse of £26,000 by a British public pleased that he had kept India under British rule. Yet pacifists in Britain, including Virginia Woolf and her friends, referred to him as the Butcher of Amritsar.[12] The word 'India' appears thirty-eight times in *Mrs. Dalloway*. In the novel Peter has just returned from spending five years in India and wants to know 'what they were doing in India—the conservative duffers' (*MD*, 144). Lady Bruton is told by the principal conservative duffer, the Prime Minister, 'what a tragedy it was—the state of India!' (*MD*, 161). This is just a small instance of how a peripheral motif can be used to identify larger discursive issues with which the novel is engaging.

New historicists reject the old literary historian's assumption that a literary text reflects a unified and coherent view shared by the society of the time. Instead they see society at any particular moment of time as the site of diverse and contradictory beliefs and practices. In their view texts enter into these complex sets of competing relations and can only be properly understood in the context of the wider culture. This chapter will explore the conflicting views of the War and the governing class that was responsible for it in *Mrs. Dalloway*. Woolf may well have been an opponent of the War from the start, but she avoided any direct representation of political positions in her fiction. Her revisions of earlier drafts of the novel show, as Jane Lilienfeld demonstrates, that she 'deleted direct statements about World War I' from these earlier manuscripts.[13] In doing so Woolf transforms Mrs. Dalloway into an ambivalent fictional construct who deplores the ruling class responsible for the War while belonging to and often admiring that class. As Woolf wrote in her Diary when she was planning the new novel, 'I want to criticize the social system, & show it at work' (*D* II, 248). When she walks down the room in which her party is being held with the Prime Minister, 'this symbol of what they all stood for, English society', her triumph nevertheless 'had a hollowness' because it was 'not in the heart' (*MD*, 154, 156). In psychological terms Woolf pits Mrs. Dalloway the society hostess, whom she suspected might be 'too glittering and tinsely' (*D* II, 272) against the too deeply feeling Septimus.[14] Clarissa's inner conflict reproduces that of post-war English society torn between external social and internal individual forces.

### War and peace

*Mrs. Dalloway* is set on a mid-June day in 1923, five years after the War ended. Yet the War still casts a haunting shadow over everyone and everything in the novel. Two mutually exclusive attitudes to the

War can be found in it: that the War changed everything, on the one hand, or on the other, that the War is best forgotten, allowing England to revert to its pre-war idyll of privilege and Imperial domination. In Woolf's early story version of the opening of the novel, Clarissa Dalloway adopts the latter attitude, reflecting that 'Thousands of young men had died that things might go on'.[15] But in the published novel Clarissa starts off taking the opposing attitude by celebrating the fact that the cataclysmic 'War was over ... thank Heaven—over' (*MD*, 4). Yet she vacillates between the two positions as the novel progresses. Septimus Warren Smith, her supposed double, acts as a living fictional embodiment of the deep wound to the collective psyche left by the War. In addition, numerous characters, major and minor—from Clarissa Dalloway to Mr. Bowley, Peter Walsh to Miss Parry—remember (and remind us of) the effects of the recent War. Woolf herself wrote in 1926, 'The war sprung its chasm at the feet of all this innocence and ignorance'.[16] Clarissa and Peter keep reverting in their minds to her childhood country home in Bourton, which comes to stand for an opposing and idealised pastoral landscape that typifies pre-war innocence and love. As Paul Fussell observes, 'Recourse to the pastoral is an English mode of both fully gauging the calamities of the Great War and imaginatively protecting oneself against them'.[17] Yet there are also representative figures of the governing class who want to forget the War, restore Britain to its past glory (as they see it), and eliminate any reminders of the toll the War took. Both Dr Holmes and Sir William Bradshaw seek to 'cure' Septimus— that is, to stop him from acting as a living reminder to the rest of the population of the continuing price being paid for the recent War. The only socially acceptable response to loss is the stoical one shown by Lady Bexborough, 'who opened a bazaar, they said, with the telegram in her hand, John, her favourite, killed' (*MD*, 4).

Repression by all except the shell-shocked Septimus has meant that the War continues to be fought deep within the psyches of the characters populating *Mrs. Dalloway*. As Woolf observed in a 1920 Diary entry, 'Our generation is daily scourged by the bloody war' (*D* II, 51). The official response is to relegate the War to the past by memorialising it, turning it into a glorious sacrifice while consigning its victims to an afterlife where they are better off. As early as 19 July 1919 (officially declared Peace Day) a temporary cenotaph was erected in Whitehall. On 11 November 1920 the permanent Cenotaph was unveiled by King George V. The inscription on the wreath he left there read, 'In proud memory of those warriors, who died unknown in the Great War—Unknown and yet well-known, as dying and behold they live'.[18] Woolf makes a point of associating this iconic war memorial with the marching boy soldiers in the novel who overtake Peter Walsh in Whitehall and who have just laid a wreath on the Tomb of the Unknown Warrior: 'Boys in uniform, carrying guns, ... their arms stiff, and on their faces an expression like the letters of a legend written round the base of a statue praising duty, gratitude, fidelity, love of England' (*MD*, 46). As David Bradshaw has shown, these boy soldiers are members of the Territorial Army established by Lord Haldane, former Secretary of State for War, who 'visualized an entire Nation in Arms'.[19] Bradshaw notes that in the phrase introducing the boy soldiers—'A patter like the patter of fallen leaves in a wood' (*MD*, 46)—'leaves are an ancient literary topos for the dead.'[20] The boys are in effect the walking dead, their 'life ... laid under a pavement of monuments and wreaths' (*MD*, 46).

Woolf herself walked down Whitehall on Remembrance Day 1920 and wrote in her Diary, 'such a lurid scene, like one in Hell. ... people marching ... women crying Remember the Glorious Dead. ... A ghastly procession of people in their sleep' (*D* II, 79–80). That last sentence hints at Woolf's objection to the traditional mind-numbing way of memorialising the War. Like the war poets Siegfried Sassoon and Wilfred Owen, she refuses to treat ameliorative mourning as the only satisfactory way of responding to the wartime dead. Rather, as Tammy Clewell has argued, 'Woolf repeatedly sought not to heal wartime wounds, but to keep them open'.[21] If *Mrs. Dalloway* is an extended elegy it is one in the modernist mode that refuses to subscribe to the traditional consolation of peace in a life after death. Mrs. Dalloway does 'not for a moment ... believe in God' (*MD*, 26); similarly, Peter is '[b]y conviction an atheist' (*MD*, 51). As Siegfried Sassoon puts it in his famous poem, 'They', the War was supposed to have been a Crusade against 'the Anti-Christ', the Kaiser, yet God did not intervene on behalf of His Crusaders. In the poem's first stanza, a Bishop describes the War in this way to a group of soldiers, who in the second stanza reply that they have not been spared physical suffering by the God on whose behalf they have been fighting:

> 'For George lost both his legs; and Bill's stone blind;
> Poor Jim's shot through the lungs and like to die;
> And Bert's gone syphilitic: you'll not find
> A chap who's served that hasn't found *some* change.'
> And the Bishop said: 'The ways of God are strange!'[22]

Septimus Warren Smith and thousands of other soldiers suffered from shell shock, a psychological condition just as debilitating as the physical wounds to which Sassoon alludes here.

Deprived of any consolatory element, we are nevertheless invited to commemorate the wartime dead and wounded because, as Erin Penner suggests, 'in a very real sense the war is not over'.[23] It is not the role of the modernist writer to lull her readers into a somnambulant state. Rather the writer needs to commemorate the past by bringing it into the post-war present. As J. Hillis Miller has suggested, *Mrs. Dalloway* 'is a novel of the resurrection of the past into the actual present of the characters' lives'.[24]

This location of the past in the present applies as much to figures like Evans and Lady Bexborough's favourite, John, as it does to the youthful Clarissa, Peter, Sally and others. And how different Clarissa and her friends were back then, rebels and visionaries, 'talking about life, how they were to reform the world' (*MD*, 30). Those younger selves now return to haunt (and taunt) the older, compromised characters, just as Evans haunts Septimus, becoming a part of his present existence. Like Septimus and the other idealistic volunteers enlisting early in the War, the earlier idealistic avatars of Clarissa and her contemporaries have suffered their own form of death. 'She had schemed,' Clarissa confesses, 'she had pilfered. She was never wholly admirable' (*MD*, 166). Similarly, the older Peter thinks of himself as 'a failure' (*MD*, 39, 45), and associates Bourton days with the 'death of the soul' (*MD*, 53). And when Clarissa first re-meets Sally she reflects, 'The lustre had left her' (*MD*, 153).

## 'The Hours' and authority

After he has visited Clarissa in her house Peter associates the chimes of St Margaret's with her. 'Some grief for the past holds it back', he decides (*MD*, 45). After remembering that with her weak heart she had nearly died of the major flu epidemic in 1919 he extends the metaphor: 'the sudden loudness of the final stroke tolled for death that surprised in the midst of life' (*MD*, 45). Clocks, as has been frequently noticed, play a significant part in the novel, which Woolf at first titled 'The Hours'. Their chimes not only help Woolf structurally move from one character's inner consciousness to another's; they also act as stark thematic reminders of the connections between imperialism, war and death. The chimes of Big Ben, 'laying down the law' (*MD*, 114), set the time for the rest of the world, just as imperial Britain aspired to control huge areas of the world. They sound '[f]irst a warning, ... then the hour, irrevocable' (*MD*, 4). It is as if warfare were written into the very idea of the British Empire. Its 'leaden circles' could as easily be those of shells fired at the Front, just as the car backfiring sounds to Miss Pym like 'a pistol shot' (*MD*, 12). Everyone who has witnessed the passage of the mysterious car 'thought of the dead; of the flag; of Empire' (*MD*, 16).

As Adam Burrows points out, Greenwich Mean Time acted as 'a powerful symbol of authoritarian control from a distance and of the management of diverse populations'.[25] On the one hand Big Ben commands masculine authority. It is like the bells of Harley Street (the centre of specialist medical practice) that 'counselled submission, upheld authority, and pointed out in chorus the supreme advantages of a sense of proportion' (*MD*, 92). On the other hand St Margaret's seems identified with the opposing private and feminine individual self that undermines masculine authority. Big Ben and St Margaret's epitomise the competing ideologies in post-war Britain and in *Mrs. Dalloway*—the social and the individual.

Both Woolf's narrative stance and Mrs. Dalloway's reactions to the novel's various figures of authority reflect two competing, irreconcilable attitudes to them. On the one hand the VIP hidden behind dark windows in the car driving down Bond Street is viewed by the 'ordinary people' it passes as 'greatness', 'the majesty of England' (*MD*, 15). Yet this symbol of authority terrifies Septimus, making him think by association that the world is once again, as in the War, about 'to burst into flames' (*MD*, 14). As it departs Clarissa 'stiffened a little' (*MD*, 16), just as the men in the window of Brooks 'stood even straighter ... ready to attend their Sovereign, if need be, to the cannon's mouth' (*MD*, 17). This introduces an interesting motif, one of gesture. On the one hand are the figures of authority all of whom sit or stand rigidly straight. There is Lady Bexborough who 'held herself upright' (*MD*, 69); Lady Bruton, with her 'ramrod bearing' that she had acquired from her association with Britannia, the goddess of Empire (*MD*, 161); the boy soldiers who 'keep their arms stiff' (*MD*, 46); and as for Sir William Bradshaw, he is so rigid that he has become statue-like, 'a fine figure-head at ceremonies' (*MD*, 85). On the other hand there are those people like Ellie Henderson or the battered old woman in Regent's Park or Miss Parry leaning on her stick, 'not even caring to hold themselves upright' (*MD*, 150).[26] Miss Parry is indifferent to Empire. She has no 'proud illusions about Viceroys, Generals, Mutinies' (*MD*, 159). She only cares about her private feelings and can only think of orchids when remembering her days in India.

At times Clarissa can be as stiff as any of the members of the governing class. But this stiffness is invariably linked with a repression of feelings. In marrying Richard instead of Peter, Clarissa had acquired from Richard 'a great deal of the public-spirited, British Empire, tariff-reform, governing-class spirit' (*MD*, 69). But beneath her social veneer still lurks the younger Clarissa who, like Othello, wanted her life to end at her most intense moment of feeling, after being kissed by Sally at Bourton (*MD*, 32). Rigidity of posture is invariably connected with repression of feelings in the novel, something that characterises all the members of the governing class, and something that soldiers were forced temporarily to assume to survive the horrors of trench warfare. Richard exemplifies this, a Conservative Member of Parliament who, Clarissa reflects, 'could not tell her he loved her' (*MD*, 106). He refers impersonally to the war dead as 'thousands of poor chaps ... shovelled together, already half forgotten' (*MD*, 103). Hugh has repressed all inner life: 'He brushed surfaces' (*MD*, 92). (By contrast Elizabeth might not care about clothes, but 'she has a heart' [*MD*, 121]).

A more extreme example is Sir William Bradshaw, who imposes these ideas on others: 'Nobody lives for himself alone,' he counsels Septimus. 'Try to think as little about yourself as possible' (*MD*, 88). This is the point in the novel when the narrator expounds in uncharacteristically didactic manner on the doctrines of Proportion and Conversion that Sir William preaches. He never refers to 'madness'; instead 'he called it not having a sense of proportion' (*MD*, 89). The narrative states that in doing this he 'made England prosper ... penalized despair, made it impossible for the unfit to propagate their views until they, too, shared his sense of proportion' (*MD*, 89). In reality his attempted conversion of the likes of Septimus, performed under a guise of duty and self-sacrifice, involves the violent imposition of his socially condoned will on the damaged psyches of war-troubled individuals. 'He shut people up' (*MD*, 92). Or, as Clarissa thinks, he is 'capable of some indescribable outrage—forcing your soul' (*MD*, 165).

### Septimus's 'insane truth'

In October 1922 Woolf conceived Septimus as representative of the 100,000 cases of shell-shock treated after the Great War. Two months earlier the *Report of the War Office Committee of Enquiry into*

'*Shell-shock*' was presented to Parliament.[27] Woolf seems to draw on the description of the causes and symptoms of shell shock in the *Report* together with her own experiences of doctors' responses to her mental breakdowns to offer her portraits of a soldier suffering from Post-Traumatic Stress Disorder (PTSD) and of the doctors who attempt to treat him. Both *The Report* and *The Times* articles that followed its publication attributed shell shock to a loss of self-control or will power. *The Report* emphasised how important it was for the physician to 'dominate the situation', just as Sir William does.[28] The reader learns what Bradshaw does not, that Septimus's illness began with his response to Evans's death when he 'congratulated himself upon feeling very little and very reasonably' (*MD*, 77). Simultaneously Septimus lost his senses of taste and feeling. In fact he became remarkably like Sir William. The War had deprived him of that sentient inner self that Woolf so prizes. By the time we encounter him at the beginning of the novel madness has allowed him to recover his feelings. But those feelings are now out of control, the expression of his madness.[29]

Yet is the madness of Septimus any worse than the sanity of Holmes and Bradshaw? Septimus lacks a sense of the separation of past and present, the War and present peacetime. The dead are still alive, a ghostly Evans tells him (*MD*, 63). But is this hallucination any worse than the entire governing class's strenuous attempts to erase all memory of the wartime dead (apart from official memorials)? Neither attitude is truly sane. When Woolf first started writing the novel in October 1922 she wrote in her Diary, 'I adumbrate here a study of ... the world seen by the sane and the insane side by side' (*D* II, 207). Yet in the finished novel Woolf offers us insanity not in contrast to sanity but as a component of it, just as she locates death within life and beauty within death. What Woolf called Septimus's 'insane truth' seems to entail those feelings of the heart (but turned excessive) that Woolf pits against the moribund social imperative that represses the promptings of the heart.[30] Septimus's thought that 'it might be possible that the world itself is without meaning' (*MD*, 79) is one that haunts the work of so many of the modernists, including Woolf. His fragmentary experience comes closer than Bradshaw's methodical thought process to Woolf's conception of what should constitute the subject matter of modern writing, recording 'the atoms as they fall upon the mind in the order in which they fall'.[31] In fact Septimus is himself a kind of modernist writer in that he writes down his thoughts on scraps of paper as they occur to him (cf. *MD*, 126).

## The ambivalence of Clarissa Dalloway

Woolf shares with the traumatised Septimus disillusionment with the ideologies of the past, just as she shares his fragmented vision of life. For *Mrs. Dalloway* she has employed irony and indirection to enable her to construct a complex modernist portrait of post-war English society, in which her stated aim was 'To give 2 points of view at once: authority vs irresponsibility'.[32] One of the ways in which Mrs. Dalloway is Septimus's double is the way in which the War has divided her into two competing personae, one an active member of the post-war governing class, and the other a victim and critic of it, 'chained to a sinking ship' (*MD*, 70). As Alex Zwerdling pointed out long ago, the novel cannot 'be called an indictment because it deliberately looks at its object from the inside', employing Clarissa's stream of consciousness to win the reader's sympathy for her conflicted feelings.[33] In the first chapter Woolf describes Clarissa as virtually two polarised personae: 'She felt very young; at the same time unspeakably aged.' She goes on to describe Clarissa as both a social insider and 'outside, looking on' (*MD*, 7–8). Clarissa is as critical of her social self as is Peter, who thinks of her as 'too worldly', someone who 'cared too much for rank and society and getting on in the world' (*MD*, 69). Sally also accuses Clarissa of being a snob who identifies with the governing class. Yet she follows this judgement with the opposing opinion that 'Clarissa was pure-hearted' (*MD*, 171). It is this quality that enables Clarissa to distance herself from the upper-class characters associated with the deathly shadow cast by a war they initiated.

Nor is Clarissa the only character to be conflicted. Peter is both an instrument and critic of British imperialism. Even though he comes from a 'respected Anglo-Indian family which for at least three generations had administered the affairs of a continent', he still finds himself 'disliking India, and empire, and army' (*MD*, 49). Yet he still has moments of 'pride in England' (*MD*, 50). He 'cared not a straw' for what the Dalloways or Whitbreads thought of him; yet he needs to get Richard or Hugh to help him obtain a job (*MD*, 45). One of the most ironical incidents in the book occurs when Peter observes the ambulance carrying away the dead body of Septimus: 'One of the triumphs of civilization', he thinks (*MD*, 135). As Wyatt Bonikowski comments, the irony consists in the way that the suicide that may 'attempt to communicate' a message to and about civilisation is efficiently tidied up by one of civilisation's 'triumphs'.[34] Even Septimus is described as a paradox, 'the happiest man in the world, and the most miserable' (*MD*, 75).

## Clarissa's party

The party that serves as the novel's climax perfectly illustrates Clarissa's ambivalent relationship to British society. Both Richard and Peter think that Clarissa likes throwing parties because she enjoys being surrounded by famous people (*MD*, 108). She has turned into the perfect society hostess, according to Peter. And she admits that she admires the Lady Brutons of her world; they stand 'for something real to her' (*MD*, 69). She might despise Sir William, but she still invites him to her party. At the same time parties are an expression of her desire to bring individuals together: 'it was an offering; to combine, to create' (*MD*, 109). Her party serves the same unifying function as do the dinners in *To the Lighthouse* and *The Waves*. This is why news of Septimus's death in the middle of her party so disturbs her. Death, like the War, negates her form of creativity. At the same time his death keeps intact that 'thing' that she and the others from Bourton days have with time 'defaced'. His death 'was defiance', she concludes, a rejection not just of Bradshaw but of the entire class that has taken Britain and him to war and now wants to forget that it had ever happened. Death is therefore 'an attempt to communicate', an 'embrace' of others as much as her party is (*MD*, 165). So she ends up feeling 'glad that he had done it' (*MD*, 167).

Death of a figurative kind is also present at Clarissa's party in the form of her privileged guests who constitute a representative sample of England's moribund governing class. They turn out to be either old and out of touch with modern life or superficial and sycophantic, like Peter's *bête noir* Hugh Whitbread, 'dancing forward, bowing and scraping' as the Prime Minister emerges from a side room (*MD*, 155). Clarissa sees the Prime Minister as 'this majesty passing'. Yet she cannot avoid admitting that he 'looked so ordinary', even as he 'tried to look somebody' (*MD*, 154). The Prime Minister is Stanley Baldwin, who had only held office for three weeks by mid-June 1923 as leader of the first non-coalition Conservative government since 1905. *The New Statesman* considered him a 'pygmy' whose government had achieved 'precisely nothing'.[35] His party was about to lose to the newly arisen Labour Party in the November elections, as Richard and Lady Bruton forecast (*MD*, 99). For ordinary English men and women, like Mrs. Walker, the cook for the party, 'one Prime Minister more or less made not a scrap of difference' (*MD*, 148). Baldwin was a junior minister in the coalition government during the Great War. So he acts as the figurehead of the old guard that was still just hanging on to power in 1923. But the end is near. As Alex Zwerdling notes, the climactic party, 'for all its brilliance, is a kind of wake', because it offers an outer display of power without its substance. The novel closes not at the height of the party, but by offering a close-up of a private moment between Peter and Sally. Why? Is it that Woolf wants to end by celebrating the personal and the deeply felt amidst the glamour and superficiality of the social and politically powerful? A few lines from the end, Lady Rosseter offers a view of life that overrides the dichotomy between war and peace, between power and impotence, the one position about which the narrative is never ambivalent: 'What does the brain matter ... compared with the heart?' (*MD*, 174).

## Notes

1   Steven Erlanger, 'The Great War: The war to end all wars? Hardly. But did it change them forever?' *New York Times* (26 June 2014), A1. Web. 29 July 2014.
2   Siegfried Sassoon, *Memoirs of an Infantry Officer* (1930; rpt. London: Faber, 1973), p. 178.
3   Steven Erlanger.
4   'First World War', *The National Archives*, UK. Web. 29 July 2014.
5   Siegfried Sassoon, *Memoirs of an Infantry Officer* (1930; rpt. London: Faber, 1973), p. 205.
6   Siegfried Sassoon, '*Journal, 26 June 1916 – 12 August 1916*', Image 22. University of Cambridge Digital Library. Web. 1 Aug. 2014.
7   Adrian Bingham, '*The Daily Mail* and the First World War', *History Today*, 63.12 (2013). Web. 29 July 2014.
8   David Roberts, *Minds at War: The Poetry and Experience of the First World War* (Burgess Hill, UK: Saxon Books, 1966). Quoted in Philippa Lyon, ed. *Twentieth-Century War Poetry* (New York: Palgrave Macmillan, 2005), p. 41.
9   'The celebration', *The Times* (19 July 1919), 15. Web. 29 July 2014.
10  Samuel Hynes, *A War Imagined: The First World War and English Culture* (Oxford: Bodley Head, 1990), p. 84.
11  Virginia Woolf, Unpublished memoir of her nephew, Julian Bell, cited in Quentin Bell, *Virginia Woolf: A Biography*, Vol. 2, (London: Hogarth Press, 1972), p. 258.
12  Nigel Collett, *The Butcher of Amritsar: General Reginald Dyer* (London & New York: Continuum, 2006), p. 380.
13  Jane Lilienfeld, 'Success in circuit lies: Editing the war in *Mrs. Dalloway*', *Ariel* 15 (2009), 116.
14  Virginia Woolf, 'Introduction', *Mrs. Dalloway* (New York: Random House, 1928), p. vi.

15  Virginia Woolf, 'Mrs. Dalloway in Bond Street', in *Mrs. Dalloway's Party: A Short Story Sequence*, ed. Stella McNichol (London: Hogarth Press, 1973), p. 292.

16  'The Cinema', in *The Essays of Virginia Woolf*, ed. Andrew McNeillie (London: Hogarth Press, 1989–2000, Vol. 4), p. 349.

17  Paul Fussell, *The Great War and Modern Memory* (New York Oxford University Press, 1975), p. 255.

18  A. Murray Smith and Lady Birchenough, *Westminster Abbey* (London: Vacher & Sons, 1922), p. 22A.

19  M. E. Howard, *Lord Haldane and the Territorial Army* (London: Birkbeck College, 1967), p. 9.

20  David Bradshaw, '"Vanished like leaves": The military, elegy and Italy in *Mrs. Dalloway*', *Woolf Studies Annual*, 8 (2002), 113.

21  Tammy Clewell, 'Consolation refused: Virginia Woolf, The Great War, and modern mourning', *MFS: Modern Fiction Studies*, 50.1 (2004), 198.

22  *The War Poems of Siegfried Sassoon*, ed. Rupert Hart-Davis (London: Faber & Faber, 1983).

23  Erin K. Penner, 'Mapping the search for consolation in *Mrs. Dalloway*', *Virginia Woolf Miscellany*, 83 (2013), 24.

24  J. Hillis Miller, 'Virginia Woolf's All Souls' Day: The Omniscient Narrator in *Mrs. Dalloway*', in *The Shaken Realist: Essays in Modern Literature in Honor of Frederick J. Hoffman*, eds. Melvin J. Friedman and John B. Vickery (Baton Rouge: Louisiana State University Press, 1970), p. 113.

25  Adam Burrows, '"The shortcomings of timetables": Greenwich, modernism, and the limits of modernity', *MFS: Modern Fiction Studies*, 56.2 (2010), 263.

26  See Louise K. Barnett, 'John Bull and *noblesse oblige*: Doing and not doing one's duty in *Mrs. Dalloway*', *Studies in the Humanities*, 5.2 (1976), 22–27.

27  See Sue Thomas, 'Virginia Woolf's Septimus Smith and contemporary perceptions of shell shock', *English Language Notes*, 25.2 (1987), 49.

28  Ibid., 53.

29  Cf. Wyatt Bonikowski, *Shell Shock and the Modernist Imagination: The Death Drive in Post-World War I British Fiction* (Farnham, UK: Ashgate Publishing, 2013), p. 152.

30  Holograph notebook dated 12 March 1922, p. 133. Berg Collection, New York Public Library.

31  Ibid., p. 132.

32  Alex Zwerdling, '*Mrs. Dalloway* and the social system', *PMLA*, 92.1 (1977), 70.

33  Wyatt Bonikowski, *Shell Shock and the Modernist Imagination, op. cit.*, p. 134.

34  'Mr. Baldwin?' *New Statesman* (26 May 1923), 188–89.

35  Alex Zwerdling, *op. cit.*, 71.

# 9

# *Mrs. Dalloway* and the Reinvention of the Novel

## H. Porter Abbott

---

### Introduction: The novel and life itself

In a letter to David Garnett in 1917, Virginia Woolf wrote that 'Novels are frightfully clumsy and overpowering of course; still if one could only get hold of them it would be superb. I daresay one ought to invent a completely new form' (*L* II, 167). Of special interest here is the way Woolf hovers between wanting to 'get hold of' the novel and wanting to 'invent a completely new form'. On the one hand, she knew that, historically, the novel itself was almost without prescribed form, a baggy genre that Mikhail Bakhtin was to describe as no genre at all but, at its best, the enemy of genre, dedicated to formal sabotage.[1] To 'get hold of it', then, was to write a novel in the same spirit as the radical innovators of the form. On the other hand, by 1917 the novel appeared to have run its course. As Woolf wrote two years later in a searing critique, 'Modern Novels', the novel had become a thing without life. The term 'novel' in other words had been so abused that it was barely viable. She was still hunting for another term eight years later: 'I have an idea that I will invent a new name for my books to supplant "novel". A new _____ by Virginia Woolf. But what?' (*D* III, 34). In 1939, a year before her death, they were still 'my so-called novels' (*MB*, 70).

There are two sides to the critique in her revised version of 'Modern Novels', 'Modern Fiction' (1925). On one side, her target authors—H. G. Wells, John Galsworthy and Arnold Bennett—are 'materialists' in the sense that their characters are all exterior with no interior, predictable material beings driven by material needs in a material world cluttered with material objects. On the other side, the novel itself had become an object, something formally pre-packaged. Were these authors to write from feeling rather than convention, Woolf wrote, 'there would be no plot, no comedy, no tragedy, no love interest or catastrophe in the accepted style' in the modern novel (*MF*, 160). These are two interconnected complaints, but I want to feature the second, since it relates to a deeper issue: the emplotment of novels, and Woolf's difficulty with this seemingly fundamental feature of narrative form—especially when it came to understanding and representing human beings.[2]

In grappling with this issue, Woolf was willing to trade away a considerable formal advantage. Her target authors may have been mechanically emplotting their novels, moulding content in predictable ways, but these plots worked in the marketplace. In this sense Wells, Galsworthy and Bennett told 'good stories'—that is, stories with sufficiently strong narrativity to bind readers in the chains of curiosity, suspense and surprise that make them keep reading. Woolf didn't know the term 'narrativity' because it hadn't been invented yet,[3] but as a great reader and prolific reviewer she certainly knew what a 'good story' was and proved she could write one with her first novel, *The Voyage Out* (1915). It was a modest success, satisfying a popular appetite primed by the good stories told in successful Victorian novels.

But with her third novel, *Jacob's Room* (1922), the spirit of her 1919 critique began quite strikingly to inflect her fiction, eating away at the strong narrativity that was working so well in the book trade. The change in her approach was so extreme that one reviewer of her fourth novel, *Mrs. Dalloway* (1925), warned that only 'readers of preternatural intellect may discover a consecutive story'.[4] But then, as she wrote in her diary, 'I'm the only woman in England free to write what I like' (*D* III, 43).[5] And this she did, stubbornly, inventively, producing, one after another, works of prose fiction that have inevitably been classified as novels but were also very new things.

The commonest accounting of why she did this is Woolf's own: to capture what she was 'prepared to call life itself' (*MF*, 162). As she put it in her most frequently cited words on the subject, 'Life is not a series of gig lamps symmetrically arranged' (*MF*, 160).[6] It is not, in other words, a linear chain of events, but rather a matter of what it feels like to live in the present, experiencing the 'myriad impressions—trivial, fantastic, evanescent'—that fall upon 'an ordinary mind on an ordinary day' (*MF*, 160). Her vagueness on the subject derived in part because 'life' or 'life itself' was at once an idea, a value and a feeling. Moreover, it not only indicated her object in writing but also how that writing best comes into being. She had criticised Wells,

Galsworthy and Bennett for writing, not freely from their hearts, but as slaves labouring under the 'tyrant' of what had become the conventional novel (*MF*, 160). Increasingly, as the writing of *Mrs. Dalloway* progressed, Woolf found herself tracking how, by releasing her craft from the market demand for a salient narrative thread, thoughts from 'deep in the richest strata of my mind' (*D* II, 323) could emerge. As she wrote in her diary and her letters, the two seemed to go together. The meandering form of her novel, *Mrs. Dalloway*, matched the meandering of Woolf's mind when she seemed most to be herself. Fortunately, she was 'the only woman in England free to write what I like'. And what she claimed to like as a drifting writer was what Clarissa Dalloway claimed to like as a drifting observer—something they both, with equal and deliberate vagueness, called 'life'.[7]

## Narrating lives

There's 'life' or 'life itself' but there is also 'a life', which has been and still is widely considered a narratable phenomenon. This brings me to a central theme of this chapter: Woolf's deep distrust, in fact fear, of emplotted narrative both as a way of representing the lives of others and as a way of shaping one's own life. The value of narrative for both these ends has been a commonplace idea since St Augustine composed his theory and practice of life narrative in his *Confessions* (400 AD). In recent years, it has been the subject of widespread cross-disciplinary theorising.[8] That narrative does, or should, participate in the construction of the self is so intuitively strong that even Galen Strawson ends his oft-referenced counterblast, 'Against Narrativity', with a celebration of lives that are lived within a projected narrative structure: 'truly happy-go-lucky, see-what-comes-along lives are among the best there are, vivid, blessed, profound.'[9]

But what Strawson meant in his argument against narrativity is that lives are, or should be, open to the future, unconstrained by the arc of narrative necessity that comes with emplotment. For a character in the plot of a novel, the arc of necessity generates narrative expectations. The narrative form that Strawson promotes, by contrast, is the simplest form of narrative: the 'and then' structure. In fiction, it is loosely the 'picaresque', in which the only expectation generated by what has gone before is that something new is coming up. In essence, it is narrative without plot.

This is, essentially, the pattern (and lack of it) that Woolf followed when she invented her signature narrative mode in *Mrs. Dalloway*. Call it the 'narrative meander',[10] it is a micro-version of Strawson's 'see-what-comes-along' picaresque, unfolding as a succession of moments over seventeen hours in the story space of London: 'now it was a bed of tulips, now a child in a perambulator, now some absurd little drama she made up on the spur of the moment' (*MD*, 70). Woolf did not abandon narrative in *Mrs. Dalloway*, or displace it for poetry as some argue, but instead relocated the generators of curiosity, suspense and surprise to successive acts of perception and imagining, distributed among the narrator and a small cast of characters, with Clarissa Dalloway at the centre. It follows a loopy course in something like a geographical circle, but extends frequently to sparks of memory scattered in the past, of which 'the most exquisite moment of her whole life' (*MD*, 32) is a kiss out of the blue. If this narrative does not have the kind of strong narrativity that would satisfy much of the novel-reading public, there is in it a subtle kind of narrativity, rendered microscopically in the movements of the focalising mind: 'that one day should follow another; Wednesday, Thursday, Friday, Saturday; that one should wake up in the morning; see the sky; walk in the park; meet Hugh Whitbread; then suddenly in came Peter; then these roses; it was enough' (*MD*, 110).[11]

Actually, there's a double meander: the succession of micro-events experienced personally by Clarissa Dalloway and the darting of Woolf's own narrative eye and ear, meandering from mind to mind and place to place. What they accomplished together was to bring into apparent harmony 'a life' and 'life itself'. This in turn creates a syllogism: that if, in this minimal form of narrative, one comes closest to capturing life as it is lived, then any greater encroachment of plot moves one away from life. In support of this idea, those characters in *Mrs. Dalloway* who lead lives in which a plot line is clearly the 'dominant' are all versions of 'the death of the soul' (*MD*, 53)—characters like Hugh Whitbread, Dr Holmes, Sir William Bradshaw, MD. Doris Kilman, for example, whose name is a dead giveaway, lives within a self-construction that maps onto the classic formula of the conversion story. One day, '[b]urning and bitter [she] had turned into a church' (*MD*, 111) and, under the influence of the choir and the sermon of the Reverend Whittaker, had burst into tears. As the Reverend explains to her later, she had undergone a conversion and been born again—an explanation the unhappy woman has clung to ever since. In a very different way, Sally Seton, for all the reckless energy and wild unpredictability of her youth, returns years later born again into a predictable narrative trajectory, married to a rich bald industrialist in Manchester, with a family of five boys (*MD*, 163).

Epitomising this condition of suffocation by life narrative is the towering figure of Sir William Bradshaw, MD, 'the son of a shop-keeper' who had 'worked very hard' and 'won his position by sheer ability' (*MD*, 85); having acquired a duchess and begotten one son along the way, he now walked hospitals, caught salmon, took excellent photographs and through continued hard work kept England safe from abnormality and excess while building 'a wall of gold ... between [the Bradshaws] and all shifts and anxieties' (*MD*, 85) of life. This contained and containing man is to Clarissa, certainly 'a great doctor yet [is] to her obscurely evil, without sex or lust, extremely polite to women, but capable of some indescribable outrage ...' (*MD*, 165). He is, in short, a walking dead man, immaculately contained within the safety of a self-constructed life narrative, which in turn makes him dangerous, capable of 'forcing your soul, that was it' (*MD*, 165).

## PTSD and the trauma plot

Woolf used the same verb, 'force', in a letter to Gwen Raverat when she described how hard it was for her to write out the episodes involving the madness of Septimus Warren Smith, the shell-shocked veteran who had seen his closest friend blown up in the war. 'You can't think what a raging furnace it is still in me—madness and doctors and being forced' (*L* II, 180).[12] And sure enough, the perceived threat of an approaching doctor literally forces Septimus to jump out of a window to his death. The doctor who scares him—ironically named Dr Holmes—doesn't have a clue why Septimus jumps out of the window except that the patient is somehow a 'coward' (*MD*, 134).[13] But Sir William, the smart doctor who is up on the research, knows exactly what is wrong with Septimus: it is a case, he says, of 'the deferred effects of shell shock' (*MD*, 164). And Sir William knows exactly what to do in such cases: put him out of sight, lock him up until he is better. In other words, the force that would have been used in committing and then concealing Septimus follows upon a diagnostic narrative into which the patient has already been forced. The diagnosis is an instance of recursive entrapment in a tight mould of narratable identity.

And yet, if the doctor's prescription is inhuman, his diagnosis is correct, and we have more than Sir William's authority to go on. The diagnostic plot line is developed by the narrator herself who tells us that when Septimus's dear friend Evans was killed, 'just before the Armistice, in Italy, Septimus, far from showing any emotion or recognising that here was the end of a friendship, congratulated himself upon feeling very little and very reasonably' (*MD*, 77). The symptomology that Woolf's narrator (not Sir William) records—Septimus's inability to feel his grief, his sense of lurking danger, his hallucinations of Evans, his Messianic fantasies of being the Chosen One—are all recognisable symptoms of what we would now call Post-Traumatic Stress Disorder, or PTSD. There actually is, in other words, a dominant and dominating narrative with a recognisable plot governing much of what Septimus does and says, and it is a valid one. It tells a linear story with a powerful traumatic event for a cause, followed by a series of events that are explicable in terms of that cause, and culminating with the self-inflicted death of the traumatised victim.

Septimus is not the only character in the novel who lives a story of trauma and its aftermath. Woolf invites us to apply the narrative of PTSD to Clarissa herself when we learn that as a child Clarissa saw her sister Sylvia killed by a falling tree (*MD*, 70). As with Septimus, this horrendous event shows up nowhere in Clarissa's thoughts, which is itself a plausible effect of trauma.[14] It also chimes with Woolf's declared intention to make 'Septimus and Mrs. Dalloway … entirely dependent on each other' (*L* II, 189), and it is underscored late in the novel when, learning of his suicide, Clarissa feels 'somehow very like him—the young man who had killed himself' (*MD*, 166). The alignment was so close in Woolf's mind that she originally planned to have Clarissa kill herself when she learns of Septimus's suicide.[15]

For our purposes in this chapter the key questions are: How thoroughly does the sense of a dominating narrative formula, the trauma plot, play out in the life of Clarissa Dalloway? How does it work on us within a prose fiction governed by the 'and then' structure—a narrative meander that in turn is an implicit critique of emplotted narrative as the perceived dominant in the life of anyone? After all, as with Septimus, so with Clarissa, the PTSD masterplot can be recursively applied to provide a causal accounting of her thoughts and behaviour. Once you learn of the trauma she suffered in childhood, it provides a new way of reading what you've already read. On the first page of the novel, an effect of this causal trauma pops like a *non sequitur* into the meandering narrative stream as Clarissa recalls herself at eighteen, plunging 'into the open air' at Bourton in the morning, 'feeling as she did, standing there in the open window, *that something awful was about to happen;* looking at the flowers, at the trees with the smoke winding off them and the rooks rising, falling …' (*MD*, 3; my italics). And, then again, five pages later, 'She had a perpetual sense, as she watched the taxi cabs, of being out, out, far out to sea and alone; *she always had the feeling that it was very, very dangerous to live even one day*'

(*MD*, 8; my italics). The probable cause of this feeling of imminent threat is referenced only once (and only in passing) a hundred pages later, when 'that horrible affair' pops into Peter Walsh's thoughts: 'To see your own sister killed by a falling tree … before your very eyes, a girl too on the verge of life' (*MD*, 70). But once this plot unfolds it gives its own meaning to the menacing sound of the bells that count the hours of this day, tolling 'for death that surprised in the midst of life' (*MD*, 45).

## Moments revisited

I noted above that Clarissa's passion for moments, which in turn comprise the novel's meandering course, is a passion for 'life itself'. But with the idea tolled in the bells, that death 'surprised in the midst of life', comes another narrative accounting of Clarissa's passion for moments. In this accounting, their appeal lies in their disconnection and with it the illusion of stepping out of time and thus out of the universal story that comes with time. Moments, in this reading, are places of safety where intense emotions can be felt without attachments: 'what she loved was this, here, now, in front of her' (*MD,* 8): her experience is of an aesthetic treasure, a 'secret deposit of exquisite moments' (*MD,* 26). Thus, the passage that I cited above as an example of this treasure is followed by a sentence that strengthens this alternative reading of Clarissa's passion for moments: 'that one should wake up in the morning; see the sky; walk in the park; meet Hugh Whitbread; then suddenly in came Peter; then these roses; it was enough. *After that, how unbelievable death was!*' (*MD*, 110; my italics). When time intrudes into Clarissa's consciousness, it brings with it not only the chance of death but a narrative arc that leads in that direction.

Narrative is, arguably, a reflex of the human mind—one that is very hard for a mind to disable. The neurologist Antonio Damasio has perhaps gone the furthest in pushing back the roots of this reflex to one's first minimal pre-linguistic encounters with the world.[16] Whether or not this is the case, he is probably right that narratable connection-making is inevitable for sentient beings like ourselves. It is an inevitability that Clarissa Dalloway tries to cancel by undoing the narrative connectors, leaving only moments:

> The cook whistled in the kitchen. She heard the click of the typewriter. It was her life, and, bending her head over the hall table, she bowed beneath the influence, felt blessed and purified, saying to herself, as she

took the pad with the telephone message on it, how moments like this
are buds on the tree of life, flowers of darkness they are, she thought (as if
some lovely rose had blossomed for her eyes only). (*MD*, 26)

If Clarissa seeks to identify these plotless moments—the cook whis-
tling in the kitchen, the clicking of her typewriter—as 'her life', there
is no mistaking the ironic bite of Woolf's portrait of her as a suppliant,
'bending her head over the hall table' where 'she bowed beneath the
influence, felt blessed and purified', nor the reference to the biblical
'tree of life'. The irony here is especially evident because Clarissa has
already picked up 'the pad with the telephone message on it' and in
the next moment she will read the message. It tells her that Lady
Bruton has invited her husband, but not her, to lunch, and she is
'rocked' as an old story starts up again.

## Parties

It remains to note that this passion for moments connects in turn to
Clarissa's passion for parties, which are in effect a concentration of
moments experienced by people who have been drawn out of their
ongoing life-narratives to enjoy what she thinks of as 'simply life'
(*MD*, 109). This is life understood not as an historical organisation
of narratable events but as an ahistorical disorganisation of random
moments. In her own terms, Clarissa's parties are given 'for no reason
whatever' (*MD*, 109). But if we have the masterplot of PTSD in mind,
then there is indeed a 'reason' for them. A party, as such, gives the illusion of an escape from narrative time into a space where moments
are not enchained like the events that make a story, but rather suc-
ceed each other in no particular course at all. The irony of this is that
her parties are themselves motivated events in a story of trauma that
Clarissa is living out. In short, the very need to escape from this story
produces events that are explicable in terms of this story.

   In *Self Comes to Mind*, Antonio Damasio uses the example of a
cocktail party to show how one can become distracted by the sudden
activation of one's meaning-making self. You may be, as one often is,
'technically *hearing* other conversations, a fragment here, a fragment
there, at the edges of the stream of consciousness' but not actually listening; and then 'all of a sudden something clicks, some fragment of a
conversation joins others, and a sensible pattern emerges, and ... [at]
that instant you form a meaning'.[17] What bonds pattern and meaning
is our narrative capability. Once it gets started, it cannot fail to go on,
for the mechanism involved is as irresistible as it is primordial. In the

party that forms the sustained climax to *Mrs. Dalloway*, this mechanism begins firing when Clarissa overhears fragments of a conversation between Sir William and her husband, and then is assisted by Lady Bradshaw, who murmurs how her husband had been notified of 'a very sad case. A young man … had killed himself.' And Clarissa thinks, 'Oh! … in the middle of my party, here's death. … What business had the Bradshaws to talk of death at her party?' (*MD*, 164). Seeking to shake it, to move on, to join up with other guests and re-enter the life of her party, she finds herself instead alone in a little room. 'There was nobody. The party's splendour fell to the floor' (*MD*, 164). Away from what she calls 'life', alone with death, she begins to narrativise. As always 'her body went through it first', rendering how the story must have felt as it happened: 'He had thrown himself from a window. Up had flashed the ground; through him, blundering, bruising, went the rusty spikes. There he lay with a thud, thud, thud in his brain, and then a suffocation of blackness.' After the How, comes the Why, the question that narrative invariably raises and often presumes to answer: 'But why had he done it?' (*MD*, 165).

This sequence is an exemplum of an idea that, in this reading, governs the novel both formally and thematically: that life figured as random moments in the present gives way to time figured as a story that can only lead to death. Clarissa Dalloway may not see, as we are led to see, her containment within a narrative of PTSD and its aftermath. But she always feels the weight of the larger story with its foreknown conclusion, knowing, I believe, that her 'secret deposit of exquisite moments' (*MD*, 26) is all a part of it, adding their momentum. That this story weighs on her more heavily than most shines with a hard cold light when, feeling 'somehow very like' Septimus, she also 'felt glad that he had done it; thrown [his life] away' (*MD*, 166–67).[18]

## Conclusion

Dorothy Richardson wrote that 'Plot nowadays, save the cosmic plot, is inexcusable. Lollipops for children.'[19] What I have tried to show is that Woolf had a more complex idea about plot in *Mrs. Dalloway*. She was certainly working against the novel as an emplotted narrative genre, but she was also working with it. She was doing both at the same time, composing a narrative meander with its celebration of moments as 'life itself' and composing a life story, dominated by trauma. On the one hand, we have the simplest of narrative structures by which life is conveyed as a continual series of surprises; on the other, we have a plotted novel internally mirrored by the story of Septimus Smith. If Sally Seton's sudden kiss is the most intense moment of the first, it is not a causal event from which the rest can be derived. But the horrific trauma of the second is, unavoidably, a causal event of immense power. This trauma in turn can be seen as generating the need for the illusion of life as a meander among moments.

The difference in salience between these two ways of reading *Mrs. Dalloway* as a narrative brings to mind Dan Shen's useful concept of a 'covert progression'.[20] A covert progression is an undercurrent of meaning that can be found in works of fiction running with or against or obliquely across the overt progression of a text and the meanings it bears. Unlike the unwitting authorial self-subversions that a whole range of analytical methods has construed from the most innocent seeming works, covert progressions are the product of deliberate craft. They are endowed by their creators with potential power that, when released into the reader's awareness, contribute to the overall depth and complexity of a text.

What I have been tracking in the latter part of this chapter is a covert progression, but with an important exception—one that plays a central part in Woolf's departure from novelistic narrative norms in *Mrs. Dalloway*. For Shen (as for most narratologists), plot is the primary progression of narrative. It is the major factor in generating the narrativity of a text, the feeling that we are reading a good story. A covert progression, by contrast, emerges in the mind of the attentive reader from beneath the overt progression and depends not on plot but on other stylistic and rhetorical means. In *Mrs. Dalloway*, however, Woolf has turned this model upside down, giving her novel a covert plot that runs beneath the meandering string of moments that lies on the surface. By extension, Woolf has made emplotment itself covert since, for her, all plots are sinister plots. They lay a course and drag one along with them, reducing one to a function, robbing one of the infinitude of possibility that seems promised by a life of moments.

The problem is that plots are not just the province of fiction. We may not see them in the ordinary course of our lives, but they work as surely as causes have effects. This is what allows Sir William to make an accurate diagnosis, despite his stunted nature and downright fear of the richness of life that both Woolf and Mrs. Dalloway treasure. He can make out the plot that has captured his patient, while remaining blind to the richness of his patient's life—the moments of rare beauty that accompany Septimus during his own short meander on this day in London.

With just a touch in a passing thought, Woolf assures us that there is a covert plot doing its work in Clarissa's life, too. For the reader, the salience of this plot depends on how fully and vividly she allows herself to enter the mind of a child witnessing the sudden crushing to death of her sister. This relation to the text is something like Clarissa's, when (guided by what necessity?) she enters the mind and body of Septimus Warren Smith as he falls on the spikes of an iron fence. The mind and body of the reader can be excused for swerving from the scene that Clarissa witnessed as a child. And yet if our minds don't swerve and the image stays with us, I wonder how thoroughly the power of this event might saturate the way we experience the moments of Mrs. Dalloway's life? How dark a shadow does it cast on the affirmation of those moments? Much depends, of course, on who is doing the reading. My own view is that these two conflicting narrative structures, each with its different view of our freedom or lack of it in this life, coexist in a kind of impossible partnership. They create an unrelieved tension that Woolf must have felt in her own life.

## Notes

1   The anti-generic, 'transcendent' character of the novel was a central focus of the unorthodox twentieth-century Russian thinker Mikhail Bakhtin (1895–1975). See especially *Problems of Dostoevsky's Poetics* [1929], ed. and trans. Caryl Emerson (Manchester: Manchester University Press, 1984).

2   'Emplotment' is, in Hayden White's words, an operation essential to the creation of narrative in that it is what gives a mere succession of data 'the formal coherency that only stories can possess' (Hayden White, 'The Value of Narrativity in the Representation of Reality', in *On Narrative*, ed. W. J. T. Mitchell [University of Chicago Press, 1981], p. 19). 'Plot', a term I use frequently in this chapter, has been used in a variety of contrasting ways. For a brief overview, see Hilary Dannenberg, *Coincidence and Counterfactuality: Plotting Time and Space in Narrative Fiction* (Lincoln, NB: University of Nebraska Press, 2008), pp. 6–10. In this chapter, I will be following one common usage of plot as story kind, as in tragic plot, comic plot, marriage plot, revenge plot, quest, pilgrimage. A plot in this sense is an over-arching narrative schema that, once cued, generates in the reader expectations about how the narrative will unfold.

3   'Narrativity' is another vexed term (see H. Porter Abbott, 'Narrativity', in *Handbook of Narratology*, revised edition, ed. Peter Hühn, et al. [Berlin/New York: Walter de Gruyter, 2014], pp. 587–607). In this chapter, I follow David Herman when he writes that narrativity is a measure by which something is deemed 'more or less prototypically story-like' (David Herman, *Story Logic: Problems and Possibilities of Narrative* [Lincoln: University of Nebraska Press, 2002], pp. 90–91). Marie-Laure Ryan has similarly used it interchangeably with 'storiness' (Ryan, *Avatars*

*of Story* [Minneapolis: University of Minnesota Press, 2006], p. 7). By
using the term 'strong narrativity' I have wedded this sense of narrativity as storiness with the force exerted on the reader that Meir Sternberg
locates in the dynamic narrative triad of curiosity, suspense, and surprise
(Meir Sternberg, *Expositional Modes and Temporal Ordering in Fiction*
[Baltimore: Johns Hopkins University Press, 1978]).

4   In the *Western Mail*, 14 May 1925 (*D* III, 21 n.24).

5   Woolf's name had already acquired a cachet that helped sales, but the
principal agent of her freedom was the Hogarth Press that she and her
husband, Leonard Woolf, founded in 1917.

6   A gig was a light two-wheeled one-horse carriage, often used as a hackney cab. Woolf has in mind how they would look of an evening, lined
up on the side of a street with their lamps lit.

7   See the following passage in her diary: 'But how entirely I live in my
imagination; how completely depend upon spurts of thought, coming as
I walk, as I sit; things churning up in my mind & so making a perpetual
pageant, which is to me my happiness' (*D* II, 315). See also: '[T]here is
no principle, except to follow this whimsical brain implicitly, pare away
the ill fitting, till I have the shape exact, & if that's no good, it is the
fault of God, after all. It is He that has made it, not we ourselves' (*D* II,
299–300).

8   For an overview of the subject of narrative and identity, including the
controversies regarding the role of narrative in identity construction, see
Michael Bamberg, 'Identity and Narration', in *Handbook of Narratology*,
revised edition, ed. Peter Hühn et al. (Berlin/New York: Walter de
Gruyter, 2014), pp. 241–52.

9   Galen Strawson, 'Against Narrativity', *Ratio* 17.4 (2004), 449.

10  See H. Porter Abbott, 'Old Virginia and the Night Writer: The Origins
of Woolf's Narrative Meander', in *Inscribing the Daily: Critical Essays
on Women's Diaries*, ed. S. Bunkers & C. Huff (Amherst: University of
Massachusetts Press, 1996). For an assessment of recent scientific research
into the nature and value of mental meandering (day-dreaming), along
with its relevance to Woolf's practice as a writer, see Melba Cuddy-
Keane's excellent chapter in this volume.

11  There were precedents for something like this micro-version of the
picaresque, particularly *A Sentimental Journey* and *The Life and Opinions
of Tristram Shandy*, both by the eighteenth-century novelist Laurence
Sterne, whom Woolf noted with praise in 'Modern Fiction'.

12  Woolf's bouts of depression could be so severe that in three instances
prior to working on *Mrs. Dalloway* she had been confined to a mental
hospital for women suffering from mental disease. Her illness has been
variously diagnosed in hindsight, but strong arguments have been made
that she had PTSD. Suzette Henke, who has made this case, has gone
meticulously through the case histories of patients in the archives of
Holloway Sanatorium for the Insane, dating back to 1895. In both what
they record and the language in which they are written, these case

histories reveal the extent to which patients were not only robbed of their freedom and dignity, but forced into misdiagnoses (Henke, *Virginia Woolf and Madness: Trauma Narrative in Mrs. Dalloway* [London: South Place Ethical Society, 2010]).

13    Cowardice was a frequent charge levelled at soldiers who became immobilised by shell shock (PTSD). For an excellent fictional treatment of Dr William Rivers's groundbreaking work on shell shock as a covert language of protest, see Pat Barker's novel *Regeneration* (1991).

14    Hemingway said the same about Nick in 'Big Two-Hearted River', who had been so traumatised by the war that he was 'unable to comment on this condition and could not suffer that it be mentioned in [his] presence. So the war, all mention of the war, anything about the war, is omitted.' (See Ernest Hemingway, 'The Art of the Short Story', in *New Critical Approaches to the Short Stories of Ernest Hemingway*, ed. Jackson J. Benson [Durham, NC: Duke University Press, 1990], p. 3). Part One of this story was published in the same month of 1925 as *Mrs. Dalloway*.

15    Virginia Woolf, 'An Introduction to *Mrs. Dalloway*,' in *The* Mrs. Dalloway *Reader*, ed. Francine Prose (New York: Harcourt, 2003), p. 11.

16    Since the publication of his *Descartes' Error: Emotion, Reason, and the Human Mind* (1995), Damasio's work on the embodied nature of cognition has had a marked influence on cross-disciplinary fields like cognitive narratology. An important, evolving, thread of his theorising has been the centrality of narrative as the primary cognitive mechanism in our engagement with the world. Before there is language or meaning, there is narrative activity in the mind that generates the 'feeling of knowing'. From its first manifestation as minimal continuities of images, narrative is a key player in a complex ontogeny from 'protoself' to 'core self' to 'autobiographical self' (Antonio Damasio, *Self Comes to Mind: Constructing the Conscious Brain* [New York: Pantheon Books. 2010]).

17    Damasio (2010), p. 173.

18    In the first American edition, Woolf added two sentences that were not in the Hogarth first edition: 'He made her feel the beauty. Made her feel the fun' (see *MD*, 354). It was a tortuous move, vaguely suggesting a Christlike Septimus who dies that Clarissa might live. My own view is that Clarissa is straining to transmute the meaning of this death and thereby resist the attractive power of Septimus's act. It may also indicate Woolf's own struggle as she tried further to soften the bleakness of what she had already softened by choosing to let Clarissa live.

19    Richardson, *Journey to Paradise*, ed. Trudi Tate (London: Virago Press, 1989), p. 139.

20    Shen, *Style and Rhetoric of Short Narrative Fiction: Covert Progressions behind Overt Plots* (New York & London: Routledge, 2014).

# 10

# *Mrs. Dalloway* and *To the Lighthouse*: The Novel as Elegy

Daniel Bedggood

## Introduction: 'A new name for my books to supplant "novel"'

Virginia Woolf lived at a time when the twentieth century's early upheavals seemed to demand new approaches and forms of expression. Writing in her diary in the midst of composing *To the Lighthouse* in 1925, she reflects that 'I have an idea that I will invent a new name for my books to supplant 'novel'. A new _____ by Virginia Woolf. But what? Elegy?'[1] Significantly, Woolf's evocation of elegy shapes the form and some of the major concerns of two of her novels, *To the Lighthouse* and *Mrs. Dalloway*, fusing her desire to make it new with the elegy's preoccupation with the past, absence and loss. While some studies have considered Woolf's adaptation of elegy with respect to its formal features, there has been a shift in recent Woolf criticism to consider the secular elegiac mode that emphasises the vicissitudes of time, silence and narrative separations in perspective. As a text that is written as a kind of suspended parallel narrative, her novels deal with fragmentary recollection and problems attendant on return and survival in the wake of the Great War. Woolf uses elegy as a mode to examine consciousness, trauma and unrealised hope at both individual and societal levels. Her focus extends to symbolic emphases on absent characters, the persistence of memory, and possibilities of art and narrative to bridge the social ruptures between generations. She blends elegiac remembrance of the familial past with a radical urge to challenge and invent, to use the concept of elegy for new purposes.

Elegy is a signal form for Woolf, useful through its distinction from the 'novel', and also demonstrative of her fascination with the examination of the past. Her comment, above, that her novels might be more aptly described as elegies dates from the time of writing *To the Lighthouse*; yet it is clear that elegy was on her mind before this, evident in her critical engagement with reading and writing about the past in the years prior to this diary entry, and in her recognition of her turn to 'poetic' register in prose form: 'What was I going to say? Something about the violent moods of my soul. How describe them, even with a waking mind? I think I grow more & more poetic' (*D* II, 304; entry dated 21 June 1924).[2] Her knowledge of past literary traditions, evident for example in her collection, *The Common Reader* (1924), suggests a very acute awareness of classical and Elizabethan poetic modes especially, though *Mrs. Dalloway* and *To the Lighthouse* demonstrate an eclectic breadth of intertextuality that goes beyond 'two years' worth of reading Homer, Aeschylus, Euripides, and Sophocles'.[3]

Yet, however much it is a feature of her writing to quote from and allude to these past traditions, it is crucial to note delight in novelty in her use of allusion, something akin to the kinds of artistic bricolage of Eliot in his poem *The Waste Land*. Like Eliot, she makes something new out of fragments of the past, and yet, unlike Eliot or James Joyce, her treatment is playful and 'feminine', reflecting her own reading practice that finds meaning when, as Jane de Gay has it, 'the words of [another] writer loom up to describe phenomena Woolf experiences'.[4] Her apparent rejection of 'novel' and choice of alternative 'elegy' goes with this practice: in *A Room of One's Own*, Woolf articulates the constraints placed on women novelists.[5] Elegy, though also a genre with a long tradition, presents a relatively open, malleable form for a Modernist experimenter, though with some conventions of its own to challenge.

Elegy, a mode fostered in classical literature, tends to take the form of a short poetic work, 'usually formal or ceremonious in tone and diction, occasioned by the death of a person … [though] it has been most often a poem of meditation, usually on love or death'.[6] While the form of elegy and its specific subject are quite elastic, allowing a large variety of treatments, the tradition tends to share features of tone and function: 'to lament, praise, and console … [encompassing] responses to the experience of loss [through]… expressing grief … idealizing the deceased … and finding solace in meditation on natural continuances or on moral, metaphysical, and religious values.'[7] By the time of Woolf's writing in the 1920s, both a post-Victorian crisis of faith in religion and the devastations of the First World War had had their impacts on Modernist poetry in general, but especially

on the 'redemptive elegiac narrative and poetic closure'.[8] Peter Sacks'
influential psychoanalytical study of elegy suggests that even while
sceptical of past elegiac modes, especially their features of idealisation
and consolation, writers of Woolf's generation nonetheless repeat or
sample 'the residue of generic strategies' of elegy to create their own
elegiac effects, albeit with less sense of redemptive closure.[9]

For Woolf, a more complex, uneven treatment of elegy is more
'truthful'. The very innovations in her particular style of writing, its
fragmentary, subjective and imagistic qualities, are related in Woolf's
view to a more honest recollection of the past and the experience
of human consciousness. In considering writing style, Woolf's choice
of a 'poetic' style of prose is defended as more responsive to a fuller
range of expression:

> [Can] prose say the simple things which are so tremendous? Give the
> sudden emotions which are so surprising? Can it chant the elegy, or
> hymn the love, or shriek in terror, or praise the rose, the nightingale,
> or the beauty of the night? Can it leap at one spring at the heart of its
> subject as the poet does? I think not. That is the penalty it pays for hav-
> ing dispensed with the incantation and the mystery, with rhyme and
> metre.[10]

Prose elegy, on the other hand, is less confined by conventions: it 'will
also give the sneer, the contrast, the question, the closeness and complexity of life. It will take the mould of that queer conglomeration
of incongruous things—the Modern mind.'[11] Connected with this is
Woolf's sense of the artistic parallels between language and image. In
an exchange of letters between Woolf and her friend, the artist Jacques
Raverat, Raverat writes of the associations triggered by his work
being akin to a rock tossed into water: 'there are splashes in the outer
air in every direction, and under the surface waves that follow one
another into dark and forgotten corners.' Woolf responds, suggesting that writers, too, try 'to catch and consolidate and consummate
... those splashes of yours; for the falsity of the past ... is precisely I
think that [some writers] adhere to a formal railway line of sentence,
for its convenience, never reflecting that people don't and never did
feel or think or dream for a second in that way; but all over the place,
in your way'.[12] In this rejection of conventional 'realistic' representations of the past, Woolf's innovations of style and form are represented
as attempts to be more true to experience; for her, an examination
of consciousness depicts the persistence of the past in the present,
admitted by demanding memory, associations and overlapping trains
of thought.

## Presenting the past as elegiac in *Mrs. Dalloway*

For a book ostensibly set in London over the course of a single day in June 1923, Woolf's fourth novel is thoroughly engaged with the past in its many forms. In extensively detailing its day in the present, as Joyce does in *Ulysses*, Woolf's text also plays with multiple perspectives and a saturation of the past provided by demanding memory that inserts itself between and in relation with current dialogue and represented thought. Early in the writing process, this was not the case; Woolf notes in June 1923 that the book 'is too thin and unreal somehow', especially problematic considering her ambitions: 'in this book I have almost too many ideas. I want to give life and death, sanity and insanity; I want to criticise the social system, and to show it at work, at its most intense.'[13] However, in August she comments on 'My discovery: how I dig out beautiful caves behind my characters; I think that gives exactly what I want; humanity, humour, depth. The idea is that the caves shall connect, & each comes to daylight at the present moment.'[14]

The 'discovery', the 'beautiful caves' behind the characters she writes, is manifest in her presentation of the past in the present narrative, where even the present day appears in the past tense, and hence a merging of temporality where 'the world waver[s] and quiver[s] and threaten[s] to burst into flames' (*MD*, 14). At moments when characters suggest otherwise, such as when Peter Walsh thinks that 'women live much more in the past than we [men] do' (*MD*, 50), Woolf undermines such claims, in this case by quickly following this with Peter's extended dream and recollection of his frustrated courting of Clarissa decades earlier. In one critic's words, 'the weight of all the past moments presses just beneath the surface of the present, ready in an instant to flow into consciousness, overwhelming it with the immediate presence of the past'.[15]

Throughout the book, mechanical time, insanity, illness and death play a counterpoint in treatment of the past, both recreating and making problematic past elegiac modes. Constant reminders of present time take the form of refrains and repetitions that mimic clockwork: 'the sound of Big Ben striking the half-hour struck out between them …, strong, indifferent, inconsiderate. … [O]verwhelmed by the traffic and the sound of all the clocks striking, her voice crying "My party to-night! Remember my party tonight!"… (The leaden circles dissolved in the air)' (*MD*, 43). The 'leaden circles' remind us that with the passage of time, we grow closer and closer to death, and the repetitive language rhythms are matched by allusive repetition that shifts

significance, as in the apparently conciliatory line from Shakespeare's
*Cymbeline*, 'Fear no more the heat o' the sun/ Nor the winter's furi-
ous rages',[16] repeated in many different contexts, but oddly consoling
as a funeral sentiment offered to one still living. Such repetitions are
part of a mode of emptied-out elegiac lyric: the present is a repetition,
offering at best a partial or ironic consolation.

Though Mrs. Dalloway is clearly mortal, feminist critics Sandra
Gilbert and Susan Gubar see her as 'a kind of queen [who] with a
divine grace ... regenerates the post-war world'.[17] This may be over-
stating her role in the novel: she may be more significantly a woman
who escapes the taxonomy of glibness. The very title, *Mrs. Dalloway*, is
fraught with a personal examination of past identity and present role,
where the present absence cancels out the former 'Clarissa':

> That she held herself well was true; and had nice hands and feet; and
> dressed well, considering that she spent little. But often now this body
> she wore ... this body, with all its capacities, seemed nothing—nothing at
> all. She had the oddest sense of being herself invisible; unseen; unknown;
> there being no more marrying, no more having of children now, but
> only this astonishing and rather solemn progress with the rest of them,
> up Bond Street, this being Mrs. Dalloway; not even Clarissa any more;
> this being Mrs. Richard Dalloway. (*MD*, 9–10)

In this reflection early in the text, 'Clarissa' is no more, personal identity extinguished when the primary functions of a woman of her time
and station are exhausted: marriage and childhood. As a menopausal
woman, she intimates that all is now past, and instead, the signature of
the husband elides the former Clarissa, and we are presented with a
pale ghost of her former self, literally pale after recent illness, and sleeping alone: 'it was all over for her. The sheet was stretched and the bed
narrow' (*MD*, 42). The presentiment of death continues, with hints
that her narrative will not go on and fantasies of her death abounding,
including those that present an autobiographical recollection of the
death of an acquaintance falling over the bannister,[18] echoed in Peter's
vision of 'the sudden loudness of the final stroke toll[ing] for death
that surprised in the midst of life, Clarissa falling. ... No! No! he cried'
(*MD*, 45), in anticipation of Septimus's suicidal plunge. Mrs. Dalloway
accepts some of these presentiments, fancying an almost vegetative
withdrawal at one point:

> Quiet descended on her, calm, content, as her needle drawing the silk
> smoothly to its gentle pause, collected the green folds together and
> attached them, very lightly, to the belt. So on a summer's day waves

collect, overbalance, and fall; collect and fall; and the whole world seems to be saying 'that is all' more and more ponderously, until even the heart in the body which lies in the sun on the beach says too, That is all. Fear no more, says the heart. (*MD*, 35-36)

What is past, then, takes on special importance for Clarissa, who relies on an elegiac rekindling of herself in recollection. Wondering whether this is insanity, she fixates and repeats passages from her earlier life, in contrast with her light-hearted former self, and past flirtations and possibilities with Sally Seton: 'had not that, after all, been love? ... The strange thing, on looking back, was the purity, the integrity, of her feeling for Sally' (*MD*, 29, 31).

In contrast to the vivid and shifting past, and alternative histories they may have emanated from it, chaste present consolations of love and a sense of herself as a 'diamond' condensed from droplets of the past mix with the image of the superficiality of her endeavours in preparing for a 'glittering' party. Observing a pair of her guests, Clarissa confirms the kind of charade being enacted at the party that is like the waxed-over-ness of 'the deeper sources of life [that] could be unsealed suddenly, inappropriately, sentimentally' (*MD*, 18): 'not that *they* added perceptibly to the noise of the party. They were not talking (perceptibly) as they stood side by side by the yellow curtains. ... They looked; that was all' (*MD*, 158). This is a party representing its age: small talk, civilities and observance of social position circulate in a static pattern, and even 'the young people could not talk. ... They would solidify young' (*MD*, 159). Against such a background, Clarissa seems doomed to fulfil the figurative 'invisibility' alluded to at the beginning of her day.

Yet, the mass death and insanity of the Great War is a primary feature of elegy in the text, providing a telling counterpoint to Clarissa's personal loss of self, and one that helps her to reflect on her continuing substance by contrast. Critics such as Mark Hussey recognise 'the centrality of war in [Woolf's] life's work',[19] and as Karen Levenback puts it, 'to Virginia Woolf, whatever the associations or connotations, after 1914 war was not a figure of speech. She saw its experience, on the front or at home, as its history—yet increasingly its constructions had replaced individual memory and become its reality.'[20] When Peter Walsh is overtaken in his walk, the rhythm of marching young men transporting a wreath 'from Finsbury Pavement to the empty tomb' (*MD*, 46) is at once a repetition of earlier elegiac war ceremony and celebration, alongside an evocation of empty repetition, like the emptiness of the tomb itself.[21]

In a more sustained fashion, Woolf explores the unpacking of past elegiac sentiment as part a more complex *new* elegiac position through examining the case of the 'shell-shocked' Septimus Smith, akin to the need to unpack the 'myth' of figures like Rupert Brooke, publicly turned into a poet-war-hero.[22] Septimus is another disenfranchised character, a double for Clarissa: under-educated due to class, and drawn to war through over-romantic cultural narratives and his desire to experience the war as a poet, but brutalised by the experience. Quite unlike Clarissa's flight between past and present, Septimus's lack of 'internal time-consciousness' signals a truly invisible wound of the war: 'he lacks conscious memory of the war, that is, memory of the war as something past.'[23] Instead, the war is part of his daily life, and Septimus hallucinates the ghost of his dead officer, Evans, trailing him through the urban-scape, talking and singing of Thessaly and hence evoking, again, the classical tradition of immortalising the 'glorious dead' warriors. At one point, the mentally-ill war veteran meanders through strange dissociated dictums, 'men must not cut down trees. There is a God. (He noted such revelations on the backs of envelopes)' (*MD*, 22), to mimic a sentiment from past elegiac war poetry: 'a sparrow ... [sang] freshly and piercingly in Greek words how there is no crime and, joined by another sparrow, they sang in voices prolonged and piercing in Greek words, from trees in the meadow of life beyond a river where the dead walk, how there is no death' (*MD*, 22). Woolf's juxtaposition of the surreal and strange oracle-like sparrows reveals Septimus as an observer and recipient of 'higher truth' (in the tradition of celebrated oracular madness from antiquity), unlike the 'war-blind' civilians who surround him;[24] such a sensibility further separates and stigmatises his elegiac viewpoint, even if he seems unable to place time in sequence.[25] Furthermore, such recollections of past poems of praise to the glorious dead are void of sincerity in a novel that also surveys self-delusions of messianic power: [26]

> Septimus cried, raising his hand ... like some colossal figure who has lamented the fate of man for ages in the desert alone with his hands pressed to his forehead, furrows of despair on his cheeks, and now sees light on the desert's edge which broadens and strikes the iron-black figure ... and with legions of men prostrate behind him he, the giant mourner, receives for one moment on his face the whole—. (*MD*, 63)

The hyperbole of his paranoid delusion strains the religious connotations of this vision: religion becomes conflated with madness, and the trappings of the 'sacred' debased in their turn as pomp.[27] Septimus, ironically, seems to sense the heroism of the natural world and care for the *life* of animals and trees (almost an animistic faith), unlike his compatriot Mr. Bowley, who only acknowledges the heroism of the dead, bronzed in statuary (*MD*, 18). As a scapegoat and oracle, Septimus acts as conscience to society, and represents a significant tract of veterans whose suffering was largely ignored. Within the novel's structure, however, his reported suicide also has the positive impetus of helping Clarissa recollect herself in the present:

> [Why] had he done it?... She had once thrown a shilling into the Serpentine, never anything more. But he had flung it away. They went on living. ... [There] was in the depths of her heart an awful fear ... one thing with another, she must have perished. She had escaped. But that young man had killed himself. ... But she did not pity him; with the clock striking the hour, one, two, three, she did not pity him, with all this going on. ... She felt somehow very like him. ... She felt glad that he had done it; thrown it away while they went on living. (*MD*, 165-67)

In an ambivalent elegiac substitution, it seems that Septimus's death reaffirms Clarissa's life, recognised as truly present at the end of the novel: 'for there she was' (*MD*, 174) are the final words, and they impart a kind of consolation and survival that cements the work as ironic elegy in the face of death.

### *To the Lighthouse*: The art of remembering

Woolf's next book, *To the Lighthouse*, is equally engaged with interrogating the past, and though some of her concerns are repeated from her prior novel, this other elegy takes a different form and has significantly distinct emphases. Death and survival are again major subjects, as is the examination of the role of women in Woolf's society, and the book straddles the Great War, so that its impact looms over the lives and action depicted. However, Woolf's focus here is also particularly personal, and all the other issues and concerns are tied up with a primary project of complex family elegy.

*To the Lighthouse* can be read as a fictionalised autobiography of her childhood experiences, of her early family life and holidays at St Ives, in Cornwall. As she noted early in the writing process, this book was to be 'all character—*not* a view of the world. Two blocks joined by a corridor.'[28] A little later, she sketches further: 'This is going to be fairly short: to have father's character done complete in it; & mothers [*sic*]; & St Ives; & childhood; & all the usual things I try to put in—life, death &c. But the centre is father's character, sitting in a boat, reciting We perished, each alone, while he crushes a dying mackrerel....'[29] Woolf's sister, the artist Vanessa Bell, certainly read the book in this way, moved by the recollection of time and place but especially the 'portrait' of their parents:

> You have given a portrait of mother which is more like her to me than anything I could ever have conceived possible. It is almost painful to have her so raised from the dead. ... It was like meeting her again with oneself grown up and on equal terms and it seems to me the most astonishing feat of creation to have been able to see her such a way. —You have given father too I think as clearly,... so you see as far as portrait painting goes you seem to me to be a supreme artist and it is so shattering to find oneself face to face with those two again.[30]

It is no surprise that this fictionalised portrait of her parents is so vivid that she worries that the narrative has become too 'sentimental'.[31] Woolf's depiction of them in the guise of Mr. and Mrs. Ramsay is of dominating figures, celestial presences at the centre of orbiting friends and family members in a manner that reflects her in thrall to her own parents, even after death. Woolf artistically embellishes them, with Mr. Ramsay a dramatic, changeable figure, charming, eloquent and charismatic, and yet also 'petty, selfish, vain, egotistical; he is spoilt; he is a tyrant; he wears Mrs. Ramsay to death' (*TL*, 23). His son James especially cherishes a mixed emotional attachment to him, repeatedly fantasising about cutting the 'tyrant' to the heart with a knife (*TL*, 150–51); yet the father's dramatic habits of walking around, flapping his hands, reciting poetry and proclaiming, on the one hand, his love of Sir Walter Scott, philosophy and the square roots displayed on railway tickets, and on the other, his anxiety about how long his work will endure, also recall features of Sir Leslie Stephen's own mannerisms and proclivities.[32] Alongside this patriarchal figure, Mrs. Ramsay is beautiful, enigmatic, magnetic, 'girlish', able to draw people out into conversation, but also prone to small talk, meddling, match-making and Victorian ideas about gender roles. Woolf hereby complicates the processes of elegiac remembrance and valorisation: her parents' flaws and the irony of observation signal Woolf's recognition both of their attractiveness to her but also of a need to break with the old order of societal values that they represent.

The year after publication of *To the Lighthouse*, Woolf notes her changed relationship to her parents which suggests some efficacy in this attempted elegiac 'break':

Father's birthday. He would have been 96, 96, yes, today … but merci-
fully was not. His life would have entirely ended mine. What would
have happened? No writing, no books;—inconceivable. I used to think
of him and mother daily; but writing the *Lighthouse* laid them in my
mind. And now he comes back sometimes, but differently. (I believe
this to be true—that I was obsessed by them both, unhealthily; and
writing of them was a necessary act.) He comes back now more as a
contemporary.[33]

Woolf goes even further in characterising the writing process as a
kind of psycho-analytical talking cure, diminishing her obsession with
her mother: 'In expressing it I explained it and laid it to rest. But what
is the meaning of 'explained' it? Why, because I described her and my
feeling for her in that book, should my vision of her and my feeling
for her become so much dimmer and weaker?' (*MB*, 81).

Yet, inasmuch as these characters may have direct real-world
counterparts in her parents, they also represent qualities and features that Woolf wants to examine beyond considerations of family.
In Gillian Beer's study of 'surviving and relinquishing' the past in *To
the Lighthouse,* Mr. and Mrs. Ramsay symbolise 'abstract thought and
social action', both philosophical markers of features of the 'human'.[34]
If this is the case, it is telling to note how the central passage of her
narrative, 'Time Passes', negates these markers of the 'human': this
section accommodates the deaths of key characters and also the Great
War itself. In narrating these individual deaths, Woolf presents them
as asides, juxtaposed against a narrative of the holiday house decaying:
a kind of elegy expressed through the rumours and play of everyday
objects abandoned by humans, and human deaths objectified through
platitude. Mrs. Ramsay is said to have died the night before Mr.
Ramsay reaches for her in the dark; Prue dies after childbirth, 'which
was indeed a tragedy, people said. They said nobody deserved happiness more' (*TL*, 108); and Andrew is 'killed in a second by a shell; he
should have been a great mathematician' (*TL*, 159).

Against such a dehumanising depiction of death, though, Woolf
juxtaposes her other main thematic consideration, art and the artist's
perspective, personified especially by Lily Briscoe, who comes to be
the key figure in the book portrayed in the acts of remembrance and
survival. Woolf's writing about 'art' is partly achieved through her use
of imagist poetic prose, combining her own psychological realism of
stream of consciousness narrative (where people think and dream 'all
over the place'), with highly sensory depiction. Patterns of light and
sound abound, and especially in the last section, the sea is not only
heard but viewed as a character in its own right. Such a treatment

is established from the first page, where James Ramsay artistically embellishes the everyday 'with heavenly bliss. It was fringed with joy. The wheelbarrow, the lawn-mower, the sound of the poplar trees, leaves whitening before rain, rooks cawing, brooms knocking, dresses rustling—all these were so coloured and distinguished in his mind' (*TL*, 7). Woolf cements the link between art, the senses and memory as facets that work against the absent figure of the past.

If, as Beer notes, there is an absence at the heart of this book,[35] then this artistic void is doubled in the manner that Woolf uses Lily Briscoe's painting as its analogue: the painting she was working on in the first section, 'The Window', includes a kind of secular Madonna and child assemblage (Mrs. Ramsay and her son). As an elegiac portrait, it remains incomplete in the first section, is abandoned (like the house itself) in the middle linking section, and is only returned to in the last section, alongside the artist's meandering memory of the past: 'so much depends … she thought, upon distance' (*TL*, 156). Lily's completion of the picture at the end serves the elegiac purposes of restoring the absent dead and placing them back in the centre of the picture. The act of 'centring' is restorative of the whole: 'with a sudden intensity, as if she saw it clear for a second, she drew a line there, in the centre. It was done, it was finished. Yes, she thought, laying down her brush in extreme fatigue, I have had my vision' (*TL*, 170). While this may seem like a fruitful resolution of an elegiac novel, a final consolation and restoration after grieving, it is important to note that this is still an artistic substitution. Lily's painting captures the presence of absence, like the photo of dead loved ones which is a token rather a full replacement: a limited immortality for the Ramsays noted alongside the 'empty' step and the 'blurred' canvas that may end up relegated to an attic.

Woolf's artistic treatment of variegated memory in *To the Lighthouse* and play on death, substitution and continuity in *Mrs. Dalloway* are equally elegiac in mode. Yet, unlike previous examples of elegy, which tended to rehearse conventions of grieving, valorisation and consolation, Woolf's new elegy complicates the retrieval of the past in the present narrative. Difficulties are demonstrated when dealing with the features of the past which cannot be wholly valorised, and processes of substitution and ironic distance from the subject of elegy result in the creation of subjective, fragmented and ambivalent pasts that defy easy resolution. Woolf's use of this more complex elegiac mode potentially unsettles the reader, who is invited to look again at subjects like life, death, war, gender inequities and memory itself, to see them anew.

# Notes

1  Virginia Woolf, *A Writer's Diary*, ed. Leonard Woolf (London: Hogarth Press, 1953), p. 80. The entry is dated 20 July 1925.

2  See Jane de Gay, *Virginia Woolf's Novels and the Literary Past* (Edinburgh: Edinburgh University Press, 2006), pp. 79–80. De Gay suggests earlier novels such as *Jacob's Room* contain an assertion of elegy in the emphasis of 'literature['s]… vibrancy': 'culture continues to thrive and survive… [crossing] "the river of death this way and that incessantly"' (quoting from *Jacob's Room*).

3  See Alexandra Harris, *Virginia Woolf* (London: Thames and Hudson, 2013), p. 84, where Harris considers Woolf's tongue-in-cheek erudition challenging accepted reading of these sources; and Jane Goldman, 'From *Mrs. Dalloway* to *The Waves*: New Elegy and Lyric Experimentalism', in *The Cambridge Companion to Virginia Woolf*, 2nd Ed, ed. Susan Sellers (Cambridge/New York: Cambridge University Press, 2010), p. 49, quoting Woolf's diary for 21 June 1924.

4  De Gay makes much of Woolf's 'lighter, more allusive engagement with literary tradition [than Joyce]… a more optimistic, feminine way of reading' (p. 87) that challenges her male characters' assumption of a totality of knowledge about a subject (p. 6). Woolf's tactical use of quotation and allusion goes with the imagistic practice I outline below.

5  Virginia Woolf, *A Room of One's Own* (London: Hogarth Press, 1929).

6  'Elegy', in *The New Princeton Encyclopaedia of Poetry and Poetics*, ed. Alex Preminger and T.V.F. Brogan (Princeton: Princeton University Press, 1993), p. 322.

7  Ibid., p. 324.

8  Melissa F. Zeiger, *Beyond Consolation: Death, Sexuality, and the Changing Shapes of Elegy* (Ithaca/ London: Cornell University Press, 1997), p. 14.

9  Ibid., pp. 3–4; 'Elegy', p. 324. Peter Sacks' *The English Elegy* is heavily influenced by Freudian theories of mourning and oedipal substitution, drawing in particular on Freud's *Mourning and Melancholia* (1917).

10  Virginia Woolf, 'Poetry, Fiction and the Future', *New York Herald Tribune* (14 and 21 August 1927), E4, 436.

11  See Jane Goldman, 'From *Mrs. Dalloway* to *The Waves*: New Elegy and Lyric Experimentalism', in *The Cambridge Companion to Virginia Woolf*, 2nd Ed, ed. Susan Sellers (Cambridge/New York: Cambridge University Press, 2010), pp. 49–69.

12  Virginia Woolf, *Congenial Spirits: The Selected Letters of Virginia Woolf*, ed. Joanne Trautmann Banks (San Diego/New York/London: Harcourt Brace Jovanovich, 1989), p.188.

13  *A Writer's Diary*, p. 57, entry dated 19 June 1923.

14  Ibid., p. 60, entry dated 30 August 1923.

15  J. Hillis Miller, '*Mrs. Dalloway*: Repetition as the Raising of the Dead', in *Critical Essays on Virginia Woolf*, ed. Morris Beja (Boston: G.K. Hall, 1985), p. 59.

16 *Cymbeline*, IV, ii, ll. 258–59.
17 See Sandra M. Gilbert and Susan Gubar, *No Man's Land: The Place of the Woman Writer in the Twentieth Century*, vol. 2, *Sexchanges* (New Haven: Yale University Press, 1989), pp. 317–18.
18 See Daniel Ferrer, *Virginia Woolf and the Madness of Language*, trans. Geoffrey Bennington and Rachel Bowlby (London: Routledge, 1990), p. 10, where Ferrer discusses the impact of the suicide of Kitty Maxse, quoting Woolf's diary: 'Kitty fell, very mysteriously over some bannisters.... I adumbrate here a study of insanity of suicide.'
19 Mark Hussey, 'Living in a War Zone: An Introduction to Virginia Woolf as a War Novelist', in *Virginia Woolf and War: Fiction, Reality, and Myth*, ed. Mark Hussey (New York: Syracuse University Press, 1991), p. 3.
20 Levenback, p. 2.
21 See Showalter, pp. xxxvi–xliv.
22 See Levenback, pp. 13–15.
23 Ibid., pp. 50–51.
24 Ibid., p. 53.
25 De Gay, p. 85.
26 See Sandra M. Gilbert, *Death's Door: Modern Dying and the Ways We Grieve* (New York; London: Norton, 2006), pp. 366–69.
27 Again, the funereal ceremonies displayed in the novel are presented as empty repetitions, glossing over the realities of war and its aftermath.
28 Woolf's writing notes, quoted in Hermione Lee, *Virginia Woolf* (London: Vintage, 1997), p. 475.
29 Ibid., pp. 475–76. Lee is quoting from Woolf's *Diary*, 14 May 1925.
30 Ibid., p. 480. Lee is quoting from a letter Vanessa Bell wrote to Woolf on 11 May 1927.
31 Woolf, *A Writer's Diary*, 20 July 1925, p. 80.
32 Lee, p. 481.
33 Woolf, *A Writer's Diary*, 28 November 1928, p. 138.
34 Gillian Beer, 'Hume, Stephen, and Elegy in *To the Lighthouse*', in *Mrs. Dalloway and To the Lighthouse: A New Casebook*, ed. Sue Reid (New York: St Martin's Press, 1993), p. 78.
35 Ibid., p. 71.

# 11

# 'What is a woman?' I assure you, I do not know': Woolf and Feminism in the 1920s

Patricia Moran

## Introduction: Woolf and Second Wave feminism

Virginia Woolf was not regarded as a major feminist thinker until the late 1960s, when Second Wave feminists proved a receptive audience for her two book-length essays, *A Room of One's Own* (1929) and *Three Guineas* (1938). In *A Room of One's Own*, Woolf argues that the successful woman writer must be in possession of the same income and degree of privacy as her male counterparts: she 'must have money and a room of her own if she is to write fiction'. In *Three Guineas* Woolf is again concerned with gender equity: here she describes being approached for a donation by a pacifist group, a women's college and a group devoted to promoting the entry of women into the professions. As a pacifist and advocate of the rights of women she decides to donate a guinea to each. But just as the pacifist movement was unable to prevent the outbreak of the Second World War, so the feminists of the 1920s and 1930s were unable to establish equal rights for women.

*A Room of One's Own*, *Three Guineas* and Woolf's other writings were of interest to Second Wave feminists because it was clear in the 1960s and 1970s that much still needed to be done in the interests of fostering gender equity. While Woolf concentrated on different aspects of women and gender at different points in her life, her works taking shape within particular political and social contexts and in response to particular audiences and readerships, her thinking remained remarkably consistent: she believed that women's experiences as second-class citizens created in them 'a difference of value' (*R/TG*, 96) and that this difference, mobilised and expressed, could transform all aspects of the social order, including education, work, family life, relationships and, of course, fiction and literary history. In the 1920s Woolf's ideas about women, writing and sexual difference found expression in *Mrs. Dalloway* (1925), *To the Lighthouse* (1927), *Orlando* (1928) and *A Room of One's Own* (1929), as well as in numerous essays on fiction and women writers. To understand how Woolf developed the views expressed in these works, it is necessary to contextualise her thinking by setting it within the wider frames of the First Wave women's movement and her own trajectory of engagement with that movement.

## Woolf and First Wave feminism

First Wave feminism refers to the efforts made by groups of women in the late nineteenth and early twentieth centuries to achieve equality with men.[1] In 1882, the year of Woolf's birth, Britain had passed the Married Women's Property Act: prior to this act married women had no legal right to their property or earnings, which were legally owned and controlled by their husbands. Battles for access to education and the professions took place throughout Woolf's lifetime: in 1919 The Sex Disqualification (Removal) Act opened many professions and public offices to women; in 1920 Oxford University agreed to award degrees to women. Cambridge University voted against awarding degrees to women in 1921: women were awarded only the titles of degrees, so that women's degrees were popularly and insultingly referred to as the 'BA tit'.[2] Male students celebrated the defeat by using a handcart to batter the gates of Newnham College, one of the university's two women's colleges. Woolf would later discuss this outrageous behaviour and the gradual accession of women to education and the professions in *Three Guineas*.[3] She was well aware of the scope and nature of women's struggles to gain access to education and the professions: many of her relatives and close associates were active in effecting reforms, and held positions of authority in both women's colleges and women's organisations.[4]

By the first decade of the twentieth century, 'feminism' had come to focus on gaining the right to vote, and in 1910, the year Woolf volunteered to address envelopes for a suffrage society, that struggle had resulted in a split between those women who continued to work for reform through conventional constitutional measures, and those who advocated more militant measures such as window-breaking and the disruption of public meetings.[5] Woolf chose to work not for the 'suffragette' but for the less militant, 'suffragist' wing of the movement. The brutality levelled against militant suffragettes and the horrific accounts and images of the force-feeding of hunger-striking women prisoners may well have played a role in Woolf's reluctant desire to participate in the movement in some way.

Woolf's stint at addressing envelopes was short-lived, and her sense that the single-minded focus on gaining the vote warped the perceptions of those dedicated to 'the cause' is reflected in a letter to her Greek tutor and mentor, Janet Case: 'Do you ever take that side of politics into account—the inhuman side, and how all the best feelings are shrivelled?' (*L* I, 441). It is also reflected in her satiric portrait of a suffrage organisation in her 1919 novel *Night and Day* (though she portrays Mary Datchett, a suffrage worker and volunteer, as an inspirational figure whose light shines as a beacon for the future at the end of the novel). When the vote was granted to women over thirty in 1918, a concession to their work on behalf of Britain during World War One, Woolf reports the victory with detachment: 'I dont [*sic*] feel much more important—perhaps slightly so. Its [*sic*] like a knighthood; might be useful to impress people one despises'—she notes (*D* I, 104). By 1924 Woolf would begin a sentence in her diary, 'If I were still a feminist', perhaps indicating her belief that the Suffrage Bill had made the label extraneous, but in any event recording her sense of detachment and distance from the activist women's movement: 'But I have travelled on', she adds (*D* II, 318). She would continue to use the term 'feminist' disparagingly the rest of her life, worrying after the publication of *A Room of One's Own* that she would be 'attacked for a feminist and hinted at for a Sapphist' (*D* III, 262). In *Three Guineas* she declared, notoriously, 'feminist' a word that should be burned.[6]

In fact, Woolf continued to take part in organised activities on behalf of women: she arranged and hosted monthly meetings of the Richmond branch of the Women's Co-operative Guild for four years (1919–1923), and both *A Room of One's Own* and *Three Guineas* grew out of talks given to women's organisations. (The former was delivered to the two women's colleges at Cambridge, the latter to the Junior Council of the London and National Society for Women's Service, an organisation dedicated to obtaining economic equality for women).[7] She also supported women's organisations in the 1930s, contributing money and books to the women's library managed by the London and National Society for Women's Service, and becoming a dues-paying member of both that group and the Women's Employment Federation.[8] In addition, the Hogarth Press, established by the Woolfs in 1917, published numerous important works concerning women's

lives and concerns.[9] But as Naomi Black observes, 'Woolf's dissocia-
tion from feminist activism is real; if more involved with feminism and
women's organisations than is usually realised, she was not a 'joiner'
like many of the women she associated with.'[10]

## Woolf's dissociation from the term 'feminist'

Why did Woolf dissociate herself from activism and specifically from
the label 'feminist'? Woolf's dislike of the term 'feminist' stems in part
from her awareness that the label is likely to alienate or antagonise
potential readers, particularly those she most wanted to reach. Hence
in a well-known diary entry in which she pondered potential titles
for what would become *Three Guineas*, Woolf rejected 'Men Are Like
That' as 'too patently feminist' (*D* IV, 77). Not long after that entry
she wrote that her new book would include 'millions of ideas but no
preaching … a summing up of all I know, feel, laugh at, despise, like,
admire hate & so on': topics were to include 'history, politics, feminism, art, literature' (*D* IV, 152). If her public repudiation of the term
may have been in part a rhetorical strategy, it is also true that Woolf's
apprehension of the patriarchy as systemic and institutional made her
sceptical of what she considered simple panaceas, such as the fervent
belief of devoted suffrage workers that the vote would solve all of
women's problems.

As Alex Zwerdling remarks, Woolf's scepticism about the power
of the vote reflects her understanding that 'human relationships and
institutions are dismayingly conservative and likely to preserve the
substance of the old in the form of the new. The psyche was much
more resistant to change than the law.'[11] Woolf's own interest in
subjectivity and the workings of the mind comes to the fore here:
her writing, fictional and non-fictional, is a sustained inquiry into
the psychology of the patriarchy—of domination and subordina-
tion, inclusion and exclusion, privilege and disadvantage. She came
to believe that her most valuable contribution to social change
inhered in her writing, in the exploration of the causes and motivations of that psychology, in the dramatisation of its consequences,
and in the formulation and positing of alternatives. She articulated
this belief most explicitly during the last years of her life, when her
life-long pacifism was challenged by the rise of fascism. Hence she
wrote in 1936, 'As I've already said, Societies seem wrong for me,
so I do nothing. … What can I do but write? Hadn't I better go on
writing—even by the light of the last combustion?'[12] And in 1940,
after Britain had declared war on Germany, she continued to defend

writing as her strongest contribution to ending fascism and war: 'This idea struck me: the army is the body: I am the brain. Thinking is my fighting' (D V, 285).

Woolf's conviction that 'thinking is my fighting' is matched, however, by her equally strong conviction that art should not be didactic: it should contain 'millions of ideas but no preaching'.[13] Deeply influenced by Bloomsbury's Post-Impressionist painters and art critics, Woolf set herself the challenge of embodying her critique of patriarchy in the form and texture of her writing.[14] Plot structure, narrative voice, characterisation, subject matter and a densely allusive style that draws upon literature, myth and history: all become part of Woolf's exploration of the ways in which questions of gender, sexuality and identity intersect with the conventions of literary and historical representation.[15] Such conventions, Woolf demonstrates, develop out of long-standing assumptions about what is 'important', even 'natural'; they thus become powerful ideological and institutional instruments that embody, transmit and authenticate patriarchal values and structures.

Yet in challenging these conventions, Woolf tends to raise questions rather than answer them: What is the relationship of writing to the sexed and gendered body? What is the proper subject of fiction? Why are women invisible in so much of (literary) history, and how do we account for their absence? In addition to posing such open-ended questions—questions which became critical points of departure and debate in feminist criticism—Woolf also offers contradictory theoretical positions. To take just one example, A Room of One's Own posits the necessity of a female tradition for the woman writer ('we think back through our mothers if we are women' [R/TG, 75]), and details the need for the woman writer to shape the sentence to her own use (R/TG, 75–76), but also sternly warns that 'it is fatal' for the successful writer to be aware of her sex while writing (R/TG, 102–103).

## Three phases of Woolf's practice as a novelist and literary historian

While consistently focused on issues of gender, sexuality, subjectivity and representation, Woolf's oeuvre shifts emphasis in response to both her personal development as a writer and her immediate historical and cultural contexts. Three distinct phases emerge in her practice as novelist and literary historian. In the first phase, from her first published review in 1905 to the publication of her first two novels, Woolf struggled with defining and claiming her vocation against the competing and seemingly contradictory claims of femininity. Her first two novels are both renditions of the marriage plot: in *The Voyage Out*, the would-be woman artist dies when it becomes clear that marriage and female artistry are incompatible; in *Night and Day* her protagonist escapes the confines of her late-Victorian family by deciding to marry a man who respects her autonomy and desire to work. Woolf's dissatisfaction with the conventional framework of *Night and Day* gave rise to the second phase of her practice, as she explored the intertwined issues of the appropriate form for modern fiction and the nature of female artistry. During this phase—the period in which Woolf produced *Mrs. Dalloway*, *To the Lighthouse*, *Orlando* and *A Room of One's Own*—Woolf's writing focuses on questions of gender identity, feminine writing and the material and cultural conditions of artistic production.

Woolf's third phase dates from her talk, 'Professions for Women', in 1931, to an audience of young professional women. Her ambitious attempt to combine fiction and fact in a 'novel-essay', combined with the growing threat of fascism in Europe, resulted in what Jane Marcus calls the 'documentary project' of the thirties, the realist novel *The Years* (1937) and Woolf's most politically vocal essay, *Three Guineas* (1938).[16] As Laura Marcus observes, these distinct phases in Woolf's *oeuvre* have engaged different types of feminist critics: 'Whereas a feminist criticism centred on feminine writing, identity and sexuality turned primarily to the poetics of *A Room of One's Own*, *Mrs. Dalloway*, *To the Lighthouse* and *The Waves*, those critics concerned with a more overtly feminist Woolf—one whose feminism is an aspect of political and social engagement with the events of her time—have tended to focus on *The Years*, *Three Guineas* and, though to a lesser extent, *Night and Day* and *Between the Acts*.'[17]

*A Room of One's Own* is the capstone of Woolf's thinking about women and fiction in the 1920s. First conceived in a spirited exchange of letters with literary critic Desmond MacCarthy in the pages of *The New Statesman* in 1920, then expanded into talks delivered to the two women's colleges at Cambridge in 1928, and finally published in 1929, *A Room of One's Own* theorises the concerns that shaped Woolf's writing of *Mrs. Dalloway* and *To the Lighthouse*.[18] The central thesis—'a woman must have money and a room of her own if she is to write fiction' (*R/TG*, 4)—develops out of Woolf's rejoinders to MacCarthy's pronouncement that 'women are inferior to men in intellectual power, especially in that kind of power which is described as creative'.[19] *A Room of One's Own* explains why there has never been a female Shakespeare—MacCarthy's clincher, and a common indictment that 'proved' women's inferior powers of intellect and creativity—by exploring the multiple factors involved in women's disenfranchisement.[20] Amongst these are economic dependence, a lack of access to education, subordinate status both within the family and within society, cultural expectations of unpaid domestic and emotional labour, familial and social constraints generally upon their behaviour (and particularly upon their sexuality), active discouragement and ridicule of their intellectual and artistic efforts, and dismissal of their concerns and experiences as trivial and unimportant. Woolf's thesis that a woman must have money and a room of her own becomes, as Susan Gubar notes, an 'elegant shorthand' that condenses the economic, aesthetic, sexual and psychological repercussions of gender into a single phrase.[21]

### Women's disenfranchisement

*A Room of One's Own* fictionalises the facts of women's disenfranchisement. Six chapters detail the speaker's 'research', conducted over the three days preceding her talk. The first two chapters explore women's exclusion from (masculine) public space and hence from access to public culture as the speaker describes lunching at a mythical men's college, Oxbridge, then dining at another mythical women's college, Fernham, then spending the next day in the Reading Room of the British Museum.[22] The following three chapters trace a female literary tradition, from Shakespeare's imaginary sister Judith through actual women writers to a hypothetical contemporary woman writer, Mary Carmichael, whose novel, *Life's Adventure*, focuses on two women who like each other 'perhaps for the first time in literature' (*R/TG*, 106). The final chapter retreats from the homoerotic implications of *Life's Adventure* to recommend the androgynous mind as an ideal, closing with a peroration in which the speaker urges her audience to work and wait for Judith Shakespeare's second coming. Structured in binary oppositions—inside/outside; public/private; wealth/poverty; presence/absence; fact/fiction; all underwritten by masculine/feminine—*A Room of One's Own* enacts the very disenfranchisement that it sets out to explore and, at the same time, privileges disenfranchisement as the site of an alternative and potentially radical 'difference of value' (*R/TG*, 96).

Men's access to and control of public space and public culture results in a world where women perceive themselves as trespassers. Driven off the turf at Oxbridge and denied entrance to the university library which serves as the repository of male canonical texts, encircled by the names of great men engraved upon its dome and barraged by male-authored publications insisting upon women's inferiority at the British Museum, the speaker retreats to her private study to contemplate how women's marginal status in public space impacts their self-expression. Men's self-confidence develops out of a material sense of well-being, qualities reinforced by the psychological crutch of believing themselves naturally superior to half the human race.

By contrast, denied access to education and the professions and thereby to economic independence until very recently, women have developed 'flattering and fawning' habits in their relations with men (R/TG, 48), underwritten by the emotions of fear, bitterness and resentment that simultaneously poison those relations. Hence her aunt's legacy of five hundred pounds a year—a private and matrilineal bequest from one woman to another 'for no other reason than that [she] shares her name' (R/TG, 48)—frees the speaker not only from the servitude of the demeaning paid jobs available to her, but also from the servile habits of mind and corrosive emotions men inspire in her. In addition, the legacy bestows the 'freedom to think of things in themselves' (R/TG, 48): economic independence translates into psychological and intellectual autonomy. This autonomy is 'infinitely ... more important' than the vote (R/TG, 48).

## Female sexuality

To these material, cultural and psychological threads that connect the web of fiction to life Woolf adds the thread of sexuality: indeed, this thread becomes inextricably tangled with all the others. For female sexuality and its policing and control undergird the entire structure of patriarchy and motivate all the other forms of constraint; the 'religious importance' accorded chastity points up its key role in determining legitimate—i.e., male-authorised—offspring. Woolf refers here to St Paul's naming of silence as an aspect of female chastity: he requires women to veil themselves if speaking publicly, 'for it is shameful' for speech to issue visibly from the female body, shameful.[23] Hence to speak publicly, to write, is akin to violating female purity, a violation that, together with all the other factors, causes intense anguish and textual distortions.[24] 'Thwarted and hindered by other people' and 'tortured and pulled asunder by [their] own contrary instincts', whatever women write is 'twisted and deformed' because it issues from a 'strained and morbid imagination' (R/TG, 64).

Judith Shakespeare's attempt to emulate her brother's 'free life' illustrates the ways in which gender impacts every stage of the writer's development: denied schooling, confined to domestic tasks, pressured to marry, she runs away from home and makes her way to London, where in short order she is seduced, impregnated, abandoned and dead by her own hand. Her suicide fittingly inaugurates a female literary tradition characterised by gaps and silences, and her illegitimate unborn child functions as a synecdoche for women's stillborn literary texts. The actual women writers Woolf examines produce for the most part 'twisted and deformed' textual offspring because they cannot concentrate on their art without being conscious of their gender. But their texts—'small, pock-marked apples' spoiled by the 'flaw in the centre' (*R/TG*, 96–97)—nonetheless constitute an important contribution to this illicit and transgressive female tradition, one that paradoxically becomes more respectable when the 'shady and amorous' Aphra Behn becomes a professional writer in the eighteenth century. '[H]ere begins the freedom of the mind, or rather the possibility that in the course of time the mind will be free to write what it likes', the speaker observes, 'Money dignifies what is frivolous if unpaid for' (*R/TG*, 84).

*A Room of One's Own* is an optimistic and forward-looking text that privileges the different values that spring from disenfranchisement. While it is true that Oxbridge possesses material wealth that the bare walls raised upon bare earth of Fernham cannot equal (*R/TG*, 29), that wealth results in pavement 'laid solidly upon the wild grasses' (*R/TG*, 12), whereas at Fernham the wild grasses blow freely, the season magically transforms from autumn to spring, and a riot of flowers attests to an exuberance and vitality missing at the men's college. Women's fiction-writing evidences a generative and vernal spirit in images of ingestion that counteract the dismal dinner at Fernham and rewrite Eve's transgressive apple-eating as a new scene of genesis: Mary Carmichael's imagination 'feasted like a plant newly stood in the air on every sight and sound that came its way' and her character Olivia 'sees coming her way a piece of strange food—knowledge, adventure, art' (*R/TG*, 110). Topically, *A Room of One's Own* enumerates the subjects available to women when they value the differences their experiences engender: 'infinitely obscure lives [that] remain to be recorded'; domestic interiors permeated by women's creative force (*R/TG*, 86). *Mrs. Dalloway* and *To the Lighthouse* take as their subjects such obscure lives—a society hostess, the wife of an academic, a spinsterish middle-aged woman who paints—and both novels celebrate the creative force of daily domesticity (parties, dinners, knitting, sewing), connecting more conventional artistic modes, such as Lily's painting, to them.

*A Room of One's Own* also celebrates the new subject of women's relationships with each other. Teasingly alluding to the male authorities who prosecuted Radclyffe Hall's *The Well of Loneliness* and deemed it obscene for its depiction of lesbianism, *A Room of One's Own* challenges not only the heterosexism of representations that depict women only in relation to men, but challenges as well patriarchal strictures on women's sexual experiences and speech. Adumbrating new landscapes of desire—'a vast chamber where nobody has yet been ... all half lights and profound shadows like those serpentine caves where one goes with a candle'—and new languages—'unsaid or half-said words ... words that are hardly syllabled yet' (*R/TG*, 110)—*A Room of One's Own* 'uses Chloe's non-specific liking for Olivia to link the woman's novel, the novel of lesbian love and the novel of the future'.[25] Both *Mrs. Dalloway* and *To the Lighthouse* foreground women's relationships and both employ similar imagery: Clarissa describes Sally Seton's kiss as an illumination 'like a match in a crocus', an image *A Room of One's Own* echoes in the torch Mary Carmichael must use to illuminate the shadowy cave of women's intimacies. Lily figures her desire for intimacy with Mrs. Ramsay as a desire for access to 'chambers of the mind and heart of the woman who was, physically, touching her', and access too 'to the tablets bearing sacred inscriptions [;] ... nothing that could be written in any language known to men' (*TL*, 44).

Yet *A Room of One's Own* offers a seemingly contradictory model of female writing in its positing of the androgynous mind as the writer's ideal. Here the imagery centres upon heterosexual marriage, a 'natural fusion' inspired by the sight of a man and woman getting into a taxi cab together (*R/TG*, 127). While this section reflects Woolf's own conviction that the fully realised work of art must transcend personal grievances and politics—'it is fatal for any one who writes to think of their sex' (*R/TG*, 136)—it retreats from the woman-centred aesthetics sketched out in the preceding chapters. The source of much critical discussion and debate, the androgynous mind, whereby the writer 'must lie back and let his mind celebrate its nuptials in darkness' (*R/TG*, 136), depicts a process in which the woman writer must subordinate the female to the male portion of the brain.[26]

Rhetorically, this closing chapter returns to the divisive scenes of its opening two chapters and to the battles for suffrage and for access to education and the professions that have contributed to the 'stridently sex-conscious' mood of the 1920s (*R/TG*, 129); it offers a gesture of reconciliation by diluting the overtly feminist tone of the preceding chapters, a gesture perhaps designed to make *A Room of One's Own* more palatable to the circle of 'intimate friends'—all men—who Woolf worried would dislike its 'shrill feminine tone' (*D* III, 262).[27] It may also reflect Woolf's own bias, hinted at in the statement that 'One has a profound, if irrational, instinct in favour of the theory that the union of man and woman makes for the greatest satisfaction, the most complete happiness' (*R/TG*, 127).[28] Its seeming contradiction of earlier positions exemplifies the ongoing debate *A Room of One's Own* has with itself: its inconsistencies and its refusal to take definitive stands have contributed to its ongoing appeal for feminist literary critics.

## *A Room of One's Own*, Mrs. *Dalloway* and *To the Lighthouse*

*A Room of One's Own* develops as polemic ideas Woolf had worked out in *Mrs. Dalloway* and *To the Lighthouse*. The two novels depict differences between men and women and, by extension, between masculine and feminine ways of thinking and viewing the world. The distinctions *Room* draws between masculine space/culture and feminine space/culture is reflected in both novels: the London of the 1920s in *Mrs. Dalloway* is dominated by emblems of Crown and Empire; men hold visible positions of social and cultural authority, whereas women's relationship to that space centres on shopping. Clarissa's reveries often unfold in the privacy of her home, even her bedroom, and return her to the female-centred pastoral world of Bourton and to her long-ago choice of a marriage partner. That choice, the most important decision a girl of her generation would make, results in a companionate marriage that allows her to maintain an independence at odds with feminine ideals of self-effacement and immersion in the needs and feelings of others. The gulf Woolf depicts between men's and women's worlds is bridged when Septimus Smith, the traumatised war veteran, commits suicide, an act Clarissa alone understands as a heroic gesture of refusing to conform to normative conventions of gender.

*To the Lighthouse* similarly draws distinctions between masculine and feminine culture. Mr. Ramsay and his associates devote themselves to academic success, a sphere *Room* delineates as an integral element of the patriarchal social and cultural system; the masculine nature of Mr. Ramsay's philosophical strivings is reflected in his habit of imagining himself engaged in a lonely heroic quest he likens to that of an explorer or military leader. Mrs. Ramsay, by contrast, occupies a generative role: she tends to the needs of others; promotes the centrality of marriage, children and family life; and busies herself with cooking and gardening. The brown stocking she knits vividly images her gift for interlacing the divergent needs and claims of others and creating social harmony, an interlacement writ large in the dinner party that closes part one of the novel ('that woman', Lily Briscoe will later reflect, remembering an unusual moment of accord between herself and her arch-enemy Charles Tansley under the aegis of Mrs. Ramsay's presence, 'resolved everything into simplicity' [TL, 132]). Cam, the youngest Ramsay daughter and a poignant self-portrait of the adolescent Woolf after the death of her mother, illustrates the division of masculine and feminine realms when, drawn to her father's study, she 'strays in from the garden', an encroachment that anticipates the narrator's trespass on masculine turf in *Room*.

Both novels embed the social and cultural break Woolf associated with World War One in their narrative structures, *Mrs. Dalloway* in its oscillation between past and present, *To the Lighthouse* in the 'Time Passes' interlude that separates the two days of the novel by ten years. In depicting the war as a narrative break, Woolf closes off the Victorian past and with it the traditional nineteenth-century plots that limited women to marriage. The marriage plot exists in the past in *Mrs. Dalloway*; Elizabeth Dalloway's voyage on the bus near the novel's end gestures towards new, uncharted possibilities for women. Lily holds an imaginary conversation with the long-dead Mrs. Ramsay in which she triumphantly puts paid to Mrs. Ramsay's 'mania' for marriage: 'Life', she tells Mrs. Ramsay, 'had changed completely' (*TL*, 143). Lily's own commitment to her painting actualises the female artistry that Woolf urges women to achieve in *Room*.

Yet in her characterisation of Lily Woolf also makes manifest the obstacles that impede the female artist. Significantly, it is not just Charles Tansley's 'Women can't paint, women can't write' that eats at Lily's confidence—a refrain picked up in the admonition, 'You can't do this and you shan't do that' that Mary Carmichael must ignore in *Room* (*R/TG*, 122)—but Mrs. Ramsay's dismissiveness towards Lily's aspirations and her conviction that the woman who does not marry has missed the best of life. That Woolf herself struggled not only with patriarchal constraints but also with the feminine ideal she would later refer to as the 'Angel in the House' is well-known;[29] she defines killing that 'phantom' as 'part of the occupation of the woman writer'.[30] Yet in what many consider her most powerful work, Woolf chose to foreground the kind of woman she herself refused to become. Thinking back through her own mother and the women of a previous generation, Woolf memorialised a way of 'being a woman' even as that way seemed irrevocably lost. Woolf recognised the enduring power of the traditional 'feminine' values she accorded Mrs. Dalloway and Mrs. Ramsay, and she hoped that women would make use of their newly won rights in a way that preserved those values. Woolf does not tell us where Elizabeth Dalloway's voyage will take her, but leaves that unwritten future open. As she told an audience of young professional women in 1931, 'What is a woman? I assure you, I do not know. I do not believe that you know. I do not believe that anyone can know until she has expressed herself in all the arts and professions open to human skill. That indeed is one of the reasons why I have come here—out of respect for you, who are in process of providing us, by your failures and successes, with that important piece of information.'[31]

## Notes

1  Women's colleges were established at Cambridge and Oxford throughout the latter decades of the nineteenth century. Elizabeth Garrett Anderson, the first woman licensed to practise medicine in the UK, established the Edinburgh School of Medicine for Women in 1886; Sophia Jex-Blake established the London School of Medicine for Women in 1874. See Carol Dyhouse, *No Distinction of Sex? Women in British Universities, 1870–1939* (London: Routledge, 1995); and *The Education Papers: Women's Quest for Equality in Britain, 1850–1912*, ed. Dale Spender (London: Routledge, 1987).

2  The titular degree meant that women did not have equal status: they had no voting rights and could not share in university governance. Jane Ellen Harrison, whom Woolf cites admiringly in *A Room of One's Own* and whose works on the classics Woolf owned and used as source material, resigned from Newnham in protest after the defeat.

3  Cambridge did not award full degree status to women until 1948, and the strict limitation on the numbers of women granted admission was not lifted until the 1970s.

4  For discussions of the women activists in Woolf's circle, see *Women in the Milieu of Leonard and Virginia Woolf: Peace, Politics, and Education*, eds. Wayne K. Chapman and Janet M. Manson (New York: Pace University Press, 1998).

5  As Alex Zwerdling notes, 'What had begun as a comprehensive movement of thought about women's nature and status—legal, educational, psychological, economic, professional, marital, and political—had been turned into a much narrower cause deliberately centered on a single issue: the vote. … The rationale for this single-mindedness was that political power would guarantee every other desirable reform' (*Virginia Woolf and the Real World* [Berkeley: University of California Press, 1986], p. 214).

6  Jane Marcus notes that the repeated references to burning words and
   buildings in *Three Guineas* invokes and alludes to fascist book-burnings
   (See 'Introduction', Virginia Woolf, *Three Guineas*, annotated and
   introduced by Jane Marcus [New York and London: Harcourt, 2006],
   pp. xxxvi–xxxvii).

7  For accounts of Woolf's involvement with women's organisations, see
   Clara Jones, *Virginia Woolf: Ambivalent Activist* (Edinburgh: Edinburgh
   University Press, 2015); and Naomi Black, *Virginia Woolf as Feminist*
   (Ithaca/London: Cornell University Press, 2004), especially Chapter
   Two of the latter, 'Feminism and the Women's Movement' (pp. 23–50).

8  Black, p. 45.

9  J. H. Willis, *Leonard and Virginia Woolf as Publishers: The Hogarth Press
   1917–1941* (Charlottesville: University Press of Virginia, 1992); and
   *Leonard and Virginia Woolf, the Hogarth Press and the Networks of
   Modernism*, ed. Helen Southworth (Edinburgh: Edinburgh University
   Press, 2010), provide a good range of critical interest in the press.

10 Black, p. 48.

11 Zwerdling, 214.

12 Woolf's letter appears in 'Some New Woolf Letters', ed. Joanne
   Trautmann Banks, *Modern Fiction Studies* 30.2 (Summer 1984), 189.

13 Laura Marcus writes that, in the 1930s, Woolf's fear of didacticism grew
   'as she saw and heard the workings of fascist ideology. Increasingly, Woolf
   seemed to link political propaganda … with the forms of masculine
   war-mongering or war-enthusiasm' ('Woolf's Feminism and Feminism's
   Woolf', in *The Cambridge Companion to Virginia Woolf*, ed. Susan Sellers,
   2nd Ed [Cambridge: Cambridge University Press, 2010], p. 156).

14 As Toril Moi observes, Woolf's textual practice *is* the location of her
   politics. See *Sexual/Textual Politics* (London: Routledge, 1985), p. 16.

15 Rachel Bowlby observes that 'issues of literary representation, historical narrative and sexual difference are inseparable throughout Woolf's
   work. She insists on the difficulty of distinguishing the question of what
   constitutes a plausible story, historical or biographical, from the question of what constitutes the difference of men and women' (*Feminist
   Destinations and Further Essays on Virginia Woolf* [Edinburgh: Edinburgh
   University Press, 1997], pp. 14–15).

16 Virginia Woolf, *Three Guineas*, annotated and with an introduction by
   Jane Marcus (1938; rpt. New York and London: Harcourt, 2006), liii.

17 Laura Marcus, 162.

18 Julia Briggs writes that 'It was characteristic of her that her insights usually came in the form of fictions; only later did she extract their theoretical lessons and argue them out as polemics' (*Virginia Woolf: An Inner
   Life* [Penguin, 2006], p. 77).

19 Desmond MacCarthy [Review of *Our Women* by Arnold Bennett], *The
   New Statesman*, (2 October 1920), 704.

20 Alex Zwerdling writes that 'the absence of great female artists … [had]
   become *the* trump card in the argument against women's equality.

The question of women's artistic achievement was thus seen in Woolf's time as a sort of last frontier in the exploration of their powers' (224). See also Patricia Moran, 'Cock-a-doodle-dum: Sexology and *A Room of One's Own*', *Women's Studies*, 30 (2002), 477–98; and '"The Cat Is Out of the Bag", and It is a Male: Desmond MacCarthy and the Writing of *A Room of One's Own*', in *Essays in Transgressive Reading: Reading Over the Lines*, ed. Georgia Johnston (New York: Mellen, 1997), pp. 35–55.

21 Virginia Woolf, *A Room of One's Own*, annotated and with an Introduction by Susan Gubar (1929; New York and London: Harcourt, 2005), p. xxxv.

22 Oxbridge is a widely-used portmanteau of Oxford and Cambridge, not a college at either university, while Fernham is a non-existent women's college whose name recalls that of Newnham College, Cambridge.

23 Although Woolf does not name St Paul in *Room*'s discussion of chastity, in her elaboration of the links between chastity and the veil in *Three Guineas* she quotes these words (*R/TG*, 392).

24 In drafts Woolf links the 'flaw in the centre' of women's fictional webs with the ruptured hymen. See Patricia Moran, '"The flaw in the centre": Writing as hymenal rupture in Virginia Woolf's work', *Tulsa Studies in Women's Literature*, 17.1 (Spring 1998), 101–21.

25 Briggs, *An Inner Life*, 230.

26 See, for example, Lisa Rado, 'Would the Real Virginia Woolf Please Stand Up? Feminist criticism, the androgyny debates, and *Orlando*', *Women's Studies*, 26 (1997), 147–69; and Ellen Bayuk Rosenman, 'Sexual Identity and *A Room of One's Own*: "Secret Economies" in Virginia Woolf's Feminist Discourse', *Signs*, 14 (1989), 634–50.

27 Woolf names Lytton Strachey, E. M. Forster and Roger Fry as the specific friends who would probably dislike the book. See 'The Cat Is Out of the Bag' for a discussion of the role an imagined male audience played in *Room*'s creation.

28 Julia Briggs reads this strategy as mirroring the one Woolf used in *Orlando* when Woolf shifts the meaning of androgyny 'from a woman with masculine traits' (such as Orlando/Vita) to its more traditional sense of a being in whom the sexes meet (such as Shakespeare might have been) (Briggs, 231).

29 Woolf took the phrase, 'The Angel in the House', from Coventry Patmore's poem of that title, first published in 1854 and expanded in 1862.

30 'Professions for Women', in *Virginia Woolf, Women and Writing*, ed. Michèle Barrett (New York and London: Harcourt Brace Jovanovich, 1979), p. 60.

31 Ibid.

# 12

## The Warp and the Weft: Homoeroticism in *Mrs. Dalloway* and *To the Lighthouse*

### Diana L. Swanson

---

### Introduction: 'The love that dare not speak its name'

In the early twentieth century in England, to engage in a male homosexual act was a criminal offence. The trials of Oscar Wilde in 1895, and his sentence to prison with hard labour, had seared this truth into the hearts and minds of homoerotically inclined men throughout Britain. Socially, homoerotic desires and homosexual acts were considered unspeakable and degenerate. For example, in E.M. Forster's novel *Maurice*, written in 1913–1914 but not published until 1971, after Forster's death, Maurice Hall's Greek tutor calls homosexuality 'the unspeakable vice of the Greeks'.[1] The family doctor to whom Maurice confides, 'I'm an unspeakable of the Oscar Wilde sort', replies, 'Never let that evil hallucination, that temptation from the devil, occur to you again' (*Maurice,* 159). Same-sex desire between women was even more suppressed in the cultural psyche. Terry Castle, in *The Apparitional Lesbian: Female Homosexuality and Modern Culture,* argues that Western culture has 'ghosted' lesbian desire and lesbians themselves. In particular, Western writing is a 'derealization machine: insert the lesbian and watch her disappear'.[2] The development of the new science of sexology laid some foundations for the decriminalisation of homosexuality decades later; however, in the 1920s this science, as popularised, mainly offered new vocabulary for condemnation of homosexuality. Radclyffe Hall's novel, *The Well of Loneliness,* which pleads for tolerance of inverts (as the sexologists called homosexuals), was banned as obscene in 1928 even though it includes no sex scenes.[3]

How, then, did 'the Love that dare not speak its name', as Oscar Wilde's lover Lord Alfred Douglas named homosexuality in his now famous poem 'Two Loves' (1896),[4] manifest nonetheless in literature? Virginia Woolf's *Mrs. Dalloway* and *To the Lighthouse* inscribe two different but related aspects of homosexual life in the early twentieth century: 1) hidden networks and 2) emotional life saturated with longing. These two novels imply that, in order to perceive homosexual reality, one must become consciously aware of the 'normal', of how society constructs heterosexuality as both real and ideal. In order fully to see one reality, you must also be aware of the other. In *Mrs. Dalloway* and *To the Lighthouse*, the representation of homoeroticism is intricately connected to the representation of gender norms, heterosexual relations and the social institutions of marriage and the family.[5]

In this essay, I argue that both novels weave homoeroticism deeply into the texture of themes, characters, images and allusions. I use the metaphor of weaving to describe this phenomenon. In a woven fabric, the warp is the threads, yarn or twine strung lengthwise and the weft (or woof) is the threads or yarn, often in a variety of colours, worked in from side to side through the warp in order to weave the fabric. In many techniques used to create tapestries or carpets, the warp can be partially or wholly invisible while the weft, in various colours, creates the pattern visible from the 'right side' of the fabric—that is, the side placed uppermost when installing the carpet or tapestry on the floor or wall. In *Mrs. Dalloway* and *To the Lighthouse*, homoeroticism and same-sex loving relationships function similarly to the warp; they are an integral part of the fabric but are usually, though not always, unseen. They are not part of the society's official, public patterns, the picture of social life seen from the 'right side' of things. However, the metaphor of weaving acknowledges that both the homosexual and the heterosexual are parts of the whole social fabric.

The narrative of *Mrs. Dalloway* gradually widens out from Clarissa Dalloway's viewpoint to encompass various social circles and perspectives. In this novel, I argue, the representation of homosexuality traces partially hidden networks of homoeroticism beneath the surface pattern of the dominant, heteronormative society. *To the Lighthouse*, in contrast to *Mrs. Dalloway*, focuses on one upper-middle-class family and several friends. This novel represents homosexuality through the emotional lives of a few characters who experience intense longing as they witness the socially sanctioned and culturally exalted heterosexual marriage and family life of the Ramsays. This homoerotic longing, in a sense, is the warp showing through in individual parts of the fabric while the family life of the Ramsays, who function as symbols of the Victorian ideal of husband and wife with children, constitutes the weft, the major pattern of the social tapestry.

## The fabric of London society in 1923: Hidden networks in *Mrs. Dalloway*

The opening pages of *Mrs. Dalloway* build up the multifarious fabric of London society in June 1923. They describe the people, places, air, traffic, products for sale in shop windows and inner thoughts of numerous characters, some of whom never appear again and others who become central to the novel. Scrope Purvis considers Mrs. Dalloway 'a charming woman'; Clarissa remembers Mrs. Foxcroft and Lady Bexborough grieving for their sons who died in the Great War; 'the King and Queen [are] at the palace' (*MD*, 4); 'whirling young men and laughing girls in their transparent muslins' are dancing and courting; Hugh Whitbread and his wife Evelyn visit town 'to see doctors' (*MD*, 5); 'the mothers of Pimlico [give] suck to their young' while 'messages [are] passing from the Fleet to the Admiralty'; Clarissa remembers Peter Walsh and thinks she was right not to marry him (*MD*, 6); Septimus thinks that his wife Rezia 'had a right to his arm' (*MD*, 14); as the motor car carries someone representative of 'the majesty of England', girls are 'buying white underlinen threaded with pure white ribbon for their weddings' and men in their clubs '[stand] even straighter ... and [seem] ready to attend their Sovereign ... to the cannon's mouth' (*MD*, 17). In addition the narrator tells us that 'the surface agitation of the passing car as it sunk grazed something very profound' (*MD*, 16). That so much of this early description and action in the novel concerns heterosexual attraction, marriage, government, empire, and commerce implies that these interwoven actions, feelings, and beliefs constitute 'something very profound', England itself—its social, economic, and political fabric—as well as the patriotism and duty that uphold that fabric: work, military service, marriage, child-bearing, and home-making.

Within this context of heteronormativity, Clarissa Dalloway feels its pressure: 'She had the oddest feeling sense of being herself invisible, unseen; unknown; there being no more marrying, no more having of children now, but only ... this being Mrs. Dalloway; not even Clarissa any more; this being Mrs. Richard Dalloway' (*MD*, 10). Now past middle age and no longer a potential bride or a potential mother, Clarissa feels that she no longer has a social identity but rather is simply an extension of her husband. Thus Woolf critiques both the heteronormativity and male dominance of the institution of marriage; coverture may have been partially dismantled by the Married Women's Property Act passed in 1882, but in many ways women still lose their independent selfhood when they marry.[6]

At the same time, Clarissa feels threads of connection among people: she is 'part of people she had never met; being laid out like a mist between the people she knew best, who lifted her on their branches as she had seen the trees lift the mist' (*MD*, 8). Later in the text, other characters repeat this notion of invisible emotional connections among people. For example, after luncheon with Lady Bruton, Richard Dalloway and Hugh Whitbread are 'attached to [Lady Bruton] by a thin thread … which would stretch and stretch … as they walk across London; as if one's friends were attached to one's body … by a thin thread' (*MD*, 101). Richard's thoughts turn toward Clarissa and he becomes 'very eager, to travel that spider's thread of attachment between himself and Clarissa' (*MD*, 103).

Thus, the text creates an interwoven fabric of 'normal' society—made up of people of all classes in the streets and buildings of London, politicians, shopkeepers, housewives, soldiers, maids—that provides the sense of the common life of England. The dominant pattern of this social fabric is clearly heterosexual. Partially hidden within that pattern lies the reality of other desires and thoughts that are not officially accepted or commonly assumed. Homoeroticism and same-sex love are part of the whole but are unnamed, often silenced, and largely invisible, showing through the dominant pattern only in a few spots, misty, ghostly or even monstrous.

Miss Doris Kilman constitutes one of the ghostly monsters and is the only overtly 'queer' character in the book. Her name (Kilman/ Kill man) is all too obvious, pointing toward homophobic stereotypes of lesbians as man-hating ball-busters. But much more about Doris Kilman implies her queer homosexuality; she transgresses conventional definitions and boundaries of gender. Both the impressions of others and her own thoughts show her to be powerful, intense, ambitious, angry, desirous, physically strong and clumsy—all characteristics much more acceptable in men than women. Descriptions of her emphasise 'her largeness, robustness, and power' (*MD*, 120). Mrs. Dalloway repeatedly thinks of Miss Kilman's ugly 'green mackintosh coat' as an example of how 'insensitive' Miss Kilman is to the sensibilities of others (*MD*, 11), how she neglects the feminine arts of pleasing. To Clarissa, Miss Kilman even has 'the power and taciturnity of some prehistoric monster armoured for primeval warfare' (*MD*, 112).

Within herself, Doris Kilman struggles with monstrous feelings of rage and resentment over her outsider status due to her poverty, German ancestry and, as she puts it, 'her unlovable body which people could not bear to see' (*MD*, 115). Finding in religion a possible sanctuary, she struggles against her carnal desires, thinking 'it was the flesh that she must control' (*MD*, 115).

Miss Kilman's homoerotic desires are directed toward both Clarissa and Clarissa's daughter, Elizabeth. First, Miss Kilman feels 'she was about to split asunder' because of her love for Elizabeth; 'if she could grasp [Elizabeth], ... if she could make her hers absolutely and forever and then die; that was all she wanted' (*MD*, 118).[7] The scene at tea with Elizabeth conveys the strength of Doris's feelings and the intensity of her struggle. Three times, at the moments when Elizabeth wants to leave, Miss Kilman's strong, large hands open and shut, conveying her intense desire and desperation and suggesting the physical as well as emotional nature of her love for Elizabeth. She yearns to 'overcome', 'unmask', and 'subdue' Clarissa (*MD*, 112), desires that could easily mask (or morph into) lust. As Eileen Barrett argues, Clarissa and Doris recognise each other's lesbian passions and that recognition disturbs their respective strategies to repress their own homoerotic desires.[8] Thus, threads run between Miss Kilman and Mrs. Dalloway beneath the social surface.

Clarissa herself realises that her hatred of Miss Kilman is based in her own insecurities and desires, but nevertheless, Doris 'had become one of those spectres with which one battles in the night', an apparition that raises within Clarissa the 'brutal monster', hatred. This hatred 'gave her physical pain, and made all pleasure in beauty, in friendship, in being well, in being loved and making her home delightful rock, quiver, and bend as if indeed there were a monster grubbing at the roots' (*MD*, 11). Miss Kilman threatens to rend the fabric of Mrs. Dalloway's life as a well-to-do, respectable wife, mother and hostess. At the same time, Clarissa thinks that 'no doubt with another throw of the dice, had the black been uppermost and not the white, she would have loved Miss Kilman! But not in this world' (*MD*, 11). In this world, Clarissa is invisibly, rather than monstrously, homosexual.

Clarissa lives what today we would call a 'closeted' life. As many critics have noted, Clarissa's teenage love for Sally Seton is clearly a sexual and romantic desire. However, brought up in a conservative Victorian family, Clarissa has, in adolescence, no way of understanding her feelings. In adulthood, she realises that, although she never fully requited her husband Richard's passion, 'she could not resist sometimes yielding to the charm of a woman. ... she did undoubtedly then feel what men felt' (*MD*, 29). The wording here implies that Clarissa usually does 'resist' and actively repress her desires. The melancholy of this extended passage in which Clarissa goes up to her closet-like room comes from the fruits of this repression. Clarissa feels that she 'had failed' Richard 'again and again' and that 'there was an emptiness about the heart of life. ... Narrower and narrower would her bed be' (*MD*, 28). Even as a girl, Clarissa recognises the hostility of her social world to same-sex love and the need for secrecy. When Sally kisses her, she 'felt that she had been given a present, wrapped up, and told just to keep it, not to look at it' (*MD*, 32). When Peter interrupts them with a mocking comment, 'it was like running one's face into a granite wall in the darkness! ... [S]he felt his hostility; his jealousy; his determination to break into their companionship' (*MD*, 32). Indeed, Peter's repeated thoughts of Clarissa as 'cold' (*MD*, 40, 46, 76) and 'impenetrable' (*MD*, 56) 'like iron' (*MD*, 61) encode a refusal, not just by him but by the whole society, to recognise lesbian passion and a determination to define women not open to men's heterosexual desire as frigid, deficient and abnormal.

In her adult life, Clarissa helps create social networks, including homosocial and homoerotic ones. According to Peter, 'she made her drawing-room a sort of meeting-place. ... But odd unexpected people turned up; ... *queer fish* in that atmosphere. And behind it all was that network of visiting, leaving cards, being kind to people' (*MD*, 69; italics mine). Clarissa herself thinks, 'But to go deeper, beneath what people said. ... Oh, it was *very queer*. Here was So-and-so in South Kensington; some one up in Bayswater; and somebody else, say, in Mayfair. ... [A]nd she felt if only they could be brought together' (*MD*, 109; italics mine). Both she and Peter describe this networking as 'behind' or 'beneath', supporting the sense of a network both embedded within and partially obscured by the dominant social pattern. Clarissa's feminine labour of weaving social networks is largely unrecognised or trivialised but nevertheless productive of social connections, including 'queer' ones.[9]

Other characters who demonstrate the network of homosexuality in the novel include Lady Bruton and Miss Milly Brush, Lady Bruton's secretary and 'good friend' (*MD*, 161). Milly Brush 'was capable of everlasting devotion to her own sex in particular, being knobbed, scraped, angular, and entirely without feminine charm' (*MD*, 95). Lady Bruton, like Miss Kilman, is spectral and masculine, 'a spectral grenadier' (*MD*, 161) who 'talk[s] like a man' (*MD*, 95) and, rather than being susceptible to men's compliments, feels that 'the difference between one man and another does not amount to much'

(*MD*, 93). Additionally, women know Lady Bruton as 'an almost silent companion, whose utterances … signified recognition of some feminine comradeship which went beneath masculine lunch parties and united Lady Bruton and Mrs. Dalloway', even if outwardly they seem 'indifferent and even hostile' to each other (*MD*, 95). Even the beautiful, nubile Elizabeth Dalloway's heterosexuality is in doubt. Not only does she have a crush on Miss Kilman, when she attends parties and receives attentions from young men, 'she [is] really awfully bored' (*MD*, 121). Other suggestive characters include Professor Brierly, 'a very queer fish' (*MD*, 157), and Miss Ellie Henderson who stays till the end of the party so she can 'tell Edith' about everything (*MD*, 173).

Clarissa's connection to Septimus Smith is the most 'spectral', becoming obvious only after Septimus's death. Prior to the party scene, the text links Septimus and Clarissa implicitly and indirectly through imagery such as trees and birds. Clarissa 'has a touch of the bird about her, the jay' (*MD*, 4), while Septimus is a 'young hawk' (*MD*, 131). Both Clarissa and Septimus use the image of a tree in their internal musings; for both the tree is important to their sense of life's connectivity, fruitfulness and sanctity. They are also linked through allusions to Shakespeare, whose sonnets Richard Dalloway says no decent man should read. Richard implies that their content, which includes expressions of admiration and love for a young man, is unacceptable (*MD*, 68). The repetition of 'fear no more the heat of the sun' from *Cymbeline* (*MD*, 8, 27, 36, for example) suggests that both Clarissa and Septimus are afraid of their own hot, passionate feelings and seek peace from them.[10]

Septimus's homoerotic desires are evident in his relationship with his commanding officer, Evans. 'Undemonstrative in the company of women', Evans feels 'affection' for Septimus. Septimus and Evans 'had to be together, share with each other, fight with each other, quarrel with each other'; 'it was a case of two dogs playing on a hearth-rug' (*MD*, 77). Not only does this description bear similarities to the homoerotic scene of Rupert Birkin and Gerald Crich wrestling on a rug before a fire in D.H. Lawrence's *Women in Love* (1920/1921), the phrase 'share with each other' echoes Woolf's friend E.M. Forster's euphemism for homosexual intercourse in *Maurice*.[11] Septimus's shell shock is attributable to his combat experiences but his love for Evans intensifies his emotional trauma. Certainly, Septimus's agony and fear are phrased in ways that suggest a sexual guilt. He 'saw faces laughing at him, calling him horrible disgusting names' (*MD*, 60); he feels 'so pocked and marked with vice that women shuddered when they saw him in the street' (*MD*, 82). And what was, and still is, a common condemnation of homosexuality? That it is 'unnatural'.

In the final scene of *Mrs. Dalloway*, many characters come together at Clarissa's party. Clarissa's party involves different levels of society, from the housemaids and cook on up. When the Prime Minister makes an appearance, the guests 'all knew, felt to the marrow of their bones, this majesty passing; this symbol of what they all stood for, English society' (*MD*, 154). Thus, the characters congregated at the party, like the crowds in the London streets earlier, stand for English society—they are a microcosm of the whole. The novel's most significant queer characters, however, attend the party invisibly.

Miss Kilman attends the party only in Clarissa's mind. After Clarissa walks down the room with the Prime Minister, she thinks 'these triumphs ... had a hollowness; at arm's length they were, not in the heart'. Then, watching the Prime Minister go down the stairs, 'the gilt rim of the Sir Joshua picture of the little girl with a muff brought back Kilman with a rush'. Clarissa feels 'that was satisfying; that was real. ... She hated her: she loved her' (*MD*, 156). But why does this picture make Clarissa think of Miss Kilman? Most obviously, the picture hangs on the landing where Miss Kilman waited earlier that day while Elizabeth tells Clarissa that she and Miss Kilman are going shopping. In addition, though, 'muff' was then, as now, according to the *Oxford English Dictionary*, slang for a woman's pubic hair and vulva. At some level, Clarissa feels a likeness to Miss Kilman; they both feel lesbian desire. Clarissa both hates and loves Miss Kilman because Miss Kilman brings her a sense of reality about her own sexual feelings, feelings she both recognises and wants to repress.

Like Miss Kilman, Septimus enters the party not bodily but in thought. When Lady Bradshaw tells Clarissa of Septimus's suicide, Clarissa imagines what Septimus might have felt as he fell and died. She compares herself to Septimus: 'She felt somehow very like him. ... She felt glad that he had done it; thrown it away' (*MD*, 166–67). She thinks:

> A thing there was that mattered ... defaced, obscured in her own life, let drop every day in corruption, lies, chatter. This he had preserved. ... Death was an attempt to communicate; people feeling the impossibility of reaching the centre which mystically, evaded them; closeness drew apart; rapture faded; one was alone. There was an embrace in death. (*MD*, 165)

This language echoes the scene in which Clarissa thinks about her desire for women: 'some pressure of rapture'; 'an inner meaning almost expressed'; 'but the close withdrew; the hard softened' (*MD*,

29). Clarissa thinks, '[H]ad he plunged holding his treasure? "If it were now to die, 'twere now to be most happy", she had said to herself once, coming down in white' (*MD*, 165). Clarissa remembers quoting this line from *Othello* when Sally Seton was staying in the house, Sally whose kiss was like 'a diamond, something infinitely precious' (*MD*, 32)—a treasure, in fact. Thus one of the things 'that mattered' but is 'defaced, obscured in her own life, let drop every day in corruption, lies, chatter', is same-sex love.

## 'To want and want and not to have': longing in *To the Lighthouse*

Critics generally view *To the Lighthouse* as a family story, often noting the resemblances to Woolf's own family of origin. Less often noted are the novel's alternatives to 'the love of man for woman': the idea that 'love had a thousand shapes' (*TL*, 157) and the representation of some of 'those unclassified affections' (*TL*, 85). Longings for different ways to live and love fill the pages of this novel. *To the Lighthouse* represents homoeroticism through the intense longing of a few characters as they witness the socially sanctioned and culturally exalted marriage and family life of the Ramsays. To return to the weaving metaphor, homoerotic longing functions as the warp which shows through in individual parts of the fabric while the family life of the Ramsays constitutes the weft, the dominant, visible pattern of the social tapestry. After discussing how the opening of the novel lays out competing visions, normative and alternative, of love and life, I focus on William Bankes, Mr. Carmichael and Lily Briscoe as sites of homoerotic longing.

The beginning of the novel introduces the Ramsay family and their house guests. It also introduces Mrs. Ramsay's devotion to the male sex and belief in the importance of male dominance and traditional gender roles for social order and happiness:

[S]he had the whole of the other sex under her protection; for reasons she could not explain, for their chivalry and valour, for the fact that they negotiated treaties, ruled India, controlled finance; finally for an attitude towards herself which no woman could fail to feel or to find agreeable, something trustful, childlike, reverential. (*TL*, 9)

Men, in Mrs. Ramsay's view, create the social, economic and political order and women must support men at home so that men can 'uphold the world' (*TL*, 94), 'insinuating ... as she did the greatness of man's intellect, … the subjection of all wives … to their husbands' labours' (*TL*, 13). Indeed, Mrs. Ramsay believes that 'they all [women] must marry, since … there could be no disputing this: an unmarried woman … has missed the best of life' (*TL*, 43). Mr. and Mrs. Ramsay, whose first names, significantly, are never given, become the 'symbols of marriage, husband and wife' (*TL*, 60) and the representatives of the conventional gender dichotomies of man/woman, intellect/emotion, work/family, public/domestic.

Against this conventional vision of gender and family arise 'infidel ideas' that Mrs. Ramsay's daughters 'had brewed for themselves of a life different from hers; … a wilder life; not always taking care of some man or other; for there was in all their minds a mute questioning of deference and chivalry, of the Bank of England and the Indian Empire, of ringed fingers and lace' (*TL*, 9). The Ramsay daughters feel the constrictions of the life their mother urges upon them and wish to rebel against these heteronormative gender norms. Yet Mrs. Ramsay's conventional vision is also compelling; to her daughters 'there was something in this of the essence of beauty, which called out the manliness in their girlish hearts, and made them … honour her strange severity, her extreme courtesy, like a Queen's' (*TL*, 10). Note, however, that their attraction to their mother's vision calls out 'the manliness in their girlish hearts'. As I have said elsewhere, their attraction to patriarchal institutions (marriage, the Bank of England, the Empire) is inspired by their mother's beauty and their desire for an active part in life and is thus coded as non-normative and potentially lesbian.[12] Thus, the opening pages of the novel suggest competing visions of love and life: on the one hand, the conventional, Victorian, idealised vision of masculinity, femininity and marriage; on the other hand, a nascent vision of gender rebellion, girlish manliness, homoerotic desire and women's independence.

This conflict between gender rebellion and attraction to the power and beauty of Mrs. Ramsay and her vision of heterosexual love and marriage is part of Lily Briscoe's inner longing as well. Lily finds herself in love with the Ramsays' family life and wanting to fling herself at Mrs. Ramsay's knee. She feels an intense desire for intimacy with Mrs. Ramsay: 'the chambers of the mind and heart of the woman who was, physically, touching her. … what art was there, known to love or cunning, by which one pressed through into those secret chambers?' (*TL*, 44). This passage, focalised through Lily's consciousness, shows her struggling to articulate the kind of intimacy she desires. She emphasises that Mrs. Ramsay is physically, not just emotionally, touching her. She uses the metaphor of pressing through into a secret chamber—a common trope for the desire to have sexual intercourse with a woman. She expresses a desire to become 'one with the object one adored'—a common trope for romantic and sexual desire (*TL*, 44). Lily's desire for intimacy with Mrs. Ramsay is a homoerotic, lesbian desire.[13] Significantly, in this same extended passage, Lily pleads for 'her own exemption from the universal law' of marriage: '[S]he liked to be alone; she liked to be herself; she was not made for that' (*TL*, 43). Lily recognises the power of the social institution that Adrienne Rich names compulsory heterosexuality, as well as its unsuitability for those who 'are not made for' marriage.[14]

Thus, while susceptible to Mrs. Ramsay's attractiveness and to the warmth of her family life, Lily is not attracted to the ideal of married life that Mr. and Mrs. Ramsay represent. Also immune to this attraction are Mr. Carmichael and William Bankes. In fact, Mrs. Ramsay feels aggrieved that Mr. Carmichael does not respond to her legendary beauty and feminine caretaking. She thinks to herself that 'he shrank from her. He never told her anything. ... It injured her that he should shrink' (*TL*, 36). Mr. Carmichael's indifference strikes at what she feels makes herself and her life worthwhile, her heterosexual femininity. So who does interest Mr. Carmichael during his visits to the Ramsays? Mr. Carmichael is 'devoted' to Andrew and 'would call him into his room, and Andrew said, "show him things"'. This sentence about Andrew is followed immediately by a description of Carmichael as a predatory poet: '[H]e reminded one of a cat watching birds ... he clapped his paws together when he had found the word' (*TL*, 79). This juxtaposition, and the vagueness of the word 'things' in 'show him things', suggests that Carmichael's interest in Andrew may be somewhat predatory and carnal.[15] Finally, after Andrew's death in the Great War, Carmichael brings out a book of poems that unexpectedly becomes popular. The narrator notes that the war revives the public's interest in poetry. An actual volume of poetry that became famous during WWI is A. E. Housman's *A Shropshire Lad*, which contains nostalgic, homoerotic poems about young men and, though first published in 1896, did not become a bestseller until the First World War. The similarity to Carmichael's book inspired by Andrew's death is suggestive.

William Bankes, unlike Carmichael, feels attraction to and affection for Mrs. Ramsay, yet he does not envy the Ramsays their mode of life: 'the truth was that he did not enjoy family life' (*TL*, 73). He does, however, feel an affinity for Lily Briscoe; he shares with her 'some need' (*TL*, 20) that brings them together each evening to look at the view, the ocean and the Ramsay family. William remembers his youthful friendship with Mr. Ramsay, which 'had ceased, there, on that stretch of road' where Ramsay admires a hen protecting her chicks. Mr. Ramsay's delight in the maternal scene creates distance between them; 'after that ... the pulp had gone out of their friendship'. But William preserves his early love for Mr. Ramsay in his memory: '[T]here, like the body of a young man laid up in peat for a century, with the red fresh on his lips, was his friendship ... laid up across the bay among the sandhills' (*TL*, 21). Thus, the 'need' William shares with Lily may be the need to reflect on homoerotic desires, in William's case for a young man with red lips, desires which find no place within the family pattern. The view he and Lily share, across the bay, is the view of the outsider to heteronormative family life. They are both on the outside looking in at the Ramsays. They both long for the social acceptance, warmth and beauty they sense in that dominant family pattern, but both feel they are not 'made for' that mode of life.

Lily responds to this affinity with William. While she usually hides her paintings from prying eyes, when William Bankes walks up to her on the lawn, she lets him look at her painting of Mrs. Ramsay and James. She takes an emotional risk: 'that any other eyes should see' her painting, 'the deposit of each day's living mixed with something more secret than she had ever spoken or shown in the course of all those days was an agony' (*TL*, 45). This painting contains a 'secret' that Lily has never before revealed, but she chooses to share it with William. After their conversation about the painting, Lily feels that 'this man had shared with her something profoundly intimate' and that 'the world' has offered 'a power which she had not suspected—that one could walk away down that long gallery not alone any more but arm in arm with somebody' (*TL*, 46). Lily has found a companion. Mrs. Ramsay thinks that Lily and William should marry, but she mistakes the nature of their connection. Lily is 'without any sexual feeling' for William (*TL*, 23); the secret they share is homoerotic love.[16]

Ten years later, in the last section of the novel, Lily appears again, still single, still painting and still longing for Mrs. Ramsay. The two passages in which Lily's pain, grief and love for Mrs. Ramsay's beauty of body and character return to her are among the most intense and poignant of the novel. As before, Lily struggles to articulate her feelings in words because 'it was one's body feeling, not one's mind'. Looking at the empty steps and window where Mrs. Ramsay had sat with James ten years before, Lily thinks, '[T]o want and not to have—to want and want—how that wrung the heart, and wrung it again and again!' (*TL*, 146). Struggling to compose herself, she asks, 'What did it mean? Could things thrust their hands up and grip one; could the blade cut; the fist grasp? Was there no safety? ... "Mrs. Ramsay!" she said aloud, "Mrs. Ramsay!" The tears ran down her face' (*TL*, 148). She feels 'the old horror come back—to want and want and not to have' (*TL*, 165). 'The old horror', I argue, is the intense and unrequited longing of those whose most intimate loves are shut out of the family home, whose love 'dare not speak its name' because the language of love was made for heterosexual love and because revelation could call down upon one shame, disgrace and worse.

In both *Mrs. Dalloway* and *To the Lighthouse*, homoerotic desires and relationships are hidden in plain sight, interwoven throughout the texts. At the same time, each novel takes a different focus. *Mrs. Dalloway*, of which Woolf wrote, 'I want to criticize the social system, & to show it at work',[17] turns more outward than *To the Lighthouse*, focusing on social networks. *To the Lighthouse* turns more inward than *Mrs. Dalloway*, focusing on intense homoerotic love and longing. In both novels, though, the representation of homoeroticism is the warp to the weft of patriarchal heterosexist norms and social institutions. This strategic textual weaving allows Woolf subtly to show homosexuality and homosexuals as integral parts of the whole social fabric as well as to show their human loves, joys, sorrows and struggles. This strategy also allows Woolf to reveal, without the didacticism and the vulnerability to censorship of a text such as *The Well of Loneliness*, the stringency of English society's judgements upon homoerotic desires. Both novels criticise the social system's silencing, excluding and scapegoating of those 'not made for' conventional romance and family life.

## Notes

1 E. M. Forster, *Maurice* (New York: W. W. Norton, 2005), p. 51.

2 *The Apparitional Lesbian: Female Homosexuality and Modern Culture* (NY: Columbia UP, 1993), p. 6.

3 See Jane Marcus, 'Sapphistory: The Woolf and the Well', in *Lesbian Texts and Contexts: Radical Revisions*, ed. Karla Jay and Joanne Glasgow (NY: New York UP, 1990), pp. 164–179; and Jodie Medd, *Lesbian Scandal and the Culture of Modernism* (Cambridge: Cambridge UP, 2012).

4 'Two Loves' was first published in *The Chameleon* in 1894: http://law2.umkc.edu/faculty/projects/ftrials/wilde/poemsofdouglas.htm. For information about the 1895 trials of Oscar Wilde, see the University of Missouri – Kansas City School of Law website 'Famous World Trials' at http://law2.umkc.edu/faculty/projects/ftrials/wilde/wilde.htm.

5 That this presentation of gender norms, heterosexual relations, marriage and the family constitutes a feminist critique has been argued by many

scholars. See, for example, Amy C. Smith, 'Loving maidens and patriarchal mothers: Revisions of the Homeric *Hymn to Demeter* and *Cymbeline* in *Mrs. Dalloway*', *Woolf Studies Annual* 17 (2011), pp. 151–172; Gabrielle McIntyre, 'Feminism and Gender in *To the Lighthouse*', in *The Cambridge Companion to* To the Lighthouse, ed. and intro. Allison Pease (Cambridge: Cambridge UP, 2015), pp. 80–91; Jane Lilienfeld, 'Where the Spear Plants Grew: The Ramsays' Marriage in *To the Lighthouse*', in *New Feminist Essays on Virginia Woolf*, ed. Jane Marcus (Lincoln: University of Nebraska Press, 1981), pp. 148–169.

6   Coverture is the legal concept that a married woman is 'covered' by her husband's identity. Under English common law, married women did not have their own separate legal identities but were considered part of their husbands.

7   Note that Clarissa herself had thought something similar about Sally Seton when she was young: "'[I]f it were now to die 'twere now to be most happy." … all because she was coming down to dinner in a white frock to meet Sally Seton!' (*MD*, 31).

8   'Unmasking Lesbian Passion: The Inverted World of *Mrs. Dalloway*', in *Virginia Woolf: Lesbian Readings*, eds. Eileen Barrett and Patricia Cramer (NY: New York UP, 1997), pp. 146–164. Barrett also provides an important and useful discussion of the contemporary discourses of same-sex desire, showing how the novel presents Clarissa's homoeroticism in terms of nineteenth-century romantic friendship and Doris's in terms of 'inversion' as defined by the sexology of Havelock Ellis. Sexology defined 'true' homosexuality as including gender inversion as well as same-sex sexual attraction.

9   Given her friendships with Lytton Strachey, E. M. Forster, Vita Sackville-West, Duncan Grant, and others active in various homosexual subcultures, Woolf certainly uses the term 'queer' with full knowledge of its double meaning. The *Oxford English Dictionary* cites an 1894 letter by the Marquess of Queensberry as the first recorded use of 'queer' to mean homosexual. Thus, this word was in active use as a slang reference to homosexuality well before the writing of *Mrs. Dalloway* and *To the Lighthouse* in the 1920s.

10  For discussion of Clarissa, Septimus, and 'the verbal network of the novel', see Emily Jensen, 'Mrs. Dalloway's Respectable Suicide', in *Virginia Woolf: A Feminist Slant*, ed. Jane Marcus (Lincoln: U of Nebraska P, 1983), pp. 162–179.

11  *Maurice* did not see publication until 1971 but the manuscript was circulated among Forster's friends. Biographer Wendy Moffat asserts that Woolf 'was not privy to the *Maurice* manuscript' (*A Great Unrecorded History: A New Life of E. M. Forster* [NY: Farrar, Straus, and Giroux, 2010], p.194). Based on Woolf's diaries and letters, however, I consider it highly likely that the term 'sharing', among others used by homosexual men at the time, came up in conversations among friends which included Woolf.

12  Diana L. Swanson, 'The Lesbian Feminism of Woolf's *To the Lighthouse*',
    in *Re: Reading, Re: Writing, Re: Teaching Virginia Woolf; Selected Papers from
    the Fourth Annual Conference on Virginia Woolf*, eds. Eileen Barrett and
    Patricia Cramer (NY: Pace University Press, 1995), pp. 38–44.
13  See also, among other critics, Donna Risolo, 'Outing Mrs. Ramsay:
    Reading the Lesbian Subtext in Virginia Woolf's *To the Lighthouse*', in
    *Virginia Woolf: Themes and Variations; Selected Papers from the Second Annual
    Conference on Virginia Woolf*, ed. Vara Neverow-Turk and Mark Hussey
    (NY: Pace University Press, 1993), pp. 238–248; and Julie Abraham,
    'Virginia Woolf and the Sexual Histories of Literature' in *Are Girls
    Necessary: Lesbian Writing and Modern Histories* (NY: Routledge, 1996),
    pp. 139–168.
14  See Rich's now classic essay, 'Compulsory Heterosexuality and
    Lesbian Existence', in *Blood, Bread, and Poetry: Selected Prose 1979–
    1985* (NY: W.W. Norton, 1994), pp. 23–75. Also see Vara Neverow,
    'Compulsory Heterosexuality and the Lesbian Continuum in *To the
    Lighthouse*: A Woman's Studies Approach', in *Approaches to Teaching Woolf's*
    To the Lighthouse, eds. Beth Rigel Daugherty and Mary Beth Pringle
    (NY: Modern Language Association of America, 2001), pp. 169–175.
15  For a more positive analysis of the relationship between Mr. Carmichael
    and Andrew, see Ruth Vanita, 'Bringing Buried Things to Light:
    Homoerotic Alliances in *To the Lighthouse*', in *Virginia Woolf: Lesbian
    Readings*, eds. Eileen Barrett and Patricia Cramer (NY: New York
    University Press, 1997), pp. 165–179.
16  For a fuller discussion of the affinity between Lily and William and of
    Woolf's own affinities with homosexual men, see Ruth Vanita, op cit.
    See also Jean Kennard, 'From foe to friend: Virginia Woolf's changing
    view of the male homosexual', *Woolf Studies Annual* 4 (1998), pp. 67–85.
17  *D II*, 248.

# 13

# The Cambridge Woolf

Jane Goldman and E. H. Wright

## Introduction: Jane Goldman on editing Woolf for Cambridge University Press

When Susan Sellers and I were commissioned by Cambridge University Press to take on the General Editorship of the works of Virginia Woolf, we followed the press's standard, rigorous procedures; set up our editorial board; and took advice at every step from the considerable expertise made available to us by senior editors and officers of this august, historic publisher. Approval of all our volumes is arrived at through the many stages of scholarly scrutiny, including that of our editorial board as well as anonymous peer review and ultimately, the Syndics—representatives of Cambridge University Press specially chosen to evaluate our work.

Woolf and her husband founded the Hogarth Press in 1917, and had in-depth experience of preparing for publication texts of every kind, whether formal and scholarly or avant-garde and creative. Her avant-garde writing is shaped as much by that experience and knowledge as by her extensive reading in every genre, including the scholarly edition. Woolf, we point out in our General Editors' Preface, 'understands the reader to be the "fellow-worker and accomplice" of the writer', and is 'scornful … of institutionalised academic literary authority: "To admit authorities, however heavily furred and gowned, into our libraries and let them tell us how to read, what to read, what value to place upon what we read, is to destroy the spirit of freedom which is the breath of those sanctuaries"' (*E*V, 573).[1] In preparing an edition to do justice to this Woolfian ethos, we have devised 'a form that provides … the fullest means possible' for the reader to follow Woolf's advice, which is 'to take no advice, to follow your own instincts, to use your own reason, to come to your own conclusions' (*E*V, 573).

For Woolf founded a new form of feminist textual editing in *A Room of One's Own*, on the very threshold of a patriarchal college library where her dogged anonymous narrator is barred from entering at the 'flutter of black gown' from 'a deprecating, silvery, kindly gentleman who regretted in a low voice as he waved me back that ladies are only admitted to the library if accompanied by a Fellow of the College or furnished with a letter of introduction' (*R/TG*, 9). Attempting to settle a matter of textual scholarship concerning an essay by Charles Lamb on his dismay over the composition of Milton's great pastoral elegy, *Lycidas*, she wants simply to 'follow Lamb's footsteps across the quadrangle to that famous library where the treasure is kept'. The narrator vows 'never' to 'ask for that hospitality again' (*R/TG*, 8–9). This is not to say she will never again enter a library, just that in future she will not bother to ask, but trespass.

As General Editors, who would have been considered scholarly trespassers not so long ago, we are all too aware of the disservices done to the democratic ethos of Woolf's writing and to the active participation it demands of her reader accomplices by the donning of 'furred and gowned' authority. Conscious that Woolf was immensely well read, and that her work is highly allusive, we have sought to be more thorough than any previous edition in providing annotations to elucidate her historical, factual, cultural and literary references. We seek to emphasise the open-endedness of our annotations, which draw on the discoveries of past and present scholars of Woolf, in the hope that we might continue the dialogues they have initiated in published criticism. Conscious, too, that some readers of Woolf will be scholars curious about the differences between earlier British and American editions of Woolf, we have provided as clear a map as possible of textual variants, with as little interference on the page as possible, and no silent emendation. Our overall aim as editors has been to provide readers with a transparent record of textual process, and a conscientious commentary on Woolf's many and varied allusions, without suggesting that we are authorities who know better than our fellow readers or than Woolf herself.

### E. H. Wright on the Cambridge *Mrs. Dalloway*

*Mrs. Dalloway* is anchored in Woolf's experience of the world, not only the people and places that she knew or the events through which she lived, but also her enormous literary knowledge and output. The Cambridge Edition of *Mrs. Dalloway* makes many of these links explicit, highlighting the novel's potential real-life connections, its intertexts and thus its potential subtexts without offering interpretations which are left to the reader to reach. It leads to what Jerome J. McGann calls 'radial reading' where 'the text is like the hub of the wheel and the spokes lead out to other versions and to other texts'.[2] It is this way of reading *Mrs. Dalloway* that the Cambridge Edition encourages so that the reader can 'respond actively' to the text.[3] In other words the reader is not, as Woolf puts it in 'On Re-reading Novels' (1922), 'sit[ting] any longer open-mouthed in passive expectation' (*E* III, 344) but is instead taking an active part in interpreting the text.

*Mrs. Dalloway*'s editor, Anne Fernald, is careful to trace as far as possible the links to Woolf's life, which she gleans from her personal writing (her diaries, letters and memoirs), and from the numerous biographies currently available. People, places, events, experiences, moments from her life are placed in the crucible of fiction and transformed in the novel. In a 1918 essay, 'Philosophy in Fiction', Woolf observed that 'the material of life is … difficult to handle and has to be limited and abstracted … before it can be dealt with by words' (*E* II, 208). Thus, although Woolf's first-hand experience of life clearly inspired numerous aspects of the novel, it is not wise to try and map Woolf's biography onto the text too closely, as Fernald is careful to emphasise when she quotes Woolf's caveat to Philip Morrell: 'There were originals for some of the people in *Mrs. Dalloway:*—but very far away—people I last saw 10 years ago and even then, did not know well. These are the people I like to write about' (*L* III, 195). Woolf was being somewhat disingenuous here, but by using her own experience as inspiration, however abstracted, she clearly helps to ground each of her novels in the life of the time in which it was set.

Certain correlations between real people of Woolf's acquaintance and her fictional characters are already well-known, such as the link between Kitty Maxse (née Lushington) and Mrs. Dalloway, or elements of Rezia Warren-Smith which were taken from Lydia Lopokova.[4] London landmarks, parks, streets, even firms and clubs are also clearly drawn from life: for example, Mrs. Dalloway uses Rumpelmayer's for her party, which was a catering firm for the gentry, or the reference to White's exclusive men's club on St James's Street with its bow window. Events from Woolf's life are also subtly woven into the fabric of the text, for example, Richard Dalloway's thought that the London traffic poses a threat to children of five (*MD,* 104) was a paragraph written just a few weeks after Woolf's niece, Angelica Bell, was run over by a car. Indeed, as Fernald says, 'To grasp how many observations stand behind a single detail, consider Clarissa's "silver-green mermaid's dress'" (*MD,* 155)—Fernald then reveals how the description of this dress connects not only with living people in her acquaintance, including Katherine Horner, Lady Ottoline Morrell, Vita Sackville-West and Vanessa Bell, but also to literary sources such as T. S. Eliot's 'The Love Song of J. Alfred Prufrock', John Donne's 'Song', Homer's *Odyssey* and Lady Anne Clifford's diary.[5] Other connections, however, are more speculative, which is where the Cambridge Edition becomes particularly interesting, in pointing out, for example, the variety of possible models for Septimus Warren-Smith, including Siegfried Sassoon, Rupert Brooke, Ralph Partridge and Gerald Brenan.[6]

The novel's allusions and intertexts, as in all of Woolf's work, extend from her experience of lived reality to her broad knowledge of literature and literary history traceable in her autobiographical writing, reading notebooks, reviews and essays. From the names that she gives to her characters, to the clothes they wear and the refrains that play on their minds which help to link the characters together, Woolf deliberately draws, mostly consciously, from her extensive reading. William Irwin points out that the word 'allusion':

> comes to us from the Latin *alludere*: 'to jest, mock, play with', and there is indeed something ludic, gamelike, in the nature of allusion. We are asked to fill in the missing piece of a puzzle, to draw on some knowledge to complete the written or spoken word in our own minds. Perhaps allusions are by their very nature incomplete and the process of completing them is a productive one.[7]

Certainly Fernald's account of how she made the link between the description of Septimus's mental state and Homer's portrayal of the shipwrecked Odysseus while reading a version of the *Odyssey* to her daughter, aptly demonstrates the 'gamelike' 'puzzle' of piecing together the tissue of Woolf's allusions.[8] The Introduction, Explanatory Notes and Textual Notes in the Cambridge Edition help the reader to 'complete' the riddle. Ziva Ben-Porat and John Campbell both argue that allusions also call on the reader to participate in the construction of the text's meaning in order to 'reconstruct a fuller text'.[9] Campbell avers that allusions are not always intentional and can be found by the reader without the writer deliberately including them. 'Allusions', he says, 'invite us to select from our mental library, knowledge which is not in the text itself and without which the writer's intention will not be fully communicated'.[10] In other words, these critics suggest that we must reconfigure the allusions in order to access not only the writer's intentions, but also to form our own active readings of the novel. This thinking echoes that of the General Editors who, in their Introduction, point out that Woolf was certainly keen to see reading and writing as inseparable to the creative process, to the construction of meaning and the reaching of a personal and private understanding of the text.[11]

The editors are also careful to remind us that Woolf was reading for and writing *The Common Reader, First Series* (1925) at the same time as she was writing *Mrs. Dalloway*. Fernald shows in the Introduction and Explanatory Notes how 'moving ... between the books creates powerful underground thematic connections between the novel and the essays' (*MD*, xlix). Not only direct quotations, paraphrases, images or symbols, but wider thematic lines are lifted from her reading for the essay collection and find their way into the novel. In her extensive knowledge of the European canon, Woolf is, according to critic Harold Bloom, in the state of *apophrades*, by which he means her writing is open to the work of her predecessors. Woolf does not imitate, but uses her literary forebears as inspiration and remoulds their texts to suit her own purposes. She is a 'strong' writer to Bloom's mind because her allusions are under her control. As Bloom argues in *The Western Canon*: 'Great writing is always rewriting or revisionism and is founded upon a reading that clears space for the self'.[12] Woolf is one of the writers whom he identifies as having gone through this process and who has in turn contributed to the canon. The Cambridge Edition helps to highlight the ways in which Woolf has rewritten and revised her reading in order to achieve her status as one of the twentieth century's most respected authors.

In her effort to trace some of these subtle and surprising connections to other writers' works, Fernald uncovers a number of interesting sources. Some of the most exciting revelations about the novel which come out of this edition are Woolf's intention to include an anonymous Greek chorus comprised of Londoners who comment on the unfolding scene; the reinstatement of the novel's twelve section breaks which were lost in the printing process; and the laborious rewriting of 'the mad scenes' leading up to Septimus's suicide towards the end of the novel.

The original idea behind the novel's choral figures was to have Mrs. Dalloway 'seen by other people' (*MD*, lviii) and to provide the novel's poetry. The first of the choral characters allowed to remain in the published text is Scrope Purvis who notices Mrs. Dalloway perched on the kerb, ready to cross the road. Here Scrope functions as a casual observer offering an outsider's perspective on Clarissa Dalloway's character. Significantly, the chorus as an idea is also found in Woolf's essay, 'On Not Knowing Greek' in *The Common Reader*, for which she was reading at the time. Many of these characters were never written or were expunged and the job of 'add[ing] poetry and depth' became 'the function of Rezia Warren-Smith and Peter Walsh' (*MD*, lix). However, traces of these figures remain in Scrope Purvis, Maisie Johnson, Mrs. Dempster and the 'elderly grey nurse' (*MD*, 50; see Explanatory Note 50: 22) in the park who observes Peter Walsh sleeping.

The origins of the novel come clearly into focus in this edition through discussion of such features as the chorus in the diaries, note-books and early drafts. Fernald draws attention to the fact that the first stirrings of *Mrs. Dalloway* appear in her 1915 novel, *The Voyage Out*, in which Mr. and Mrs. Dalloway take cameo roles and for whose appearance she received the coveted praise of Lytton Strachey, who pronounced the 'satire' on the Dalloways '*extremely* good' (*D* II, 65). Comparisons with earlier incarnations of the novel also help to illuminate the many transformations that the text went through before publication. These versions include not only drafts of the novel itself, but also the series of short stories that Woolf wrote surrounding the composition of the novel.[13] Fernald highlights 'Mrs. Dalloway in Bond Street' (published 1923) in particular, noticing that this Clarissa Dalloway, who is buying gloves, not flowers, is more closely linked with the snobbish, class-focused, nationalistic Clarissa of *The Voyage Out* (1915) than to the subtle and reflective Clarissa in *Mrs. Dalloway* (1925).

Most interesting, perhaps, is the charting of the rewriting of Septimus's shell-shock. All three elements of the edition (Introduction, Explanatory Notes and Textual Notes) help to highlight the many changes Woolf made to this section of the novel in the summer of 1924. In her Introduction Fernald tells us that 'thirty pages of Notebook 3 are devoted to drafting the eleven pages that make up that scene in the novel (*MD*, 125–35), and that many of the 'themes and ideas' tested in this draft remain only as 'echoes' in the final version (*MD*, lxxi). The Explanatory Notes then connect the text in the light of factual evidence from Woolf's personal and literary life, while the Textual Notes trace the specific alterations Woolf made to the section—her additions, restructurings and deletions, which give a much more detailed or indeed different version of Septimus's state of mind. In the Textual Notes Fernald points out how in Notebook 3 Septimus calmly discusses care homes (see Textual Note 131:32, *MD*, 131) and how carefully he considers his method of suicide, as well as introducing 'thoughts about his habit of procrastination and a longer hesitation at the window itself' (see Textual Note 133:21; *MD*, 133); or how in the proofs for the British and American editions she was still making alterations by 'cross[ing] out seventeen lines' and adding 'Septimus's meditation on other possible methods of suicide' (see Textual Note 133:19–134:32; *MD*, 133). As Fernald shows in her Introduction, these alterations have led various scholars, including Julia Briggs and Helen Wussow, 'to a variety of different hypotheses about the relative ease or difficulty of drafting them [these sections], especially in comparison to the rest of the book' (*MD*, lxxi).

Different editions published within Woolf's lifetime introduce further alterations to the text, not only Woolf's own corrections and mistakes, but errors and misprints introduced by the printer. The most notable of these are the loss of several of the novel's twelve line breaks which arguably signal the passage of the novel's twelve hours in the first American edition. In this edition, three of the breaks disappear simply because of the page layout. Fernald notes that certain of these spaces, very deliberately highlighted to the printer by Woolf, fall on the last line of particular pages thus rendering the spaces invisible (see Textual Notes 84:22, 135:8–9 and 167:4, *MD*, 84, 135 and 167). Indeed, it is '[t]he first British edition's handling of these breaks [that] tips the balance strongly in its favour as a copy text' (*MD*, lxxxvi) for this edition. Certainly recording these variations in drafts, proofs and published versions helps the reader to confront, as Gerard Genette suggests: 'what the text is, with what it was, with what it could have been, with what it almost became'.[14]

Introductions, Explanatory Notes, Textual Apparatus and Textual Notes are, as Shari Benstock points out 'innately referential':

> reflecting on the text, engaged in dialogue with it, and often performing an interpretive and critical act on it, while also addressing a larger, extra-textual world in an effort to relate this text to other texts, to negotiate the middle ground between this author and other authors, between this author and the reader.[15]

However, what this edition does not do is tell the reader what to make of these pieces of information, how to interpret them or what the definitive explanation might be. The Explanatory Notes provide unbiased information which the reader is left to do with what they will, though pointers are given to other scholars who *have* offered opinions and analysis. In her online blog, through which she reflects informally upon the process of editing, Fernald is allowed to ask more questions of the novel than the edition can ask or answer.

For example, she connects allusions to Shakespeare's 'The Rape of Lucrece', *Cymbeline*, *Hamlet* and *Othello* with Richardson's *Clarissa* and Pope's 'The Rape of the Lock' and asks:

> So why, I want to know, is Clarissa Dalloway's happy memory of love also Othello's feeling? Why, when she remembers feeling in love, does she remember the feeling of a lover who will become a murderer, a man who will go mad from suspicion of his wife's infidelity?[16]

The answers to such questions are assisted, but not found, in this edition, which appeals to 'readers in need of access to a transparent record of textual process' (*MD*, xiii). In many ways this allows the contemporary reader to engage with *Mrs. Dalloway* as a text that is always 'becoming'. The novel is, as Jacques Derrida would have it, 'no longer a finished corpus of writing, some content enclosed in a book or its margins, but a differential network, a fabric of traces referring endlessly to something other than itself'.[17] By providing a clean text (i.e., a text of the novel which does not contain the footnote numbers within the narrative or the footnotes at the bottom of the page), this edition does not allow the extra material surrounding the novel provided by Fernald and the General Editors to, as Shari Benstock worries, 'wren[ch] away the inherent supremacy of the text by setting up a countertext in their commentary'.[18] In other words the reader is allowed to read the novel in any way he or she likes, thus creating new versions of *Mrs. Dalloway*, which is always in a process of becoming.

## Jane Goldman on the Cambridge *To the Lighthouse*

Preparing *To the Lighthouse* for a scholarly edition is challenging in all the ways our General Editors' Preface makes clear—and then some! Even categorising this work as a 'novel' is problematic. For it was conceived and received as a semi-autobiographical work that somehow performs the poetic work of elegy—in this case it is understood firstly as an elegy for Woolf's parents, Leslie Stephen and Julia Stephen. The UK and US first editions were published simultaneously on 5 May 1927, the anniversary of Julia Stephen's death. And its semi-autobiographical qualities have to be factored in to Explanatory Notes and the Introduction but not, of course, to the exclusion of the less immediately personal cultural valences, references and allusions that abound in this novel.

Preparation of the Explanatory Notes is for many editors of scholarly editions the most compelling and exciting of tasks as well as the most unlimited and therefore most exhausting. The Cambridge Woolf seeks to do justice to the richness of Woolf's densely allusive writing and to its openness and playfulness. Collation of extant states of the text and preparation of the Textual Apparatus and Textual Notes appears a more finite task, yet there is always the possibility that a previously undiscovered and assumed lost proof suddenly surfaces which throws further light on the text's genesis and needs careful collation and analysis. And, as I have indicated above, there are very different approaches to preparing a text and to the role of the editor. The Cambridge Woolf has developed a democratic and feminist ethos of transparency and mapping. In what follows I will give two examples of the challenges facing the editor of *To the Lighthouse*, and show how my Cambridge edition attempts to meet them.

The semi-autobiographical, familial landscapes in *To the Lighthouse* have proved so powerful that the Hebridean setting has been almost entirely overlooked by generations of its readers, critics and editors. Because Mr. and Mrs. Ramsay are understood as models for Woolf's parents Leslie and Julia Stephen, the novel's setting on the 'Isle of Skye' (*TL*, 10 ), a place Woolf did not visit until eleven years after the publication of *To the Lighthouse*, is assumed to be a cipher for Cornwall where the Stephen family spent their summers. My work as editor of this novel has uncovered a reach seam of Hebridean material on which it draws, so rich indeed that it spurred me to write the recent monograph for Cecil Woolf's Bloomsbury Heritage series: *'With You in the Hebrides': Virginia Woolf and Scotland* (2013). My Cambridge edition of *To the Lighthouse* attempts to mend the past deficit of serious attention to its numerous and significant allusions to its Scottish setting—without in turn setting or fixing it too dogmatically or simply in any one place. 'I'm so glad that you like some of the Lighthouse', Woolf wrote to her friend Violet Dickinson, mischievously adding: 'People in the Hebrides are very angry. Is it Cornwall? I'm not as sure as you are' (*L* III, 389).

As editor it is my job, then, to supply Explanatory Notes to this playful novel where every name and allusion resonates with numerous points of reference, and I would not wish to reduce anything in the novel to 'simply one thing'.[19] My research has already thrown up ample evidence that, contrary to the influential assertions of the Scottish critic David Daiches, the surnames of the characters McNab and Macalister do have strong Skye connections. In my first ever published essay (1992), I showed that McNab (spelled MacNab in the MS) and Macalister are names connected with the Jacobite Uprising of 1745 and with Bonnie Prince Charlie's time on Skye when he was assisted by the Macalister family, and Flora Macdonald bade him farewell in MacNab's Inn (now the Royal Hotel), in Portree.[20]

## Jane Goldman on variants in the 'Time Passes' section of *To the Lighthouse*

As with several other novels by Woolf, the variants between the first UK and first US editions are of great interest. There are many fascinating examples, not least the crucial parenthetical sentence(s) in the middle part of the book where its central character, Mrs. Ramsay, dies. The UK first edition reads: '[Mr. Ramsay stumbling along a passage stretched his arms out one dark morning, but Mrs. Ramsay having died rather suddenly the night before he stretched his arms out. They remained empty].' The US first edition reads: 'Mr. Ramsay, stumbling along a passage one dark morning, stretched his arms out, but Mrs. Ramsay having died rather suddenly the night before, his arms, though stretched out, remained empty.]'[21] Both versions convey that death in stumbling and awkward syntax, yet neither one should eclipse the other, both being simultaneously available on either side of the Atlantic. Both versions also demand the reader's repeated attention, catching us in a looping process that enacts and perpetuates a sense of loss. A digital edition or a parallel edition of the text might well resolve the dilemma of which version to plump for, but then making both simultaneously available also corrupts and detracts from both. The Cambridge edition takes the first UK as copy text, but the US variant is available in the Textual Apparatus, and readers can supplement our mapping out from the first UK edition by accessing both versions online too. What such attentive reading enacts is not only Mr. Ramsay's sense of uxorious loss forever in process, then, but the textual editor's and reader's realisation that there is no single, stable originary utterance with which to furnish those fatal editorial square brackets.

But there is a further complication for editors and readers of this work, in that a draft of 'Time Passes', the middle part of *To the Lighthouse*, was published in French translation as a short story a year in advance of the novel; and following that publication in French, Woolf made further revisions to it in English right up to final proof stage. So the Cambridge edition takes into account various states of the text between Woolf's early drafts and simultaneous first editions (British and American) of the novel's 'Time Passes' (1927), along with the typescript of the short story, 'Time Passes', which Woolf provided for Charles Mauron's French translation, 'Le Temps Passe', published in *Commerce* in 1926. Neither Woolf's typescript, nor Mauron's translation communicate Mrs. Ramsay's death in parentheses (round or square-bracketed). Rather we learn of it in Woolf's slippery free indirect discourse interweaving first- and third-person narration in the gossiping point of view of Mrs. McNab: 'They had the moth in them—Mrs. Ramsay's things. Poor lady! She would never want *them* again. She was dead they said; years ago in London. There was the old grey cloak she wore gardening (Mrs. McNab fingered it).'[22] This passage survives into the text of *To the Lighthouse* ('Time Passes' subsection 8), albeit pre-empted now by the earlier intrusion of Mrs. Ramsay's square-bracketed death notice ('Time Passes' subsection 3). Mrs. McNab here may be understood to be touching the redundant cloak or pushing her finger through a moth hole in its fabric, the round bracketed sentence in which she does so itself an intrusion into the fabric of the text. A few lines later, there is a further hole marked by round brackets where a parenthetical resumé of Mrs. Ramsay's rumoured death is inserted into the account of Mrs. McNab amongst the Ramsays' abandoned objects: '(She had died very sudden at the end, they said [*TL*, 111]).' This round bracketed parenthetical statement survives too into the 'Time Passes' of *To the Lighthouse*, and it too reverberates with the square bracketed announcement that now precedes it.

The digital archive, Woolfonline.com, gives twenty-first century readers the opportunity to pass time between all extant states of *To the Lighthouse*, including those of 'Time Passes'.[23] The Cambridge edition will be cross-referenced to this resource, directing readers to its source documents, thereby underpinning our editorial ethos of transparency by making visible to the reader the evidence behind our systematic collation of the extant published states of the text (from proofs to all editions published in Woolf's life-time), and behind our analysis of its conception and drafting. Moving between formal collation in the Textual Apparatus of the Cambridge edition and this invaluable online resource challenges us to rethink the stakes of reading and editing as well as translating modernist writing. Mauron's translation into French is not merely of arcane bibliographical interest, but a significant stage in Woolf's composition process— 'an intermediary text', as James Haule has it. Woolf's typescript of 'Time Passes' sent to Mauron is counted by Mark Hussey and Peter Shillingsburg as the *second* extant variant text of *To the Lighthouse*, but they count Mauron's 'Le Temps Passe' as the *third* extant variant. As editor I take this point as axiomatic. The Cambridge edition of *To the Lighthouse* will provide a further resource in its Appendices in the form of an especially commissioned translation of Mauron's French 'Le Temps Passe' back into English.

Kath Swarbrick's translation of Mauron's 'Le Temps Passe' has been most illuminating for me in pointing up for Anglophone readers Mauron's departures from Woolf's typescript. Restricting myself to just one example, I would draw attention to his translation of the passage relating Mrs. Ramsay's death just cited: 'La moissure les attrapait—les choses de Mrs. Ramsay. Pauvre dame! Elle n'aurait jamais plus besoin de tout ça. Elle était morte, qu'ils disaient, depuis des années, à Londres. Il y avait ce vieux manteaux gris qu'elle portait en travaillant son jardin (Mrs. McNab le soulevait du doigt)' (*WO* Commerce 29/46). Swarbrick shows in English the loss of the moth as agent of destruction as well as of the possibility of Mrs. McNab's hole-poking finger in Mauron's French: 'They were going mouldy—Mrs. Ramsay's things. Poor lady! She wouldn't be needing any of them again. She died, years ago, they said, in London. There was that old grey coat she used to wear when she was gardening (Mrs. McNab lifted it with a finger).'[24] Woolf ignores Mauron's damp and restores her moth in both first editions.

Woolf herself, in revising 'Time Passes' for publication as the middle part of *To the Lighthouse*, tidies up her own text, reorganising it at late proof stage to include those death-dealing square brackets enclosing the announcement of Mrs. Ramsay's death (and then of her son's and her daughter's). And in doing so she is mimicking the clearing and sorting actions of Mrs. McNab, the charwoman/chthonic goddess presiding over all versions of 'Time Passes' from the initial outline ('Old woman/Cleaning up'), to its five-sectioned holograph draft ('Mrs. MacNab'), to its nine-sectioned typescript and French publication, and to its ten-sectioned final bifurcated published version in the novel ('Mrs. McNab'). The already edited Mrs. McNab is a literary editor of sorts, I have argued elsewhere, and perhaps she is a translator too (another form of editor in effect), as she lurches and leers around the house with the knowledge of how its former mistress liked to arrange its furniture and objects; taking on the daunting task of restoring it and its contents to a semblance of the 'surface glitter' (as Woolf has it in 'On Not Knowing French') of that lost and bereaved household.

*To the Lighthouse* is a challenge to edit, then, precisely because it everywhere betrays a sense of its own to-be-edited-ness, not only in its use of editorial square brackets but also in its numerous other representations of acts of editing, not least by Mrs. McNab. This is more than the merely self-reflexive autotelic, textual self-consciousness that critics have identified from its long acknowledged status as a modernist *Künstlerroman*. This novel's sustained engagement with visual art and its tracking of the artist Lily Briscoe's composition of her painting of the deceased Mrs. Ramsay as co-terminus with a novel in which it is represented have certainly attracted ekphrastic critical readings, including my own. But editing *To the Lighthouse* has been revealing to me of a much deeper set of textual processes at work that return us to pressing questions of how one should edit this very text, how one should edit Woolf, how one should edit any multiplicitous, multivalent modernist work.

Woolf's texts demand of their editors, I am suggesting, not only a conventional 'gowned and hooded' (*TL*, 13) academic scholarly brain (to which Charles Tansley aspires), with the systematic alphabetical abstractive qualities of Mr. Ramsay's splendid mind, but also the indefatigable powers of the materially rooted yet visionary Mrs. McNab, restoring the house to order yet alert to all its prior and simultaneous material states.

## Notes

1 The General Editor's Preface appears at the start of each volume in the Cambridge University edition of Virginia Woolf's works. The above quotation is taken from the CUP *Mrs. Dalloway*, p. xii.
2 Jerome J. McGann, *The Textual Condition* (Princeton University Press, 1991); and Ted Bishop, 'The Alfa and the *Avant-text*: Transcribing Virginia Woolf's Manuscripts', in *Editing and Interpreting Virginia Woolf*, ed. James Haule (London: Palgrave, 2002); reproduced http://www.tedbishop.com/essays/the-alfa-and-the-avant-texte [accessed 28 June 2015].
3 McGann, *The Textual Condition*, p. 122.
4 Kitty was an old acquaintance of the Stephen family who belonged to Hyde Park days. See conscious links to Kitty Maxse (*D* III, 32 and *L* I, 349) and the moment when Woolf 'observes Lydia as a type for Rezia' (*D* II, 265) and when she miscalls Lydia Rezia (*D* II, 310).
5 See *MD*, liii–liv.
6 See *MD*, lvi–lvii.
7 William Irwin, 'What is an allusion?', *Journal of Aesthetics and Art Criticism*, 59.3 (Summer, 2001), 292.
8 See Explanatory Note 61:25 (*MD*, 251) and The Introduction, p. l, for Fernald's discussion of: 'His body was macerated until only the nerve fibres were left. It was spread like a veil upon a rock' (*MD*, 61). See also http://fordhamenglish.com/news1/2015/1/7/fernald-edits-authoritative-edition-of-virginia-woolf-novel for a description of how Fernald came upon this buried allusion.

9   Ziva Ben-Porat, 'The Poetics of Literary Allusion', *PTL: A Journal for Descriptive Poetics and Theory of Literature*, 1 (1976), 127.

10  John Campbell, 'Allusions and Illusions', *French Studies Bulletin*, 53 (1994), 1.

11  See Jane Goldman and Susan Sellers, 'General Editors' Preface', *MD*, p. ix.

12  Harold Bloom, *The Western Canon* (New York/San Diego/London: Harcourt Brace, 1994), p. 11.

13  The stories, 'Mrs. Dalloway in Bond Street', 'The Man Who Loved His Kind', 'The Introduction', 'Ancestors', 'Together and Apart', 'The New Dress' and 'A Summing Up' appear in *Mrs. Dalloway's Party: A Short Story Sequence*, ed. Stella McNichol (London: Hogarth Press, 1973).

14  Gerard Genette, *Paratexts: Thresholds of Interpretation* (Cambridge: Cambridge University Press, 1997), p. 402.

15  Shari Benstock, 'At the Margin of Discourse', *PMLA*, 98.2 (1983), 204.

16  http://www.annefernald.com/https/anne-fernaldsquarespacecom/blog/?offset=134366200000.

17  Jacques Derrida, 'Living On: Border Lines', in *Deconstruction and Criticism*, ed. Geoffrey Hartman, (New York: Seabury, 1979), pp. 83–84.

18  Benstock, 'At the Margin of Discourse', 220. Of course there are critics who find the privileging of the published text in this way. As Ted Bishop, for example, says, a 'clear text militates against an awareness of alternatives' ('The Alfa and the *Avant-text*: Transcribing Virginia Woolf's Manuscripts', in *Editing and Interpreting Virginia Woolf*, ed. James Haule (London: Palgrave, 2002), reproduced online as: http://www.tedbishop.com/essays/the-alfa-and-the-avant-texte [accessed 28 June 2015]). However, as this edition contains so much extra material and is careful to draw attention to the textual variants and makes a clear case to avoid what Bishop calls an iconic text which reproduces the manuscripts, I think the reader is made aware of alternatives to the British first edition.

19  See *TL*, 152, where James Ramsay famously reflects that 'nothing is simply one thing'.

20  Jane Goldman, *'With you in the Hebrides': Virginia Woolf and Scotland* (London: Cecil Woolf, 2013), Bloomsbury Heritage Series No. 70. *ISBN 978-1-907286-33-9*. [See the catalogue at https://bloggingwoolf.files.wordpress.com/2015/05/bh-catalogue-may-2015-3-final4.pdf].

21  Woolf, *To the Lighthouse* (London: Hogarth Press, 1927), p. 200; *To the Lighthouse* (New York: Harcourt, Brace, 1927), p. 194.

22  *Woolf Online*, Typescript 17/27. Woolf Online is to be found at http://www.woolfonline.com/. Hereafter, quotations from Woolf Online will be given in the text, preceded by *WO*.

23  See note 28.

24  Swarbrick's translation is forthcoming as an Appendix to my Cambridge University Press edition of *To the Lighthouse*.

# Further Reading

## Editions

For a complete list of Virginia Woolf's writings, see *A Bibliography of Virginia Woolf*, ed. B. J. Kirkpatrick and Stuart N. Clarke, 4th edition (Oxford: Oxford University Press, 1997). Amongst the many editions of Woolf's writings, The Cambridge University Press edition, ed. Jane Goldman and Susan Sellers, is especially well annotated, and seems destined to become the definitive edition for the foreseeable future. All quotations from *Mrs. Dalloway* are from Cambridge UP edition, ed. Anne E. Fernald (1925; rpt. 2015). The Cambridge UP edition of *To the Lighthouse*, ed. Jane Goldman, has yet to be published; the Oxford's World Classics edition of *To the Lighthouse*, ed. David Bradshaw (1927; 2008) has, on the recommendation of Jane Goldman, been used to provide page references throughout.

## Biographies of Woolf

Caramagno, Thomas. *The Flight of the Mind: Virginia Woolf's Art and Manic-Depressive Illness.* Berkeley: University of California Press, 1992.
Lee, Hermione. *Virginia Woolf.* London: Chatto & Windus, 1996.

## Books and Essay Collections

Armstrong, Karen. *The Gospel According to Woman.* London: Harper Collins, 1996, pp. 212–13.
Bell, Quentin. *Bloomsbury Recalled.* New York: Columbia University Press, 1995.
De Gay, Jane. *Virginia Woolf's Novels and the Literary Past.* Edinburgh: Edinburgh University Press, 2006.
Dunn, Jane. *Virginia Woolf and Vanessa Bell.* London: Hachette Digital, 1990.
Ellis, Steve. *Virginia Woolf and the Victorians.* Cambridge: Cambridge University Press, 2007.
Froula, Christine. *Virginia Woolf and the Bloomsbury Avant-Garde: War, Civilization, Modernity.* New York: Columbia University Press, 2004.
Fussell, Paul. *The Great War and Modern Memory* New York: Oxford UP, 1975.
Gillespie, Diane. *The Sisters' Arts: The Writing and Painting of Virginia Woolf and Vanessa Bell.* Syracuse: Syracuse University Press, 1988.
Goldman, Jane. *The Feminist Aesthetics of Virginia Woolf: Modernism, Post-Impressionism and the Visual.* Cambridge: Cambridge University Press, 1998.

_____. *The Cambridge Introduction to Virginia Woolf.* Cambridge: Cambridge University Press, 2006.

Hägglund, Martin. *Dying for Time: Proust, Woolf, Nabokov.* Cambridge, MA: Harvard University Press, 2012, pp. 56–78.

Henke, Suzette and David Eberly, eds. *Virginia Woolf and Trauma: Embodied Texts.* New York: Pace University Press, 2007.

Hussey, Mark, ed., *Virginia Woolf and War.* Syracuse, NY: Syracuse University Press, 1991.

Hynes, Samuel. *A War Imagined: The First World War and English Culture.* Oxford: Bodley Head, 1990.

Lazenby, Donna J. *A Mystical Philosophy. Transcendence and Immanence in the Works of Virginia Woolf and Iris Murdoch.* London, New York: Bloomsbury Publishing, 2014.

Levenback, Karen L. *Virginia Woolf and the Great War.* Syracuse, NY: Syracuse University Press, 1999.

Lewis, Pericles. *Religious Experience and the Modernist Novel.* Cambridge: Cambridge University Press, 2010.

Meisel, Perry. *The Absent Father: Virginia Woolf and Walter Pater.* New Haven: Yale University Press, 1980.

Nicholls, Peter. *Modernisms: A Literary Guide.* London: Macmillan, 1995.

Pease, Allison, ed. *The Cambridge Companion to To the Lighthouse.* Cambridge: Cambridge University Press, 2015.

Phillips, Kathy J. *Virginia Woolf against Empire.* Knoxville: University of Tennessee Press, 1994.

Rosenbaum, S. P. A. *Bloomsbury Group Reader.* Oxford: Blackwell, 1993.

_____. *The Bloomsbury Group: A Collection of Memoirs and Commentary.* Revised edition. Toronto: University of Toronto Press, 1995.

Spalding, Frances. *Vanessa Bell.* London: Weidenfeld and Nicholson, 1983.

Stape, J. H., ed. *Virginia Woolf: Interviews and Recollections.* Iowa City: University of Iowa Press, 1995.

## Essays in Books and Journals

Cuddy-Keane, Melba. 'Narratological Approaches', in *Virginia Woolf Studies*, ed. Anna Snaith. New York: Palgrave Macmillan, 2007, pp. 16–34.

Detloff, Madelyn and Brenda Helt, ed. 'Queering Woolf', a special issue of *Virginia Woolf Miscellany* 82 (Fall 2012); available at http://www.home. southernct.edu/~neverowv1/VWM_Online.html.

Flint, Kate. 'Virginia Woolf and Victorian Aesthetics', *The Edinburgh Companion to Virginia Woolf and the Arts.* Edinburgh: Edinburgh University Press, 2010, pp. 19–34.

Gillespie, Diane. 'The Gender of Modern/ist Painting', in *Gender in Modernism: New Geographies, Complex Intersections*, ed. Bonnie Kime Scott. Urbana: University of Illinois Press, 2007, pp. 765–808.

Goldman, Jane. 'From *Mrs. Dalloway* to *The Waves*: New Elegy and Lyric Experimentalism', in *The Cambridge Companion to Virginia Woolf*, ed. Susan Sellers. Cambridge/New York: Cambridge University Press, 2010, pp. 49–69.

—————. 'The Novel's Use of Language and Form', *The Cambridge Companion to To the Lighthouse*, ed. Allison Pease. Cambridge: Cambridge University Press, 2014.

Henke, Suzette A. 'Virginia Woolf and Post-Traumatic Subjectivity', in *Virginia Woolf: Turning the Centuries*, eds. Ann Ardis and Bonnie Kime Scott. New York: Pace University Press, 1999, pp. 147–52.

—————. '*Mrs. Dalloway*: The Communion of Saints', in *New Feminist Essays on Virginia Woolf*, ed. Jane Marcus. Lincoln: University of Nebraska Press, 1981, pp. 125–47.

Howard, Douglas L. '*Mrs. Dalloway*: Virginia Woolf's Redemptive Cycle', *Literature and Theology*, 12.2 (1998), 149–58.

Hussey, Mark. 'Introduction,' *To the Lighthouse*. Annotated with an introduction by Mark Hussey. Orlando: Harcourt, 2005.

Swanson, Diana L. 'Lesbian Approaches', in *Palgrave Advances in Virginia Woolf Studies*, ed. Anna Snaith. Basingstoke: Palgrave Macmillan, 2007, pp. 184–208.

Wolfe, Jesse. 'The Sane Woman in the Attic: Sexuality and Self-Authorship in *Mrs. Dalloway*'. *Modern Fiction Studies* 51.1 (2005), 34–59.

Wright, E.H. 'Woolf and Theatre', in *Woolf in Context*, ed. Jane Goldman. Cambridge: Cambridge University Press, 2011.

—————. Ed. *Bloomsbury Inspirations* (Newcastle: Cambridge Scholars Publishing, 2014).

—————. *Virginia Woolf* (London: Hesperus, 2011).

# Index

Apostles, The, 60, 72n1
Auerbach, Erich, 21–22, 30n24

Bakhtin, Mikhail, 149n1
Bell, Clive, 61, 62, 63, 77, 79, 87n6,
    127
Bell, Quentin, 62, 72n2, 73n7,
    137n11, 209
Bell, Vanessa (*see also* Stephen,
    Vanessa), 58, 60, 62, 63, 66, 76,
    77–78, 79–80, 81, 86, 87n3,
    87n6, 87n7, 87n9, 160, 164n30,
    198, 209, 210
Bennett, Arnold, 5, 53, 64, 87, 125,
    126, 139, 140–41
Bergson, Henri, 38, 39, 45n12
Bloomsbury Group, The, 6, 60, 63,
    64, 66, 72n2, 72n3, 73n4, 73n6,
    73n10, 126, 210
Brooke, Rupert, 125, 158, 198

Cameron, Julia Margaret, 55, 78

Domasio, Antonio, 145, 146,
    151n16
Dyer, General Reginald, 127,
    137n12

Einstein, Albert, 38–39
Eliot, T.S., 38, 60, 66, 72n3, 73n16,
    153, 198

First Post-Impressionist Exhibition
    (1910), 6, 62, 79
Forster, E.M., 60, 179n27, 180, 186,
    192n1, 193n9, 193n11
Freud, Sigmund, 1, 8, 13, 14, 29n7,
    67, 89, 106–11, 112, 113,
    114, 115, 117, 121, 122n4,
    122n5, 122n9, 123n13,
    163n9

Fry, Roger, 6, 11, 60, 62, 64–65,
    68, 69, 73n8, 73n9, 73n15,
    77, 79–81, 87n6, 87n13, 115,
    123n26, 179n27

Galsworthy, John, 5, 53, 126, 139,
    140–41
Garnett, Duncan, 60, 61, 63, 127
Grant, Duncan, 60, 61, 63, 79, 127,
    193n9

James, William, 1, 2–3, 14n1, 14n3,
    14n7, 39, 45n13
Jung, Carl, 1, 8–9, 13, 15n14, 89–92,
    101–2, 104, 104n1, 104n3,
    104n5, 104n6, 104n7, 104n8,
    104n9, 105n11

Keynes, John Maynard, 60, 70, 127
Klein, Melanie, 8, 107, 111–12, 121,
    123n13, 123n31

Milner, Marion, 8, 112–20, 123n16,
    123n17, 123n19, 123n20,
    123n21, 123n23, 123n24,
    123n27, 123n29, 123n30
Montaigne, Michel de, 44, 114,
    123n18, 123n19
Moore, G.E., 6, 61, 73n5

Nietzsche, Friedrich, 15n17, 116

Pater, Walter, 37, 53, 59n2
Pre-Raphaelite Brotherhood, 55, 78
Proust, Marcel, 17, 29n4, 37, 45n16,
    81, 111
Post-Traumatic Stress Disorder
    (PTSD), 134, 143–44, 146,
    147, 150n12, 151n13

Russell, Bertrand, 61

Sassoon, Siegfried, 11, 126, 130–31, 137n2, 137n5, 137n6, 138n22, 198
Sydney-Turner, Saxon, 60
Schopenhauer, Arthur, 4–5, 15n8–9, 15n10–11
Second Post-Impressionist Exhibition, 80
Shakespeare, William, 42, 102, 104, 156, 170, 171, 173, 179n28, 186, 202
Sickert, Walter, 7, 81
Stephen, Adrian, 60, 61, 106, 108, 113, 117, 121, 122n5, 123n31, 107
Stephen, Julia, 54–57, 78, 202, 203
Stephen, Sir Leslie, x, 2, 50, 54–57, 59n2, 59n5, 60, 66, 78, 79, 109, 122n8, 160, 202, 203
Stephen, Vanessa (see also Bell, Vanessa), x, 7, 60, 62, 63, 66, 78, 79, 82
Strawson, Galen, 141, 150n9
Strachey, Lytton, 47, 60, 61–62, 106, 110, 114, 122n1, 127, 179n27, 200

Underhill, Evelyn, 38

Vipond, Dianne, 20, 59

Watts, George Frederic, 55, 78
Wilde, Oscar, 63
Wells, H.G., 5, 126, 139, 140
Woolf, Leonard, 2, 15n19, 60, 61, 63, 69, 72n2–3, 80, 106, 127, 150n5, 163n1, 177n4, 178n9
Woolf, Virginia, Essays, 47, 87n12, 138n16
  'Modern Fiction', 1–3, 5–6, 13, 17, 64, 73n13, 115, 139, 150n11, 178n12
  Moments of Being, 25, 31, 37–39, 43, 44n7, 89
  'Mr. Bennett and Mrs. Brown', 1, 4–6, 13, 73n14, 87n12
  Room of One's Own, A, 7–8, 60–61, 75, 90, 95, 113, 153, 163n4, 166–67, 169–75, 177n2, 179n20–21, 179n26, 19
  Three Guineas, 7, 8, 34, 36, 62, 125, 165–68, 170, 178n6, 178n15, 179n23
  Wormholes, 20–21
Wyler, William, 119